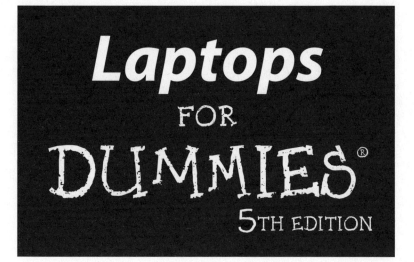

Laptops

FOR

DUMMIES®

5TH EDITION

Laptops
FOR
DUMMIES®
5TH EDITION

by Dan Gookin

WILEY

John Wiley & Sons, Inc.

004.16
Goo

Laptops For Dummies,® 5th Edition

Published by
John Wiley & Sons, Inc.
111 River Street
Hoboken, NJ 07030-5774

www.wiley.com

Copyright © 2013 by John Wiley & Sons, Inc., Hoboken, New Jersey

Published by John Wiley & Sons, Inc., Hoboken, New Jersey

Published simultaneously in Canada

For general information on our other products and services, please contact our Customer Care Department within the U.S. at 877-762-2974, outside the U.S. at 317-572-3993, or fax 317-572-4002.

For technical support, please visit www.wiley.com/techsupport.

Wiley also publishes its books in a variety of electronic formats and by print-on-demand. Not all content that is available in standard print versions of this book may appear or be packaged in all book formats. If you have purchased a version of this book that did not include media that is referenced by or accompanies a standard print version, you may request this media by visiting http://booksupport.wiley.com. For more information about Wiley products, visit us www.wiley.com.

004.14

Library of Congress Control Number: 2012949808

ISBN 978-1-118-11533-6 (pbk); ISBN 978-1-118-22426-7 (ebk); ISBN 978-1-118-26248-1 (ebk); ISBN 978-1-118-23242-2 (ebk)

Manufactured in the United States of America

10 9 8 7 6 5 4 3 2 1

WILEY

About the Author

Dan Gookin has been writing about technology for over 25 years. He combines his love of writing with his gizmo fascination to create books that are informative, entertaining, and not boring. Having written over 130 titles with 12 million copies in print translated into over 30 languages, Dan can attest that his method of crafting computer tomes seems to work.

Perhaps his most famous title is the original *DOS For Dummies,* published in 1991. It became the world's fastest-selling computer book, at one time moving more copies per week than the *New York Times* number-one bestseller (though, as a reference, it could not be listed on the *Times'* Best Sellers list). That book spawned the entire line of *For Dummies* books, which remains a publishing phenomenon to this day.

Dan's most popular titles include *PCs For Dummies, Word For Dummies, Laptops For Dummies*, and *Android Phones For Dummies.* He also maintains the vast and helpful website www.wambooli.com.

Dan holds a degree in Communications/Visual Arts from the University of California, San Diego. He lives in the Pacific Northwest, where he enjoys spending time with his sons playing video games indoors while they enjoy the gentle woods of Idaho.

Publisher's Acknowledgments

We're proud of this book; please send us your comments at http://dummies.custhelp.com. For other comments, please contact our Customer Care Department within the U.S. at 877-762-2974, outside the U.S. at 317-572-3993, or fax 317-572-4002.

Some of the people who helped bring this book to market include the following:

Acquisitions and Editorial

Sr. Project Editor: Mark Enochs

Acquisitions Editor: Katie Mohr

Copy Editor: Rebecca Whitney

Editorial Manager: Leah Michael

Editorial Assistant: Leslie Saxman

Sr. Editorial Assistant: Cherie Case

Cover Photo: © Damir Cudic / iStockphoto.com

Cartoons: Rich Tennant (www.the5thwave.com)

Composition Services

Project Coordinator: Sheree Montgomery

Layout and Graphics: Jennifer Creasey

Proofreaders: Melissa Cossell, Jessica Kramer, Christine Sabooni

Indexer: Potomac Indexing, LLC

Publishing and Editorial for Technology Dummies

    Richard Swadley, Vice President and Executive Group Publisher

    Andy Cummings, Vice President and Publisher

    Mary Bednarek, Executive Acquisitions Director

    Mary C. Corder, Editorial Director

Publishing for Consumer Dummies

    Kathy Nebenhaus, Vice President and Executive Publisher

Composition Services

    Debbie Stailey, Director of Composition Services

Contents at a Glance

Table of Contents

· ·

Introduction

• •

*1*t's lightweight, high-tech, and portable; the product of years of research, a longtime dream of engineers and scholars, something people all over the world crave. It's wireless. It's about communications. And it will help you become the ultimate mobile computer user. Of course, I'm talking about this book: *Laptops For Dummies*.

This is the fifth edition of *Laptops For Dummies*, updated and spiffed up for the latest in PC laptop hardware and software as well as Microsoft's latest operating system, Windows 8.

Don't let that scare you.

Even though this book was updated to cover Windows 8, there's still plenty of information here for older versions of Windows. This book includes full information on Windows 7, which is still popular, as well as Windows Vista (still unpopular) and the everlasting Windows XP. It's all covered here.

This book covers your portable computer from laptop to lap-bottom, inside and out, on the road or resting at home. The information here runs the gamut, from introducing your laptop to making your first wireless connection at your favorite swanky cybercafé. You'll find this book useful whether you want to go laptop shopping or you consider yourself an old hand.

About This Book

I'm glad that you're still reading this introduction. Most people stop reading after a few paragraphs, or they don't even bother reading the introduction. Consider yourself special.

This book covers laptop computing, from buying and setting up, to going on the road to networking and the Internet, to power management to security, and everything in between. There's a lot of laptoppy advice to be had between this book's yellow covers.

I don't intend for you to read every chapter in sequence. That's because this book is organized as a reference: Find the tidbit of information, the knowledge nugget you need to know, and then be on your merry way. Everything is cross-referenced, so if you need to look elsewhere in the book for more information, you can easily find it.

In writing this book, I assume that you may know a bit about computers, as most folks do today. But you may be utterly fresh on the idea of *portable* computing. Despite what they tell you, a laptop computer isn't merely a desktop computer with a handle attached. There's more to it, and this book is here to show you the ropes — and to let you take full advantage of what the laptop has to offer.

I divide the laptop experience into seven handy parts:

Part I contains an overview of laptop computing — plus, a handy how-to guide for buying a laptop to sate your portable computing lusts.

Part II introduces you to your laptop computer, covering basic operation and hardware orientation.

Part III discusses how to use your laptop and gives you important information on power management and printing with a laptop as well as laptop expansion.

Part IV is about laptop communications, which includes networking and the Internet. The idea is to let your laptop talk with the rest of the world and with a desktop computer (in case you still use one).

Part V deals with taking your laptop on the road and provides a special chapter on the hot topic of laptop security.

Part VI covers laptop troubleshooting in addition to various ways to upgrade your laptop's hardware and software.

Part VII is the traditional *For Dummies* Part of Tens — various lists for review or to help you get on your way.

I also offer you the Cheat Sheet, which can be found at www.dummies.com/cheatsheet/laptops. There, you'll find tips and places to write down important info about your laptop that you might need in the future should anything go wrong.

And Just Who Are You?

Let me jump to the conclusion that you're a human being, not a cleverly disguised owl. Furthermore, either you own a laptop PC or you want to buy one. You may already have a desktop computer, or perhaps you had a laptop a long, long time ago and noticed that things have changed.

I use the word *laptop* to refer to all types of portable computers, including traditional laptops, notebooks, ultrabooks, teensy netbooks, and those things I call Tablet PCs. Where these creatures have individual differences, I note them in the text. For example, Chapter 8 talks completely about Tablet PCs and their unique features and abilities. Otherwise, unless specifically noted, a laptop is a notebook is a netbook in the text.

Tablets, such as the Windows Surface or any device similar to the iPad or one of its many clones, aren't covered in this book. Even though these gizmos may run Windows and look a lot like laptop computers, they really aren't.

This book assumes that your laptop is PC-compatible, that it runs the Windows operating system. The current version of this operating system is Windows 8, though this book also covers Windows 7, Windows Vista — and even Windows XP (though if you're still using Windows XP on your laptop, it's probably time for a new laptop).

I don't cover Macintosh laptop computers. And the mere thought of addressing any PC laptops running the Linux operating system, or any other operating system known or unknown, from this or any parallel universe or dimension, has never occurred to me.

This book doesn't describe the basic operations of a computer, Windows, or your software. I've tried to keep the information here specific to the portable aspects of the laptop computer. Beyond that, if you need more information about running your computer, any standard PC or Windows reference works fine.

Icons Used in This Book

The Tip icon notifies you about something cool, handy, or nifty — or something that I highly recommend. For example, "Most people don't seek out good financial advice at a bowling alley."

Don't forget! When you see this icon, you can be sure that it points out something you should remember or something I said earlier that I'm repeating because it's very important and you'll likely forget it anyway. For example: "There is no need to touch the electric fence a second time just to be sure that it's on."

Danger! Ah-oogah! Ah-oogah! When you see the Warning icon, pay careful attention to the text. This icon flags something that's bad or that can cause trouble. For example: "The enormous sea monster slithering toward your village won't be using the legal system to settle its grievances."

This icon alerts you to something technical, an aside or a trivial tidbit that I simply cannot suppress the urge to share. For example: "My first laptop was a steam-powered, 8-bit 6502 that I breadboarded myself." Feel free to skip over this book's technical information as you please.

Where to Go from Here

You can start reading this book anywhere. Open the table of contents and pick a spot that amuses you or concerns you or piques your curiosity. Everything is explained in the text, and stuff is carefully cross-referenced so that you don't waste your time reading repeated information.

For additional information, you can visit my website:

```
www.wambooli.com
```

When updates for this book are available, the information can be found at

```
www.wambooli.com/help/laptops
```

Finally, I enjoy hearing feedback. If you want to send me e-mail, my personal address is dgookin@wambooli.com. I'm happy to answer questions specific to this book or just say hello. Please be aware that I don't list my e-mail address here to offer free troubleshooting or support for your laptop. If you need support, contact your laptop dealer or manufacturer. Thank you for understanding.

Enjoy your laptop computer. I'll see you on the road!

Part I
This Laptop Thing

The 5th Wave — By Rich Tennant

"He saw your laptop and wants to know if he can check his Gmail."

In this part . . .

*O*ne word truly sums up the entire laptop experience: freedom. The modern laptop gives you all the computer power you need, minus the cumbersome bulk and tethers that keep a desktop PC in one place. Even if you never plan to take the thing anywhere, you have the freedom to do so.

It has taken a while for the state of laptop technology to get to where it is. This part of the book explains the journey taken in the quest for portable computing. It also includes a useful guide for finding a laptop that fits perfectly in your very own lap.

Chapter 1

The Portable Computing Quest

*I*t was Eugene's idea. One summer day, in his 42nd year, he discovered that the weather was nice outside during the summer. His brilliant idea was to attach wheels to his room-size, vacuum tube computer. Then he and the other three computer scientists, despite their utter lack of muscle tone, would push the 17-ton beast out of the lab and work outside. It was this crazy notion that sparked the portable computer revolution.

The revolution continues. Computers are not only shrinking, they're becoming more portable. There are laptops, notebooks, netbooks, Ultrabooks, tablet PCs, and convertibles. It wasn't always this way. This chapter explains the history of portable computing, from the first dreams and desires to the panoply of options now available.

Laptop History

You can't make something portable simply by bolting a handle to it. Sure, it pleases the marketing folk, who are more interested in things that sound good as opposed to things that are practical. For example, you can put a handle on a boulder and call it portable, but that doesn't make it so.

My point is that true portability implies that a gizmo has at least these three characteristics:

- ✔ It's lightweight.
- ✔ It needs no power cord.
- ✔ It's practical.

In the history of portable computing, these three things didn't happen all at once, and definitely not in that order.

The Xerox Dynabook

The desire to take a computer on the road has been around a long, long time. Back around 1970, when Bill Gates was still in school and dreaming of becoming a chiropodist, Xerox PARC developed the Dynabook concept.

Today, you'd recognize the Dynabook as an eBook reader, similar to the Amazon Kindle: The Dynabook was to be the size of a sheet of paper and only a half-inch thick. The top part was a screen; the bottom, a keyboard.

The Dynabook never left the lab, remaining only a dream. Yet the desire to take a computer on the road wouldn't go away. For the next three decades after the Dynabook concept fizzled, many attempts were made to create truly portable computers.

The Osborne 1

The first successful portable computer was the Osborne 1, created by computer book author and publisher Adam Osborne in 1980. Adam believed that in order for personal computers to be successful, they would have to be portable.

His design for the Osborne 1 portable computer was ambitious for the time: The thing would have to fit under an airline seat — and this was *years* before anyone would even dream of using a computer on an airplane.

The Osborne 1 portable computer (see Figure 1-1) was a whopping success. It featured a full-size keyboard and two 5¼-inch floppy drives but only a teensy, credit-card-size monitor. It wasn't battery powered, but it did have a handy carrying handle so that you could lug around the 24-pound beast like an over-packed suitcase. Despite its shortcomings, 10,000 units a month were sold; for $1,795, you got the computer plus free software.

The ancient portable computer

Long before people marveled over credit-card-size calculators, there existed the world's first portable calculator. Presenting the *abacus,* the device used for centuries by merchants and goatherds to rapidly perform calculations that would otherwise cause painful headaches.

Abacus comes from the Greek word meaning "to swindle you faster." Seriously, the abacus, or *counting board,* is simple to master. Many kids now learn to use the abacus in elementary school. In the deft hands of an expert, an abacus can perform all the same operations as a calculator — including square and cubic roots.

In his short story *Into the Comet,* science fiction author Arthur C. Clarke wrote of stranded astronauts using many abacuses to plot their voyage home when the spaceship's computer wouldn't work because the Internet was down and their version of Windows couldn't be validated.

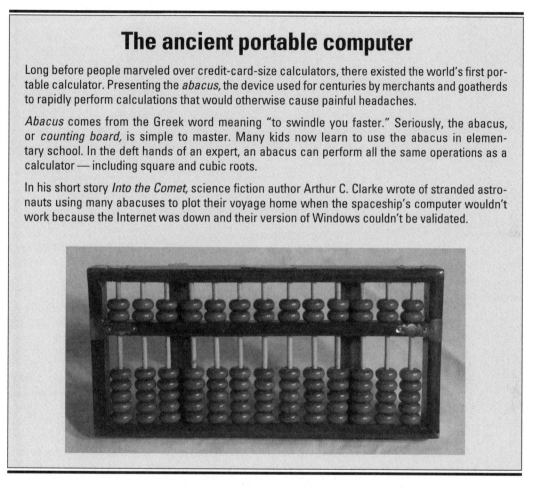

The loveable luggables

The Osborne computer was barely portable. Face it: The thing was a *suitcase!* Imagine hauling the 24-pound Osborne across Chicago's O'Hare airport. Worse: Imagine the joy expressed by your fellow seatmates as you try to wedge the thing beneath the seat in front of you.

Figure 1-1:
A late-model
Osborne.

Computer users yearned for portability. They wanted to believe the advertising images of carefree people toting the Osborne around — people with arms of equal length. But no hip marketing term could mask the ungainly nature of the Osborne: Portable? Transportable? Wispy? Nope. Credit some wag in the computer press for dreaming up the term *luggable* to describe the new and popular category of portable computers ushered in by the Osborne.

Never mind its weight. Never mind that most luggable computers never ventured from the desktops they were first set up on — luggables were the best the computer industry could offer an audience wanting a portable computer.

In the end, it wasn't the Osborne computer's weight that doomed it. No, what killed the Osborne was that in the early 1980s the world wanted IBM PC compatibility. The Osborne lacked it. Instead, the upstart Texas company Compaq introduced luggability to the IBM world with the Compaq 1, shown in Figure 1-2.

The Compaq 1, introduced in 1983 at $3,590, proved that you could have your IBM compatibility and haul it on the road with you — as long as a power socket was handy and you had good upper-body strength.

Yet the power cord can stretch only so far. It became painfully obvious that for a computer to be truly portable — as Adam Osborne intended — it would have to lose its power cord.

Figure 1-2:
The luggable
Compaq 1.

The Model 100

The first computer that even remotely looked like a modern laptop, and was
fully battery powered, was the Radio Shack Model 100, shown in Figure 1-3. It
was an overwhelming success.

What's a PC?

PC is an acronym for *politically correct* as well
as for *personal computer.* In this book, the
proper choice is personal computer. The term
refers to the early *microcomputers* from back in
the late 1970s and early 1980s. These computers were smaller and less powerful than other,
larger, more intimidating computers of the era.
They were, in fact, personal.

When IBM entered the microcomputer market
in 1982, it called its computer the *IBM PC.*

Though it was a brand name, the term *PC* soon
referred to any similar computer and eventually
to any computer. A computer is basically a PC.

As far as this book is concerned, a PC is a personal computer that runs the Windows operating system. Laptop computers are also PCs,
but the term *PC* more often implies a desktop
computer model.

Portability and communications

Long before the Internet came around, one thing that was deemed necessary on all portable computers was the ability to communicate. A portable computer had two communications duties. First, it had to be able to talk with a desktop computer, to exchange and update files. Second, it needed a *modem* to be able to communicate electronically over phone lines.

Nearly every portable computer, from the Radio Shack Model 100 onward, required a modem, or at least an option for installing one. This was before the Internet era, back when a modem was considered an optional luxury for a desktop computer. Out on the road, away from a desktop at the office, early proto-road-warriors needed that modem in order to keep in touch.

Figure 1-3:
The Radio Shack Model 100.

The Model 100 wasn't designed to be IBM PC compatible, which is surprising considering that PC compatibility was all the rage at the time. Instead, this model offered users a full-size, full-action keyboard plus an eensie, eight-row, 40-column LCD text display. It came with several built-in programs, including a text editor (word processor), a communications program, a scheduler, and an appointment book, plus the BASIC programming language, which allowed users to create their own programs or buy and use BASIC programs written by others.

The Radio Shack Model 100 was all that was needed for portability at the time, which is why the device was so popular.

✔ The Model 100 provided the *form factor* for laptops of the future. It was about the size of a hardback novel. It ran for hours on standard AA batteries. And it weighed just 6 pounds.

✔ So popular was the Model 100 among journalists that it was common to hear the hollow sound of typing on its keyboard during presidential news conferences in the 1980s.

✔ Despite its popularity and versatility, people wanted a version of the Model 100 that would run the same software as the IBM PC. Technology wasn't ready to shrink the PC's hardware to Model 100 size in 1983, but the Model 100 set the bar for what people wanted in a laptop's dimensions.

The lunch buckets

Before the dawn of the first true laptop, some ugly mutations slouched in, along with a few rejects from various mad scientists around the globe. I call them the *lunch bucket* computers because they assumed the shape, size, and weight of a typical hardhat's lunch box. The Compaq III, shown in Figure 1-4, was typical of this type of portable computer.

Figure 1-4:
The
Compaq III.

- ✔ The lunch box beasts weighed anywhere from 12 to 20 pounds or more, and most weren't battery powered.

- ✔ The lunch bucket portables were the first PCs to use full-screen LCD monitors. (The Osborne and Compaq portables used glass CRTs.)

- ✔ Incidentally, around the same time as the lunch bucket computers became popular, color monitors were becoming standard items on desktop PCs. All portables at the time, even those with LCD monitors, were monochrome.

- ✔ Honestly, the lunch bucket did offer something over the old transportable or luggable: less weight! A late-model lunch bucket PC weighed in at about 12 pounds, half the weight and about one-eighth the size of the suitcase-size luggables.

Dawn of the PC laptop

The computer industry's dream was to have a portable computer that had all the power and features of a desktop computer yet was about the same size and weight as the Model 100. One of the first computers to approach this mark was the Compaq SLT, back in 1988, as shown in Figure 1-5.

Figure 1-5:
The
Compaq SLT.

Calculating laptop weight: The missing pieces

When computer companies specify the weights of their laptops, I'm certain that they do it under ideal conditions, possibly on the moon or at another location where gravity is weak. The advertised weight is, as they say, "for comparison purposes only."

Commonly left out of the laptop's weight specs is the *power brick,* the AC adapter used to connect the laptop to a wall socket. When the laptop isn't running on batteries, you need the power brick to supply the thing with juice, so the power brick is a required accessory — something you have to tote with you if you plan to take the laptop on an extended trip.

Back when laptops were novel, the advertisements never disclosed how much the power brick weighed — sometimes half as much as the laptop itself! Either that or the power brick was even bulkier than the laptop, as shown in the figure, in the obnoxiously big Dell 320LT power brick (and its cumbersome 30-minute batteries). Lugging around those items isn't convenient. Things are better today.

The Compaq SLT was the first portable computer to resemble one of today's laptops: A hinged lid swings up and back from the base, which contains the keyboard. This design is known as the *clamshell.*

Feature-wise, the SLT had what most PC desktop users wanted in a portable system: a full-size keyboard, full-size screen, floppy drive, and 286 processor, which meant that the computer could run the then-popular DOS operating system. The computer lacked a hard drive.

Weight? Alas, the SLT was a bowling ball, at 14 pounds!

What the Compaq SLT did was prove to the world that portability was possible. A laptop computer was designed to feature everything a desktop computer could, and run on batteries for an hour or so. Yeah, believe it or not, people were *delighted*.

The search for light

Just because the marketing department labeled the computer a *laptop* didn't mean that it was sleek and lightweight. For a while there, it seemed like anyone could get away with calling a portable PC a laptop, despite the computer's weight of up to 20 pounds — which is enough to crush any lap, not to mention kneecaps.

In the fall of 1989, NEC showed that it could think outside the laptop box when it introduced the UltraLite laptop, shown in Figure 1-6.

The UltraLite featured a full-size screen and keyboard but no disk drives or other moving parts! It used battery-backed-up memory to serve as a *silicon disk*, similar to today's solid-state drives (SSDs). The silicon disk stored 1 or 2MB of data — which was plenty back in those days.

As was required of all laptops, the UltraLite featured a modem, and it could talk with a desktop computer by using a special cable. Included with the UltraLite was software that would let it easily exchange files and programs with a desktop PC.

The weight? Yes, the UltraLite lived up to its name and weighed in at just under 5 pounds — a feather compared to the obese laptops of the day. And the battery lasted a whopping two hours, thanks mostly to the UltraLite's lack of moving parts.

Figure 1-6:
The NEC
UltraLite.

Modern Laptops

As technology careened headlong into the 21st century, it became apparent that computer users were desperate for three things from their laptops — in addition to the basic PC compatibility, portability, and communications features that had long ago been deemed must-have items:

- ✔ Light weight
- ✔ Long battery life
- ✔ Full hardware compatibility with desktop systems

Over time, all these qualities were achieved — at a price. Today, the holy grail of a lightweight, PC-compatible laptop that boasts a long battery life isn't elusive; it's just expensive!

The notebook

The modern PC laptop is dubbed a *notebook*. It can sport a full-size keyboard and numeric keypad but often has a compact keyboard. The notebook weighs in anywhere from 2 to 6 pounds, and the battery lasts somewhere between 4 to 6 hours.

The rest of the typical notebook is similar to a desktop PC: LCD screen, wired and wireless networking, optical drive (CD and DVD), and various expansion options as covered elsewhere in this book. Putting all these features into a laptop computer gives you today's notebook.

The Tablet PC

Computer manufacturers have long attempted to create the electronic equivalent of a pencil and pad of paper — a very *expensive* pencil and pad of paper. Basically, what they're after is a portable computer with a monitor but no keyboard. Data is input by using a digital stylus to write directly on the screen.

Over the years, this digital triptych has had various names attached to it: the PenGo computer, the Apple Newton, Pen Windows, and eventually the Tablet PC.

The *Tablet PC* began life a few years back as its own computer category. The machine was about the same size as a laptop, but it didn't fold open; the monitor was "face up" all the time. That model failed miserably. The Tablet PC now exists as a laptop hybrid, often called a *convertible laptop*: The machine can be used like any other laptop, but the display can be pivoted and laid flat over the keyboard, as shown in Figure 1-7. The result is a flexible computer system that is a laptop with Tablet PC features.

Figure 1-7:
A Tablet PC.

✔ Don't confuse the Tablet PC with popular tablets such as the iPad or Samsung Galaxy Tab or the Windows Surface devices. A Tablet PC differs from these gizmos in that it offers features associated with traditional computers.

✔ Even as a hybrid, Tablet PC sales haven't taken off. Apparently, writing on the screen isn't a feature that laptop users are eager to use.

✔ Tablet PCs are discussed throughout this book and specifically in Chapter 8.

✔ The ancients used something called a *tabulae ceratea* to write temporary messages. Every Greek or Roman schoolboy took with him to class a folding wooden tablet. Its insides were coated with a black wax. Using a stylus (basically a stick), the student would write into the wax, again and again. Oh, we've truly come such a long way.

The subnotebooks

Human laps aren't getting any smaller. Human eyes can comfortably read text that's only so big. Most important, human fingers have trouble with keyboards that are too tiny. Despite these limitations, the most recent step in laptop evolution is the *subnotebook,* which is the smallest, lightest, and most portable computer.

Several kinds of subnotebooks are available:

The **Ultrabook** isn't light on power or ability, but it's much lighter and sleeker than the typical laptop. The idea behind the Ultrabook is to give you power and portability, but not all the bells and whistles of a full-on notebook-style laptop.

The **netbook** is not powerful, concentrating instead on being portable. It lacks an optical drive, for instance, and many netbooks lack the computing horsepower to run advanced programs. What they do provide, however, is an inexpensive and highly portable platform for using the Internet, accessing e-mail, and performing simple tasks, such as word processing. Figure 1-8 illustrates a typical netbook computer.

The **ultramobile PC,** or **UMPC,** is an attempt to cram everything you'd find in a desktop computer into a portable device about the size of a cell phone. These gizmos aren't common, given the popularity of cell phones, tablets, and other similar devices. The people in that audience don't seem to desire full PC compatibility in their mobile gizmos.

Figure 1-8:
The eensy-
weensy
netbook PC.

Chapter 2

A Laptop of Your Own

*W*hen you go out to buy something new and scary, like a computer, there are two things to know. First, it helps to identify what you want to do with the new thing. For a laptop, you probably want freedom and portability, if not the social status that comes with being a smart, handsome laptop owner. Second, it helps to know as much as possible about the thing you're buying.

For the first part, you probably already know why you want a laptop, and if you're like anyone who's read my books, you're already smart and handsome. For the second part, you need to bone up on laptop-buying issues, which is exactly the information you find in this chapter.

Do You Need a Laptop?

The dream of portable computing has been realized. Laptops, and all their variations, are everywhere.

As a consumer, and as someone who needs a computer in order to survive in the 21st century, the question is simple: Do you need a laptop?

Why you need a laptop

I can think of several reasons for getting a laptop computer:

Have a laptop as your main computer

Why dither over saving money with a desktop when you really want the portability of a laptop?

A desktop computer cannot pretend to be a laptop, but a laptop can certainly fake being a desktop: You can use a full-size keyboard and monitor with your laptop. You can also connect any number of popular desktop peripherals, such as a printer, a scanner, or an external hard drive. The advantage is, unlike with a desktop system, that you're free to disconnect the laptop and wander the world whenever you want.

Use a laptop as a space-saving computer system

Unlike with desktops, you don't have to build a tabletop shrine to your laptop computer — that is, you don't need a computer desk. If space is tight where you live or work, store the laptop on the shelf or in a drawer. Then set it up on the kitchen table or coffee table whenever you're ready to work. Forget about the constant mess and clutter that orbit the typical desktop computer station. Viva Adam Osborne!

Get a laptop as a second computer

Why buy a second desktop computer when you can get a laptop and enjoy not only the presence of a second computer but also the ability to make that computer system portable? Furthermore, you can network the two computers, allowing them to share the Internet connection and printers as well as each other's data and files. And you still have the luxury of having one system that's portable.

Take the laptop on the road

Laptops let you take your work on the road. After a few moments of *synching* (transferring current files between your desktop and laptop, covered in Chapter 19), you're off and running to anywhere you like — although being in direct sunlight can make it difficult to see the laptop screen.

When you return from your "road warrior" trip, you perform another sync and both computers get all caught up for the day.

Mr. Laptop goes to college

Setting up a computer in a college dorm room in the 1980s was the sure sign of being a nerd. Today, not setting up a laptop computer in a college dorm room is the sure sign of being a social outcast. I implore future students to pester their parental units early — say, starting in the seventh grade — to ensure that they leave for college armed with the best portable computing power possible.

No, I'm not being silly. Some colleges *require* students to arrive with laptops in tow. Those institutions may even publish laptop guides so that campus compatibility is guaranteed and

issues such as viruses and spyware are dealt with before classes start. My advice: Follow those guidelines. Look for a laptop based on the school's recommendations. But there's still more you need to do.

Be sure to prepare a college-bound laptop for the onslaught of malware. See Chapter 17 for vital information about laptop security. Also see Chapter 21 for dealing with another college laptop issue: theft. You've probably spent a lot of time preparing for college; you should prepare the laptop for college as well.

- ✔ Laptops let you escape the confines of your office and work anywhere you like for a few hours. Or, if there's power at your location, you can plug in and work all day.

- ✔ The laptop lets you take your work with you when you travel. It lets you experience the reality of using a computer on an airplane (which isn't as cool as it sounds).

Why you don't need a laptop

Laptops aren't cheap. They're also expensive to fix. Forget about upgrading the hardware. They can easily get stolen. The battery life never lives up to the printed specifications. It's tough to get work done on a jet or in a café unless you're really, really motivated to do so — *ack!* But these are minor quibbles.

You can dither about whether to get a laptop or a tablet, à la the iPad. It's a legitimate debate: If all you want to do is read e-mail, browse the web, engage in the social networking thing, take pictures, watch films, or listen to music, you don't need a laptop. Sure, the laptop can do all that, but if you don't plan to create anything or do anything else requiring a full-on PC, get a tablet instead.

Or you can get a convertible laptop, or Tablet PC, as covered in Chapter 8. Bottom line: With a laptop, you have far more options for the future. It gives you light weight, long battery life, and increasing computing power. Laptops make ideal computers for just about anyone. If you don't own a laptop now, you will someday.

Laptop Shopping

The best computer you can buy is the one that does what you need it to do. To find this computer, you have to familiarize yourself with some issues and deliberately ignore others.

Things to ignore when buying a laptop

When it comes to spending your money on a useful computer, especially a laptop, feel free to ignore these items:

Slick marketing campaigns: You'll never be as cool as the person in the ad, no matter how much effort you put into it. All laptops are tools, and they should be judged by whether they offer features that you need, not by how nifty their advertising looks.

Brand name: Too many people consider brand name first and don't even know which components they need. Similarly, you don't need to buy a laptop from the same manufacturer as the one who made your desktop PC. As long as the laptop runs the software you need, you're fine.

Low price: An abundance of cheap laptops are available. In haste, you may buy a laptop, thinking that you're getting a deal — but get stuck with a brick instead.

High price: It's easy to be duped into believing that the most expensive laptop is the best. Buying too much is not a wise buying decision.

Internal expansion: Rare is the laptop with upgradable hardware or external expansion options. Because of that, you need to know ahead of time what you plan to do with the laptop (which software you'll run) so that you can buy all the hardware you need at one time. That way, your laptop will serve you for a good, long time.

Things to heed when buying a laptop

In addition to all the regular hardware that comes with a computer (see the following section), you need to consider four key items when choosing a laptop:

Weight: Nearly all laptops weigh between 2 and 7 pounds. The heavier laptops, the notebooks, have more features, such as a larger display or a numeric keypad next to the keyboard. The lighter models, or ultrabooks, don't necessarily have fewer features; they might actually have more light-weight or advanced features, which makes them more expensive. The exception is the netbook, which weighs less on purpose but lacks many standard laptop features, such as an optical drive.

Size: Most laptops are less than 1-inch thick and about as tall and wide as a small coffee-table book. Ultrabooks are thin. Netbooks are the smallest.

Display: Recently, manufacturers have discovered that people love the larger LCD display on a laptop — even though the larger display adds to the laptop's size and weight (and consumes more battery power). For a laptop being used at one location and only rarely going on the road, a huge display is wonderful. If you want portability, though, and a longer battery life, consider a smaller display.

Battery life: Despite their manufacturers' claims, most laptops run anywhere from three to five hours unplugged. Netbooks hold the record, with some of them lasting as long as six hours. Regardless, it's possible and necessary to manage the laptop's power; see Chapters 10 and 26.

- ✔ Stuff that's important to the overall weight of the laptop — the power brick and cord, extra batteries, portable storage, and other gizmos — aren't included in the basic tonnage calculation. Keep these items in mind when weight is important to you.

- ✔ Tablet PCs are thicker than standard laptops because of the extra circuitry required for their touchscreen displays. See Chapter 8.

- ✔ If you desire both a large display and portability, consider getting an external monitor for your laptop. That way, you can enjoy the big, roomy screen when the laptop is at your workstation and still have the portability you need when taking the laptop on the road.

- ✔ A popular trick that's used to make the battery life seem longer is to specify the time used by two batteries. On some laptops, you can swap a drained battery with a fresh one, thereby extending your portable time. Although there's nothing wrong with this trick, the extended battery time shouldn't be used for comparison, *and* the extra battery's weight needs to be added to the total laptop weight.

Software for Your Laptop

A computer system is composed of two parts: hardware and software. When you buy a new computer, you probably pay more attention to the hardware. That's understandable, but it isn't the reason you bought the computer: Computers exist to run *software*. If you want a laptop computer that does everything you need, I recommend looking for software first and then finding hardware to match that software.

The operating system

The main program that controls your laptop is the *operating system*. It's the computer's brain, giving the laptop its personality and giving you, the human, a way to control the computer.

On the majority of PC laptops, the operating system is Microsoft Windows. This book covers Windows 8, Windows 7, and Windows Vista. Because some netbooks are sold with Windows XP, that operating system is covered as well.

- ✔ There's no special Windows laptop version. Windows has features specific to your laptop or Tablet PC, but otherwise it's the same Windows you would use on a desktop computer system.

- ✔ See Chapter 7 for more information on Windows.

- ✔ If you're daring, you can consider another operating system for your laptop, such as Linux. Installing this operating system is a task you may need to do yourself, which is technical and potentially frustrating. If you want to use Linux on your laptop, either buy the laptop with Linux preinstalled or have one of your Linux nerd friends do the installation for you — and reward that person handsomely so that they will be available to you in the future when you need help.

Other software

Laptop computers run the same software as desktop computers. Most major computer applications, such as Microsoft Office, are commonly used on laptops and might even come preinstalled. Just about everything you can run on a desktop PC runs on a laptop.

✔ Laptops are okay for playing computer games, but you need to ensure that your laptop has the graphics horsepower to run high-end computer games, such as *Call of Duty* or *Mass Effect*.

✔ If you plan to run graphics editing programs, get a laptop with a high-end video card, larger display, and lots of memory.

✔ If you plan to edit video on your laptop, you need the maximum amount of hard drive storage; videos use a lot of computer storage.

✔ Also see Chapter 9 for information on installing new programs, as well as removing some of those "free" programs that are included on a new laptop.

Laptop Hardware Buying Decisions

In the balance between computer hardware and software, it's the software that determines what type of hardware, and how much of it, you need. After you know what the software needs, choosing the matching hardware is a snap. This section describes some hardware considerations for buying a new laptop.

Important laptop hardware guts

Beyond weight, size, and battery issues are four core parts of a computer that play a special role in choosing a laptop:

Processor: Spend the extra money to invest in a fast processor. Doing so extends the useful life of your laptop by ensuring that you can run tomorrow's software before tomorrow comes, but not before yesterday. You'll be thankful later.

Memory: *Memory* is where the action happens in a computer, where the work gets done. Not having enough memory in your laptop limits its performance. Having enough (or way too much) memory makes Mr. Laptop very happy indeed.

Mass storage: The mass storage device is the electronic closet where the laptop stores your stuff. The mass storage device is either the traditional *hard drive* or a *solid-state drive* (SSD). It must have room for the computer's operating system, all the software you get and later install, all the data files and junk you collect, plus room (lotsa room) to grow.

Optical disc: Most notebooks feature an optical drive, capable of using CDs and DVDs and maybe even Blu-Ray discs. Ultrabooks lack optical drives, which add weight and bulk to their sleek design. Netbooks also lack optical drives, mostly to save cost. The lack of an optical drive shouldn't be discouraging, though; external optical drives are available for when you need them.

✔ The *processor* is the main chip inside a computer. It's not the computer's "brain." The computer's brain is the software you run. No, the processor is more like the computer's muscle.

✔ Laptop processors are more expensive than their desktop counterparts. That's because laptop processors must be designed to use less power and generate less heat. That takes time, so their development cycle is longer; hence the added cost.

✔ How do you know how much memory or storage is enough? Easy: Look at the software you want to use. For example, if the software states that it wants 2GB of memory, get a laptop with at least that much memory. If the software requires at least 100GB of disk space, factor that amount into your laptop's mass storage capacity requirements.

✔ If you cannot afford a faster processor, get more RAM.

✔ The things that consume huge amounts of hard drive storage space are graphics image files (such as digital photographs), music or audio files, and video files. If you plan to collect any of these files on your laptop, get a humongous hard drive!

✔ I recommend a laptop with at least 160GB of mass storage. If you need more storage, you'll have to go with a traditional hard drive because high-capacity SSDs are expensive.

✔ By investing in the latest, fastest processor, lots of RAM, and copious amounts of mass storage now, you're extending the life of your laptop. That's a good thing. You want your laptop investment to last for years. Pay more now, and you earn it back down the road, when you're still using your laptop while others are forced to buy a new one.

✔ Your laptop needs a multi-touch display to get the most from Windows 8. A single-point display is okay, but you need a five-point display for Windows 8. (The number of *points* refers to how many fingers at a time can be detected touching the screen.)

✔ GB is the acronym for *gigabyte*. It means 1 billion characters of computer storage. A GB is approximately 1,000MB. MB is the acronym for megabyte, or 1 million characters of computer storage. One MB stores about one minute of music or a 3-by-4-inch digital photo of low quality.

Communications choices

Your laptop must have gizmos that quench its communications thirst. This includes several, if not all, of the following items:

Modem: It's the traditional telecommunications device, not a broadband or satellite modem. Notebooks and Tablet PCs come with dialup modems, but some ultralights and netbooks do not. Discover how to use the modem in Chapter 16.

Networking: As with desktops, every laptop comes with a standard networking hole, called an *Ethernet port* by people who want to win that green pie slice in a game of *Trivial Pursuit.* General networking information is in Chapter 13.

Wireless networking: It's a given that your laptop must come with some type of wireless Ethernet adapter. The current wireless networking standard is 802.11g or 802.11n. You can read more about this topic in Chapter 14.

The green laptop

As human beings, it is our duty to be good stewards of the environment. Though everyone's favorite mom (that would be Mother Earth) doesn't need a computer, you can be wise about how you spend the planet's resources when you make your laptop buying decision. I have two issues to discuss: power usage and materials.

In power usage, laptops have always been ahead of the computer desktop curve when it comes to getting the most from our planet's energy resources. See Chapter 10 for information on power management.

Beyond power usage, you can check the greenness of your laptop's materials: Some laptops are designed from environmentally friendly materials or at least contain no lead, mercury, plutonium, or other poisonous materials. Even better, some laptops are designed to be recycled. The only way to know is to check with the manufacturer; they love boasting about such things.

Service, Support, and Warranty

The issue of service and support is much more important for a laptop than for a desktop computer. A laptop is a unit. It lacks the components of a desktop. As such, it's not an item that just anyone can fix. Off-the-shelf replacement parts can't simply be found in the Nerd Bin at Fry's Electronics.

To ensure that you start out your laptop experience on the best foot possible, I have three recommendations.

First, determine where your laptop will be repaired. Odds are good that it won't be in the back room at the local Mega Price Mart where you purchased the thing. The laptop will probably take a trip through the mail. If that's not what you want, ensure that you buy an on-site support option when you buy the laptop. (Yes, some manufacturers offer this service.)

Second, research how the support for your laptop is offered. Most manufacturers offer phone support. Is it good? Terrible? In your native tongue? Maybe a superior support option is available for an extra price. If you need it, buy it.

Finally, definitely get a long-term warranty with your laptop. Most manufacturers offer a standard one-year warranty — I recommend at least a three-year warranty. That's because when the laptop breaks, generally the *entire unit* must be replaced. That's not cheap!

- Some manufacturers offer you a replacement laptop by way of mail-in service while yours is being fixed. That's a bonus.

- A lack of service and support is one reason that some dealers (and large department stores and discount houses) offer laptops at ridiculously cheap prices. Don't ever expect the employees in such a place to be able to help you, and the guy who cuts meat in the back can't fix your laptop, either.

- Avoid the service contract! It's not the same thing as a warranty. A service contract is basically a way for the big box store to make *even more* money from suckers. The extended warranty that I recommend you purchase will cover your laptop just fine and dandy. The service contract is a waste of money.

The Final Step: Buying Your Laptop

When you're ready to buy your laptop, buy it!

Don't sit and wait for a better deal or a lower price. You can *always* find a better deal and a lower price. Hardware gets better and better. The price always comes down. Therefore, when you're ready to buy, take the plunge and buy! Waiting gets you nowhere.

If possible, pay for your laptop by using a credit card. The law offers far more protection to credit card users than to people who pay by check or — don't even think about it — cash.

Part II
Say Hello to Your Laptop

The 5th Wave   By Rich Tennant

"Okay, have we all signed in on our Tablet PCs? Good. I see we have Barge, Teabag, Dink, and Boob with us today."

In this part . . .

For all its promise, computer technology hasn't yet reached the point where your laptop pops out of its box and bounds — happy and cheerful and ready to use — into your lap. Even if you've seen such a thing on a television commercial (or secretly dreamed of it), it just isn't going to happen in real life. That doesn't mean that the laptop is being rude — it's just that the laptop-human thing is still a partnership. The laptop has things to do, and you have things to do. Consider this part of the book as that to-do list in addition to a formal introduction to your laptop.

Chapter 3

The Out-of-the-Box Experience

After being awarded a huge government grant, scientists have proven that any computer works best when you first remove it from its shipping box. Yes, I was surprised. Even more so, I was surprised that removing a laptop from its box and setting the thing up can be more of an ordeal than you would otherwise believe. After opening many such boxes, and experiencing the pain and frustrating anguish of not knowing what to do next, I sat down and wrote this chapter. The goal: to get a laptop computer out of its box and into your lap.

Basic Box Unpacking

I write this section with the full knowledge that it's probably too late: The box that your laptop came in is open. The foam packing material has been removed. Plastic has been peeled off. The laptop most likely sits in front of you. Great! Now you can get to the real point of this section: things to observe and pay attention to regarding that box and all the goodies inside.

✔ When you're lucky enough to find instructions on how to unpack the box, heed them! I refer specifically to labels such as Open Other Side and Remove First.

✔ Be sure to open and free the packing slip if it's attached to the outside of the box. The slip contains the shipping invoice, which you should examine to confirm that what was shipped is exactly what you ordered. If the packing slip isn't on the outside of the box, look for it on the inside.

✔ Always open computer equipment boxes with your hands. Never use a box cutter, because you can slice into something important.

✔ Beware of those big, ugly staples often used to close cardboard boxes. They can go a-flyin' when you rip things open, poking out eyeballs or just lying in wait on the floor for a bare foot.

✔ Be sure to look for boxes within boxes. Also be on the lookout for items stuck in the sides or ends of the foam packing material.

✔ Do not eat the foam packing material. When people say that rice cakes taste like foam packing material, they're being facetious.

✔ Fill out warranty and registration cards only after you're certain that the laptop works.

Step-by-step unpacking directions

Laptops, like all computers, come with lots of bits and pieces. Some of that stuff isn't junk, and you want to keep it for as long as you own the laptop. Other stuff is junk, and you can throw it away. The problem: It's difficult to determine what's worth keeping and what to toss. My advice is to keep everything for now.

Here's a handy way to approach this unpacking and pre-setup stage of your laptop's introduction to your lap:

1. **Unpack the laptop.**

   Remove the laptop from any plastic bag or shrink-wrap. Don't worry about opening the laptop's lid yet (though the temptation may be great). Just set the thing on a table by itself. When you do this, say "There."

2. **Find all the various hardware pieces that came with the laptop.**

   Look for the power adapter, power cord, battery, extra batteries (if any), cables, connectors, weird, tiny gizmos that you'll probably lose eventually, and other mystery junk.

   A handy trend for many manufacturers is to include a "road map" with the laptop. It's often the first thing you find when you open the box. Unfold the map to see a visual guide to your laptop, including setup directions.

3. **Make a pile for any optical discs that came with the laptop.**

   Some laptops come with discs; most don't. The discs may contain programs that are already installed or ready for installation. Some discs might contain *device drivers* or special software required to run your laptop's hardware. Plus, you may see an operating system disc or a system recovery disc. These discs are important!

Ultrabooks, netbooks, and other laptops that lack optical drives probably don't come with optical discs. (If they do, consider it a big plus.)

4. Make a pile for all the paperwork.

There are four categories of paperwork: manual, warranty, special offer, and weird piece of paper, the importance of which cannot be determined.

5. Place all packing material back into the box.

This material includes plastic bags, twist-ties from the cables, and those silica pouches they tell you not to eat (probably because the stuff inside would give you superhuman powers).

Later, after your laptop is all set up and you're starting to become familiar with it, you can further organize the detritus from the box. As you work, you need to keep various items with the laptop at all times — for example, the power cord, extra batteries, and other objects, depending on how you use the laptop. You need a place, such as a laptop case, for those items.

Other stuff that comes with your laptop you might want to keep for as long as you own the laptop, such as discs and manuals. These things don't need to stay with the laptop all the time, so storing them in a drawer or on a shelf is okay.

Only after using the laptop for a while should you consider throwing stuff away, such as the special-offer cards you don't need. Often times, you can just toss those things in the laptop box. See the next section to find out what to do with the box.

- ✓ If the laptop comes with a how-to manual, consider yourself lucky. Most laptops have no how-to material whatsoever.

- ✓ Sometimes, the only manuals that come with the laptop are directories listing the locations where you can get it fixed. Sometimes, that material is in English.

- ✓ Software discs are included even though the software may already be installed on the laptop. Don't toss away the discs! They were given to you so that you can reinstall the software, if you need to.

- ✓ See Chapter 20 for information on finding the best laptop case. Even though your laptop may come with a genuine imitation-leatherette case, you want to see what else is out there.

- ✓ I have a shelf in my office where I store important material that comes with every computer I own. Each computer has its own container, and each container holds all the stuff included with the computer that I want to keep: spare parts and manuals and other documentation. I suggest that you have a similar shelf or location for a container or special box for your laptop's extra stuff.

"How long should I keep the box?"

I recommend keeping the box and the packing material for as long as you own the laptop. That way, if you need to ship the laptop to a repair center or return it to the dealer, you have the original box.

When the laptop dies, you can then bury it in its original box, throwing out both at the same time or using them for recycling purposes.

- ✔ Many dealers and repair centers accept only laptops packed in their original boxes.

- ✔ You might actually have *two* boxes: the laptop box and the shipping box that the laptop box comes in. Feel free to toss out or recycle the shipping box.

- ✔ If you don't have the original box, you can order another one — but why pay for it when you can just save the original?

- ✔ Where possible, either recycle your old laptop or dispose of it properly, per the recycling or waste disposal guidelines in your community. Rarely should you throw a laptop in the trash.

- ✔ No, you don't need to pack the laptop in a box when you take it on the road; slipping the laptop into a briefcase or any quality carrying case is fine for that purpose. You need the boxes only if you plan to mail or ship the laptop.

When to send in the warranty

Wait a week to ensure that the laptop works and that you have everything you ordered. When you're satisfied, fill out and send in the warranty card. Or, as is popular today, fill out the warranty or registration (or both) online. Often, doing so is part of the setup process you complete when you first turn on the laptop. (See the next section.)

- ✔ When you order a computer directly from the manufacturer, you usually don't need to fill in and return a warranty card.

- ✔ In some cases, filling out and returning the warranty card sets the start date for the warranty period. Otherwise, the warranty may start on the day the laptop was manufactured, which could have been three months ago! Read the card to be sure.

Set Up Your Laptop

All laptops have a generic look to them. At first glance, you might even say that all laptops look alike. Even so, they have subtle differences. Anyone who replaces an older laptop with a newer model probably recognizes instantly that the power button isn't in exactly the same place. The optical drive may be on the right, left, or front of the laptop — or not even there!

When your laptop has come with specific setup directions, follow them. If not, or in addition to those directions, follow the information in this section to get your laptop all set up and ready for use.

Find a place for the laptop

Yes, you can put the laptop in your lap. But what happens to your lap when you stand up?

Ah-ha!

Unlike desktop PCs, laptops can go anywhere or be put anywhere. No wonder they're popular! With a fully charged battery, your laptop has a home wherever you are. Beyond that, you can place your laptop anywhere you like: on the kitchen table, the coffee table, a real desk, or a computer desk — or in bed with you.

Here are some general laptop-location tips:

- ✔ Use the laptop on a flat, steady surface.

- ✔ Yep: Your lap is not a flat, steady surface. It's okay for short spells, but, otherwise, I recommend that you find something more stable.

- ✔ The flat surface is a must: The laptop has air vents to help keep it cool. Setting the laptop on a pillow or another nonflat surface makes the laptop run hotter than it should.

- ✔ Keep the laptop away from the sun, if possible. Heat isn't good for any computer, and you can't see the screen in direct sunlight (or else you'll waste battery power turning up the screen brightness level).

- ✔ Likewise, use your laptop in a well-ventilated area. Don't cover the laptop while it's on.

- ✔ Keep Mr. Laptop away from, or out of spilling range of, any drinks or food you might be consuming.

✔ If possible, try to find a place to plug in the laptop while you use it.

✔ Have a place to store your laptop when it's not in use: in a drawer or on a shelf. Keeping it in the same place means that you can always find it when you need it.

✔ Although you can use the laptop anywhere, be aware of ergonomics! For example, when you're using the laptop on a coffee table, if you start to feel a pain in your back from hunching over, stop! Find a better, more comfortable place to work.

Charge the battery!

Your laptop may or may not have a fully-charged battery when you first take it out of the box. Therefore, one of the things you need to do after finding a place for the laptop is to install and charge the battery.

If necessary, insert the battery into the laptop. Plug in or attach the battery per the directions that came with the laptop or, quite handily, etched into the bottom of the laptop case.

After installing the battery, plug in the laptop, as illustrated in Figure 3-1.

Attach the power cord to the laptop's back or side: The power cord connector may be color-coded yellow. The yellow hole is where the power cord plugs in.

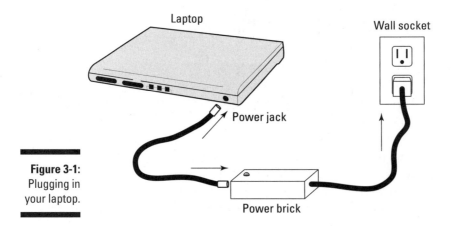

Figure 3-1:
Plugging in
your laptop.

Attach the power cord to the power brick, if necessary. Plug the power brick into the wall. Note that the power brick may also contain the plug that connects directly to the wall.

That's it. The laptop's battery is now charging. Yes, the battery charges even when the laptop's power is off.

- ✔ Every laptop has a different method for inserting, installing, or attaching its battery. Clues can be found on the laptop's case or on the battery itself. You might even find an instruction sheet, but don't count on it.

- ✔ Quite a few ultrabooks and netbooks don't come with removable batteries.

- ✔ It usually takes a few hours to charge a laptop's battery. The length of time depends on the type of battery and power management hardware and on whether you're using the laptop at the time. Even so:

- ✔ The good news is that you can start using your laptop right away — just keep it plugged in so that the battery can charge.

- ✔ Refer to Chapter 10 for more information on using the laptop's battery and power-management system.

"Should I plug the laptop into a UPS?"

I advise my desktop computer readers in *PCs For Dummies* (John Wiley & Sons, Inc.) to consider investing in an uninterruptible power supply, or UPS — specifically, one with both surge and spike protection. This device serves to protect the computer from nasty intruders that can come through the power lines and to provide emergency power if the electricity goes bye-bye.

A UPS for a laptop is unnecessary. The main reason is that your laptop already has a battery for backup power. If you're running your laptop from an electrical outlet and the electricity goes off (or some doofus unplugs it), the laptop quickly and happily switches its power source to the internal battery. Nothing is lost!

- ✔ Although you don't need a UPS for your laptop, I still highly recommend plugging your portable 'puter into a power strip that has surge protection and line filtering. Such a gizmo helps keep your laptop's power source clean and steady.

- ✔ Generally speaking, if a lightning storm is nearby, don't plug your laptop (power, network, or phone cord) into the wall unless you're using a spike protection filter. If you aren't, just run the laptop from its battery until the storm passes.

What to Do Next

My guess is that after setting up your laptop, you'll want to turn it on and see how it works. That's understandable, but it's a separate task from unpacking the laptop, so I've put that information in Chapter 4. Here are some other spots in the book you should consider visiting to help start out your laptop journey on the proper foot:

- ✔ You can find information in Chapter 4 about turning off the laptop. Turning it off can be an interesting adventure, especially if you've never used a battery-powered computer.

- ✔ Chapter 6 helps you overview the various parts of your laptop.

- ✔ For a Tablet PC, check Chapter 8 to review the special tablet features.

- ✔ Power management on a portable computer is a big deal, so consider putting Chapter 10 on your homework reading list.

- ✔ Whether you're new to the concept of wireless networking or just eager to set things up, visit Chapter 14. There you find a rundown of the basic wireless networking ordeal for a laptop computer.

- ✔ Before taking your laptop on the road, read Chapter 20, which covers a few nifty things you might want to consider before you venture out into the cold, cruel world with your new computer companion.

Chapter 4

To Turn On a Laptop

. . . .

In This Chapter

▶ Opening the laptop's lid

▶ Finding the power button

▶ Turning on the laptop

▶ Logging in to Windows

▶ Observing the Windows desktop

. . . .

Oh, please! How tough can it be to turn on a laptop computer? Do I really need to write an entire chapter on the topic? Apparently so.

There's more to turning on a laptop computer than simply flipping a switch. First, it's not a switch: It's a *power button*. Second, the power button is typically under the lid, which is something you're not used to if you're a desktop PC user. Finally, you need to contend with Windows. That's too much information for a sentence to convey, more than a paragraph can hold, and with lovely illustrations, more than a few pages can handle. Yes, it's a chapter — *this* chapter, about turning on your laptop computer.

Turn On Your Laptop

Turning on a laptop computer involves four steps: Open the lid, adjust the lid for optimal viewing, find the power button, and then push the power button. This section explains the details. Yes, there are details.

Step 1: Open the lid

Of all the laptops I've owned, it seems that no two open the same way. Sometimes there's a latch, sometimes there's no latch. Sometimes there are two latches. The latches may be in front or on the sides. The latch may be a slider or a button. Use Figure 4-1 as your guide to finding the latch.

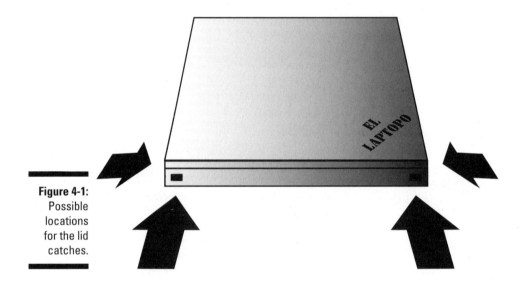

Figure 4-1:
Possible
locations
for the lid
catches.

After you find the latch, you press or slide it to release the lid. Or when there's no latch, simply lift the lid.

- ✔ The front side of the laptop is the side opposite the lid's hinge.

- ✔ You can configure the laptop to remain on when the lid is closed — for example, when you're using the laptop with an external monitor, a keyboard, or a mouse. See Chapter 12 for details.

- ✔ Some laptops allow you to play a music CD when the lid is closed, and they even sport special buttons to control the CD player.

- ✔ It's possible to leave the laptop on or off with the lid open. If so, continue with Step 2 in the following section.

Step 2: Adjust the lid for optimal viewing

Raise the lid to an angle best suited for viewing; use Figure 4-2 as your guide.

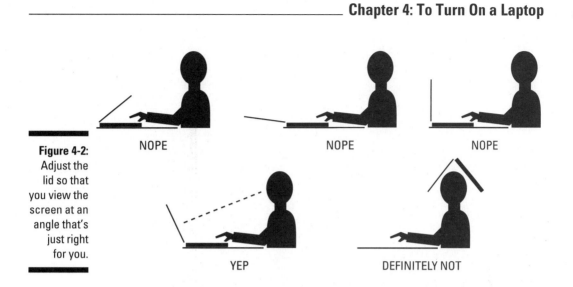

Figure 4-2:
Adjust the
lid so that
you view the
screen at an
angle that's
just right
for you.

NOPE   NOPE   NOPE

YEP   DEFINITELY NOT

Tablet PCs might allow you to open, twist, and reset the lid so that the monitor faces up when you lay the laptop flat. Hey! That's like a tablet! See Chapter 8 for more Tablet PC information.

Employees at the Apple Store adjust the lids on all the demo laptops to precisely 70 degrees. The idea isn't to present the laptop at the perfect viewing angle but to encourage potential buyers to touch the machine by adjusting the lid.

Step 3: Locate the power button

Laptop designers have grown adept at hiding or masking the power button. I've seen it on the side of older laptops, though to keep the computer from being turned on inside a briefcase, most manufacturers now put the power button inside the laptop, up near the lid hinge. Look for it there.

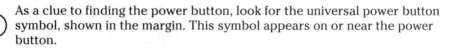 As a clue to finding the power button, look for the universal power button symbol, shown in the margin. This symbol appears on or near the power button.

✔ Sometimes, the symbol is different from the circle/slash icon, shown in the margin: The symbol can be a solid dot, a line-and-a-circle for On and Off, respectively, or, occasionally, the crescent moon symbol.

✔ The power button may be a spring-slide switch that you must push in one direction and then release.

✔ Some power buttons are tiny push buttons, or what I call *press-and-pray* buttons. There's no click or bump to the button's feel; you press it in with your finger and then pray that the laptop obeys you.

✔ On a Tablet PC, the power button is most likely located on the monitor. That way, it can be accessed when the monitor is folded flat, when the laptop is in Tablet mode. In that case, look for a special power-button lock. The lock prevents the power button from being punched accidentally when the tablet laptop is in full Tablet mode.

✔ Some laptops have both a power button and a crescent moon button. In that case, the moon button is most likely the *sleep* button.

✔ You can put a red-dot sticker near the power button's location, in case the button is easy to overlook. Even so, I find that after opening the case and turning on the system a few times, I remember where the button is. Of course, this doesn't help you use anyone else's laptop, because the power button is never in the same location twice.

Step 4: Punch the power button

To turn on your laptop, press the power button.

Sometimes, you can turn on the laptop by opening the lid. Sometimes, you can *wake up* a laptop by tapping a key on the keyboard. Whether these tricks work depends on how the laptop was shut down. But for all intents and purposes, punching the power button does the job most of the time.

✔ It's a *power button,* not an On–Off switch.

✔ If nothing happens when you punch the button, the battery is most likely dead: Plug the laptop into a wall socket by using its AC adapter cord (or module or power-brick thing).

✔ Check all power cables! The power brick may wiggle loose from the wall socket cable.

✔ When everything is plugged in and nothing happens, you have a problem. Contact your dealer or laptop manufacturer for assistance.

It's Windows!

When your laptop starts up, you see some initial messages and perhaps a logo or graphic, and then the computer's *operating system* — its main program — comes to life. For nearly all PC laptops, this program is Windows.

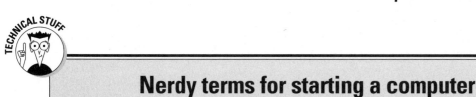

Nerdy terms for starting a computer

Despite years of effort to come up with better words, the computer industry continues to use antique and obscure jargon to say, "Start the computer." Among the lingo, you find these terms:

boot: To turn the thing on, or to "pull it up by its bootstraps." In fact, *bootstrap* is an even older version of this term. *Boot* is the oldest and most mysterious computer term.

cold boot: To turn on the computer when it has been off for a while. *See also* warm boot.

cycle power: To turn off the computer, wait a few seconds and then turn it on again. This process is often required when you're trying to fix something.

Das Boot: Not a computer term; rather, the title of a German film about a World War II U-boat.

power up, power on: More human terms for "Turn on the computer."

restart, reboot, reset: To shut down a computer and then start it without turning off the power.

start, turn on, switch on: Additional human terms for "Turn on the computer."

warm boot: Another term for *restart, reboot,* or *reset.*

The version of Windows that's used on laptops is identical to the one that's used on desktop computers. Extra options are included for laptops, specifically for power management and battery monitoring. Plus, other utilities and fun junk may have been installed by the laptop manufacturer. Otherwise, it's the same Windows you know and hate.

✔ This book covers the popular versions of Windows, which includes Windows 7 — plus, a little Windows Vista and even some Windows XP. It also covers unpopular versions of Windows, which at this time includes only Windows 8.

✔ Chapter 7 covers a few of the places in Windows that laptop computer owners should be familiar with.

✔ Messages may appear before Windows starts, especially when the laptop was improperly shut down or the laptop's battery expired the last time you used it. These messages are expected as the laptop recovers from mishaps and improper shutdowns.

Running Windows for the first time

When you first turn on a brand-new laptop, Windows completes some gyrations and prompts you to set up and configure some system settings. These include items such as the language you'll use on the laptop (I'm guessing English), the time zone, and your name. It's routine computer housekeeping stuff.

You're also prompted to create a *user profile* for yourself, which includes an account name and a password.

After you answer the questions, Windows is fully installed. More configuration may be necessary, such as specifying networking options and customizing the Windows environment. You can mess with these options later.

✔ When you're asked to create user accounts, create only one, for yourself. Don't bother creating them yet for every member of the whole fam-damily as well as for your pets. You can do that later, and then only when other people *really* need to use the laptop.

✔ The main Windows account is known as *Administrator.* This account is the one that's used to modify the computer, add new software, and tend to other administrative chores. Even when you don't intend it, when you're the only person using the computer, *you* are the administrator.

✔ Do not forget the administrator's password! The password cannot be recovered if it's lost.

✔ Entering an organization name is optional, though it's fun to specify fictitious or "borrowed" organizations, such as KGB or MI6.

✔ See Chapter 21 for more information on passwords and Windows security issues.

Activating Windows

Soon after you complete the initial setup, you're asked to "activate" Windows. Activation requires an Internet connection so that your laptop can chat with the Microsoft mothership. The purpose behind activation is to ensure that your laptop is running a legitimate copy of Windows. If it isn't, or if you elect not to activate, Windows won't function on your laptop. My advice: Activate when prompted.

Logging in to Windows

After the initial setup, and every time you start your laptop after that, you're greeted with the graphical fun and folly of the Windows operating system.

The first step is to log in to Windows. *Log in* is computer jargon for identifying yourself to the warden, er, to Windows. It involves supplying a user account name and a password to verify that you are who you claim to be.

In Windows 8, you see the lock screen when you first turn on your laptop. You need to summon the login screen, which is done by swiping upward on a touchscreen monitor or by tapping any key on the keyboard.

If you're the only person using your computer, the *login screen* appears with your account picture on it, similar to the one shown in Figure 4-3. Type your password in the box. Press Enter. When the stars are aligned in your favor, you're granted access to Windows. Otherwise, choose your picture from the list, and then type your password.

User account picture   User account name   Type password.

Dan Gookin
dangookin@live.com

Figure 4-3:
The
Windows 8
login
screen.

Accessibility options   Shutdown options

Figure 4-3 illustrates the Windows 8 login screen. In earlier versions of Windows, the login screen (or *Welcome screen*) is similar.

  ✔ The Accessibility Options button (shown in Figure 4-3) displays options for folks needing physical assistance when using the laptop.

  ✔ The Shutdown options button in the lower-right corner of the screen displays a menu with various choices for turning off the laptop. See Chapter 5 for a description of these options.

✔ The term *log on* means to identify yourself. A *logon* is the name of your account or the word you use to log on.

✔ The terms *log in* and *login* can be used instead of *log on* and *logon.* They did that just to keep you confused.

✔ By the way, it's *log,* as in *to write down.* It has nothing to do with timber.

Logging in to Windows in unusual ways

One Windows quagmire is that it offers several different ways to do the same thing. In the case of logging in to the computer, there are multiple ways as well, most of which I encourage you to ignore. So stop reading now if you value your sanity.

If your laptop comes with a fingerprint reader, you can use it to identify yourself: Simply swipe your finger (or thumb) over the reader bar, or press your finger or thumb into the reader. That's all you need to do.

In Windows 8, you can also log in by using a PIN or by swiping a touchscreen (if your laptop has one) over an image, or *picture password,* that you select. The PIN method is easy: Just type in your secret number. The touchscreen method requires you to smear the screen with your finger: Touch the screen in the manner you specified earlier, when you configured the picture password.

✔ To set a PIN or picture password for your Windows 8 laptop, go to the PC Settings screen and choose the Users item. See Chapter 7 for information about the PC Settings screen.

✔ I find the traditional password method of locking a laptop to be the most secure.

✔ When your laptop lacks a fingerprint reader, you can buy a handy, external, USB fingerprint reader.

✔ All fingerprint readers must be trained. After you initially set up Windows, software specific to your laptop's fingerprint reader is used to configure it. Configuration must be done before you can use the fingerprint reader to log in to your laptop. It also sets a finger as the "proper" one to use as a login ID.

✔ Yes, the fingerprint reader works whether your finger is attached or not. And, yes, you watch too many spy movies.

✔ A fingerprint reader is a *biometric* device.

Introducing the Windows 8 Start screen

Unlike earlier Windows versions, Windows 8 splashes up the Start screen after you log in. A typical Start screen is shown in Figure 4-4. You can click or touch a tile on the Start screen to run a program. The screen can be scrolled right or left, as illustrated in the figure.

Swipe screen to scroll.

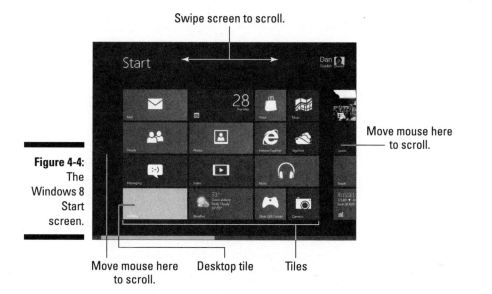

Move mouse here to scroll.

Figure 4-4: The Windows 8 Start screen.

Move mouse here to scroll.   Desktop tile   Tiles

Traditional Windows programs are started from the desktop, which is covered in the next section. To display the desktop, touch the desktop tile, shown in Figure 4-4.

- ✔ You scroll the Start screen by moving the mouse to the far left or far right edge of the Start screen. You can also use your finger to *swipe* the screen left or right, as long as your laptop has a touchscreen.

- ✔ Some Tablet PCs require that you use a stylus to swipe the screen.

- ✔ See Chapter 7 for more discussion on Windows features, such as the Start screen in Windows 8.

Beholding the desktop

The desktop is the traditional place where Windows programs lurk, the spot where you get your work done. Windows 8 is trying to change that, but for now the desktop is where the action is, as shown in Figure 4-5.

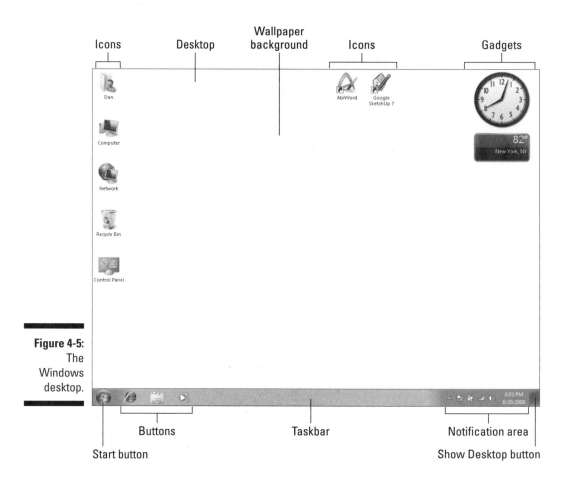

Figure 4-5:
The
Windows
desktop.

There are a few important things to note on the desktop, as illustrated in
Figure 4-5. Here are the ones you should pay attention to:

- **The desktop:** This area is the starting point for your adventures in
  Windows. The main screen. Home plate.

- **Wallpaper, or background:** The wallpaper is the image you see on the
  desktop, or it may be a solid color, such as the famous polar-bear-in-a-
  snowstorm photo used in Figure 4-5. You change the background when
  the mood hits you; see Chapter 7.

- **Icons:** These tiny pictures represent files, folders, or programs.

- **Gadgets:** These tiny programs that float on the desktop serve to distract
  you from getting work done. In Windows Vista, the gadgets appeared
  in the Sidebar area of the desktop, on one side of the screen. (Refer to
  Figure 4-5.)

✔ **The Start button:** This button is the main control on the desktop. Clicking the Start button pops up the Start button menu. This menu contains options for controlling the computer or for starting programs. In Windows 8, the Start button is replaced by the Start screen. (Refer to Figure 4-4.)

✔ **The taskbar:** This doohickey displays a host of buttons. Those on the left are used to start programs or to switch to running programs.

✔ **The notification area:** This annoying little thing contains teensy icons that pester you with pop-up balloons from time to time. The icons can also help you do things or monitor events and show you the date and time.

✔ **The Show Desktop button:** In Windows 7, clicking this button hides all open windows and shows you the desktop background.

Take a moment to find each item on your laptop screen right now. Don't touch the display! Just find them and point (and maybe even say, "Oh, there it is!").

What's Next?

After Windows starts, you can begin using your laptop. See Part III for more information about using your laptop. Check out Chapter 5, which covers the important task of properly shutting down Windows and turning off the laptop.

Chapter 5

To Turn Off a Laptop

*Y*our laptop has all sorts of features and interesting things. One thing it doesn't have is an Off switch. Yep: Using logic found only in the computer industry, the same button that turns on a laptop also turns off a laptop. Even worse, that button — the power button — may not even turn off the laptop. It can do other, mysterious, power-related functions, all covered in this chapter.

O the Ways to Turn Off a Laptop

There are several options for dismissing your laptop. You can turn off the laptop completely, or you can put the laptop to sleep, which is like turning it off just a little bit. You can log out. Or you can lock the computer while you step away. This section describes the various ways to turn off (or not turn off) a laptop computer when you're done using it.

Finding the Shutdown menu

Whether you choose to shut down the computer or any of the other non-shutdown or almost-shutdown options, you find them all in one place. In Windows 8, that place is found by following these steps:

1. **Summon the Charms bar.**

   The easiest way to bring up the Charms bar is to drag the mouse pointer to the upper-right corner of the screen.

2. **Choose Settings.**

   The Settings panel appears on the right side of the screen.

3. **Choose Power.**

   The Shutdown menu appears.

In Windows 7, the Shutdown menu is found on the Start button's menu, in the lower-right corner, as illustrated in Figure 5-1. To get there, pop up the Start button menu: Click the Start button with the mouse, or press the Win key on your laptop's keyboard. You can see the Shutdown button itself visible on the Start button menu. Other shutdown options appear when you click the Shutdown menu button, as shown in Figure 5-1.

There are several shutdown options, not all of which might appear on the Shutdown menu:

- Shutdown or Shut down
- Restart
- Sleep
- Hibernate
- Log off
- Lock
- Switch User

The following sections describe these options in detail and when and how to use them.

Some shutdown options can also be found on the Start, or Welcome, screen. They're accessed by clicking the Power icon, shown in the margin.

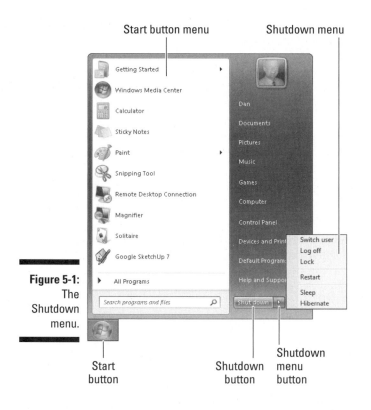

Start button menu   Shutdown menu

Getting Started
Windows Media Center
Calculator
Sticky Notes
Paint
Snipping Tool
Remote Desktop Connection
Magnifier
Solitaire
Google SketchUp 7

All Programs

Search programs and files

Dan
Documents
Pictures
Music
Games
Computer
Control Panel
Devices and Prin
Default Program
Help and Suppor

Switch user
Log off
Lock
Restart
Sleep
Hibernate

Shut down

Figure 5-1:
The
Shutdown
menu.

Start
button

Shutdown
button

Shutdown
menu
button

Shutting down your laptop

Here are the steps you need to take to properly shut down Windows and turn off your laptop when you're done for the day:

1. **Save your work and close all programs.**

   The generic Save command is Ctrl+S. The command to close most windows and programs is Ctrl+W, although often the weirdly obscure Alt+F4 is needed. In Windows 8, apps are closed by dragging their windows to the bottom of the screen.

2. **Summon the Shutdown menu.**

   Refer to the preceding section for details.

3. **Choose the Shut Down item from the menu.**

   In Windows 7, you can click the Shut Down button found on the Shutdown menu. The laptop turns itself off.

Yes, that's correct: The laptop turns itself off. When the screen goes dark and the power lamp is dimmed, you can shut the laptop's lid and put away the laptop.

- ✔ If you don't follow directions, and you somehow avoid Step 1, you still have an opportunity to save any unsaved files before the laptop shuts down.

- ✔ A Windows 8 *app* is a program you start from the Start screen. Apps are represented by tiles on the Start screen. They close automatically when you shut down Windows.

- ✔ In Windows XP, you must choose the command Turn Off Computer from the Start button menu and then click the button labeled Turn Off from the window that appears.

- ✔ Shutting down certain versions of Windows triggers updates to install. If so, note the little Shield icon over the Shutdown button on the Start menu. (See the margin.) In that case, the software updates are installed as the laptop shuts down. (They might continue to be installed when the laptop starts up again.)

Restarting Windows

Occasionally, you're directed to reset the laptop, which is often referred to as *restarting Windows*. To do so, heed these steps:

1. **Save your work and close all your programs.**

2. **Summon the Shutdown menu.**

   Refer to the earlier section "Finding the Shutdown menu" for details.

3. **Choose the Restart command.**

After you choose the Restart command, the laptop seems to be turning itself off, but just before it does, it starts right back up again. It's kind of like trying to put a toddler to sleep.

- ✔ In Windows, XP, you restart by choosing the Turn Off Computer command from the Start button menu and then clicking the Restart button from the window that appears.

- ✔ Sometimes, restarting Windows happens automatically, such as when installing software, adding hardware helpers called *device drivers*, or performing Windows updates. You're generally given a choice: "Would you like to restart Windows now?" If so, click the Yes button or Restart button, and things happen automatically. Otherwise, follow the steps in this section and you'll be fine.

✔ Shutting down Windows and then starting your laptop (described in Chapter 4) also qualifies as a restart, though this process doesn't work as fast as the procedure described in this section.

Putting Mr. Laptop to sleep

All laptops have a special low-power mode. In this mode, the computer is still on, but the monitor goes dark, the hard drives spin down, and the processor enters a special low-power mode. The idea is to keep the laptop ready but not waste power. This low-power mode is officially called *hybrid sleep,* but everyone knows it as *Sleep mode.*

The method for putting your laptop to sleep varies.

When your laptop is blessed with the sleep button, identified by the moon icon (see the margin), pressing the button puts the laptop to sleep instantly. But, hang on! The sleep button's function can be changed, so pressing it may not always put the laptop to sleep. Before you use this method, see the later section "Power Button, What's Your Function?"

One of the most assured ways to put the laptop to sleep is to choose the Sleep command from the Shutdown menu. Refer to the earlier section "Finding the Shutdown menu" for information on locating the Shutdown menu.

The laptop might also be thrust into Sleep mode when you close the laptop's lid. See the section "Shutting the laptop's lid," later in this chapter.

Finally, the laptop may simply go to sleep after a period of inactivity — say, 30 minutes or so. Setting this time-out is part of the laptop's power management scheme, which is covered in Chapter 10.

✔ There's no need to be quiet while your laptop is sleeping.

✔ The moon lamp might be on when the laptop is in Sleep mode. See Chapter 6 for information on this lamp and other lights on your laptop.

✔ If you're going to close all your programs before putting your laptop into Sleep mode, shut down the laptop instead.

✔ The laptop may beep just before it goes to sleep. That's okay.

✔ In Windows XP, put the laptop to sleep by choosing the Turn Off Computer command from the Start button's menu, and then click the Stand By button in the Turn Off Computer window. In Windows XP, Sleep mode is referred to as *Stand By.*

Waking up from Sleep mode

To revive a snoozing laptop, simply press a key on the keyboard, tap the mouse pad, or touch the screen (on a touchscreen laptop). These actions wake the sucker up, bringing it back to active duty.

If the laptop is conditioned to sleep when you close its lid, opening the lid wakes it up.

If the laptop still doesn't rouse itself, press the power button.

After waking up the laptop, you may have to unlock Windows: Log in again. That's okay — in fact, it's what you want; Windows should be locked after the laptop wakes up from Sleep mode. (See Chapter 21 for more information on laptop security.)

- ✔ I generally push the Ctrl key on the keyboard to wake up my sleeping laptop.

- ✔ One reason a laptop may not wake up is that the battery is probably dead. Check the laptop's power-on lights. If they're off, the battery is dead. Plug in the laptop and try again.

- ✔ If the laptop still doesn't wake up, you may have a problem with the system's power management software. Try pressing (and holding) the power button until the unit turns either off or on again. Then try starting up the laptop as you normally do. Ask your dealer or laptop manufacturer for updated power management software.

Using hibernation

There's a laptop option that lies between Sleep mode and turning off the laptop: *hibernation*. What it does is turn off the laptop, but before doing that, everything you're doing is saved. That way, when you turn on the laptop again, all that saved information is reloaded and, after logging in to Windows again, you see all your stuff, just as you left it.

Before you use hibernation, determine whether it's activated: Look for the word *Hibernate* on the Shutdown menu. (Refer to the earlier section "Finding the Shutdown menu" for information on the Shutdown menu.) If you don't see the Hibernate option, you can assign the Hibernate function to one of the laptop's power buttons. See the later section "Power Button, What's Your Function?" for details.

When Hibernation is available on the Shutdown menu, hibernate the laptop by choosing that option. The laptop saves everything you're doing and then turns itself off.

In Windows XP, click the Shut Down Computer button on the Start button menu. When you see the Shut Down Computer window, press and hold the Shift key. The Hibernate button replaces the Stand By button; click the Hibernate button. (When the Hibernate button doesn't appear, your laptop lacks the ability to hibernate.)

To recover from Hibernation mode, turn on the laptop, although in some cases the laptop may recover from hibernation when you press a key or touch the mouse pad. I try that trick first, before I punch the power button.

- ✔ It may take the laptop a wee bit longer to hibernate your laptop than it does to shut it down completely.

- ✔ Hibernation mode saves power because, obviously, the laptop's power is turned off. But unlike turning off the laptop completely, when you turn on the system again, it comes on much faster.

- ✔ I prefer to put my laptop into hibernation when I know that I won't be using it for longer than a half-hour or so.

- ✔ The laptop recovers from Sleep mode faster than from hibernation, so I recommend using Sleep mode for brief pauses in your work and using hibernation for longer respites.

- ✔ Unlike when you put your laptop in Sleep mode, you can leave your laptop in a hibernated state for as long as you want. Even if the batteries eventually drain, the system returns to where you left it after the computer is plugged in and started again.

- ✔ You can set up the laptop to automatically hibernate when the battery power gets way too low. See Chapter 10.

- ✔ Note that Hibernation mode requires storage space. When storage space runs low, it's possible that Hibernation mode won't work. But this probably won't happen to you, because you followed my advice in Chapter 2 and have a laptop with a nice, roomy hard drive.

Logging off

One not-quite-shutdown option for Windows is to *log off*. What it does is end your computer session without turning off the computer or restarting it.

In Windows 8, log off by following these steps:

1. **Summon the Start screen.**

   Press the Windows key on the laptop's keyboard to quickly jump to the Start screen.

2. **Click the mouse on your account picture.**

   Or you can touch the account picture, if you have a touchscreen laptop.

3. **Choose the Sign Out command.**

   Sign Out, Log Off — same thing.

To log off in older versions of Windows, choose the Log Off option from the Shutdown menu. (Refer to Figure 5-1.)

When you log out, Windows begs you to save any unsaved documents, and then it proceeds just like it's shutting down Windows. Eventually, you find yourself back at the Start, or Welcome, screen.

- ✔ In Windows XP, you log off by clicking the Log Off button on the Start button menu.

- ✔ Another option you can choose instead of Log Off is Switch User. Choosing Switch User logs you off without ending your Windows session. It allows another user to log on and use the computer and then have you return to your session when the user is done (and logs off).

- ✔ Logging off exists as an option for when folks with other accounts want to use the computer. Because most laptops are single-user PCs, logging off is rarely necessary, and, in fact, I do not recommend having multiple users on a single laptop.

Locking Windows

A quick way to protect your computer when you're away for a spell is to lock Windows. When you lock Windows, the desktop goes away and hides behind the main Windows Welcome screen. It's not the same as logging off (see the preceding section), but it prevents anyone from using the laptop or even seeing the screen while you step away. The quickest way to lock Windows is to press the Win+L key combination on the keyboard, where Win is the Windows key and L stands for Lock.

The Lock command in Windows 8 is found on the Start screen: Click or touch your account picture to choose Lock from the pop-up menu that appears.

In some versions of Windows, you can also choose the Lock command from the Shutdown menu, as shown earlier, in Figure 5-1.

 In Windows Vista, you can click the padlock icon button on the Start button menu to lock the laptop.

Shutting the laptop's lid

One of the great mysteries of mankind is whether the light inside the refrigerator goes out when you close the refrigerator door. Does it? Well, you have to buy a copy of *Refrigerator Lights For Dummies* to find out the answer. For your laptop, what happens when you close the lid depends on what *you* want to happen. To see how to set things up, refer to the later section "Power Button, What's Your Function?"

Shutting down when the laptop doesn't want to

Unlike with a desktop computer, you can't just yank that power cord from the wall to deliberately force a laptop into electronic submission. The reason it doesn't work is that with the AC power gone, the laptop immediately starts using its battery. This can be disconcerting when the system is locked up and you really, badly, want to turn the sucker off.

If the laptop just utterly seems to be ignoring you, press and hold the power button. Continue holding it down, usually for five to ten seconds. Eventually, the laptop turns itself off.

See Part VI of this book for laptop troubleshooting information.

Power Button, What's Your Function?

The power button always turns on your laptop, but remember that it's not an On–Off switch. That's because it's a real mystery what happens when you punch the power button while the laptop is on.

Well, no, it's not a mystery. The truth is that the laptop's power button can be programmed by you, the laptop's master, to do a number of things when it's punched. Obey these steps:

1. **Open the Control Panel window.**

   In Windows 8, right-click the mouse in the lower-left corner of the screen. Choose the Control Panel item.

   In older versions of Windows, choose the Control Panel item from the Start button menu to open and view the Control Panel window.

2. **Choose the Hardware and Sound category.**

   Or if you prefer to view the Control Panel in the icon manner, simply open the Power Options icon, and from the left side of the Power Options window choose the option labeled Choose What Closing the Lid Does. Skip to Step 4.

3. **From beneath the Power Options title, click the link labeled Change What the Power Buttons Do.**

   You see the Power Options System Settings window, shown in Figure 5-2. It has two columns — one for when the laptop is battery powered and another for when it's plugged into the wall. One row is for the power button, one for the sleep button, and another for closing the laptop's lid.

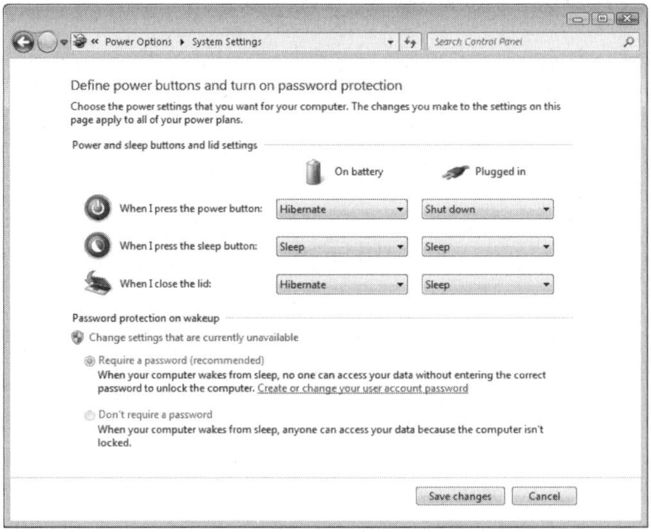

Figure 5-2:
Setting options for various power buttons and the lid.

4. **Choose what happens when you press the power button.**

   Each column has four options:

   Do nothing: Pressing the button or closing the lid doesn't change anything. If the laptop is on, it stays on.

Sleep: The laptop immediately enters Sleep mode, saving vital battery power.

Hibernate: The laptop hibernates, saving important information to disk and then turning itself off.

Shut down: The laptop turns itself off.

5. **Choose what happens when you press the laptop's sleep button (if it has a sleep button).**

6. **Choose what happens when you close the laptop's lid.**

    Refer to Figure 5-2 to see how I configured various options for my own laptop.

7. **After choosing the various options, click the Save Changes button.**

8. **Close the window.**

When the laptop is off, pressing the power button turns it back on again. There's no way to change that, nor would you really want to.

- ✔ See Chapter 6 to help determine whether your laptop features a sleep button.

- ✔ In Windows XP, the power button options are found in the Power Options Properties dialog box, which you open by double-clicking the Power Options icon in the Control Panel. Click the Advanced tab in that dialog box to configure what happens when you close the laptop's lid.

Chapter 6

Around Your Laptop in 16 Pages

*Y*our laptop has the same capabilities as, and most of the features of, a standard desktop computer, plus a handful of its own, unique traits. All this stuff is jammed into the smallest space possible: Ringing your laptop is a smattering of bumps, holes, lights, and buttons. The laptop is festooned with a festival of features. In fact, there's so much going on about your laptop that I thought I'd cobble together this chapter to go over what's what, where it is, and why it's important.

The Standard Laptop Tour

Most desktop computers look the same. Aside from minor design differences in its case, your typical desktop PC has on its face an optical drive, a media card reader, USB and headphone connectors, a power button, and blinking lights. Ho-hum. But forget about consistency when you want to locate these common items on a laptop computer, because no typical laptop exists.

Go grab your laptop. Gently. Take a moment to look it over. Then read this section to discover where its key items are located.

Optical drive location

If your laptop has an optical drive, locate the spot where the optical disc is inserted. You have two methods for inserting optical discs: slot and tray.

For the slot type of drive, you insert the disc into the slot. At some point, the laptop "grabs" the disc and pulls it all the way in.

For the tray type of optical drive, push a button to eject the tray. Place the optical disc into the tray and push the tray shut.

✔ I've used laptops where the disc ejects on the right side and used other laptops where the disc ejects on the front. The only place I've not seen discs eject is in back of the laptop, which would be silly.

✔ For the pop-out tray, be sure that you find and recognize the tiny button you press to eject the disc.

✔ See Chapter 9 for more information on how to properly eject an optical disc from your laptop.

Removable storage

Locate the spot on your laptop where media cards are inserted. Several types of media cards exist: Compact Flash, Memory Stick, and Secure Digital, for example. Each card slides into its own, special slot. Your laptop may sport one type of slot or two types or all four types.

A popular feature of larger laptops is to offer removable mass storage devices. For example, the laptop's optical drive might be removed and replaced by a second hard drive, a solid-state drive (SSD), or a media card reader. Having this type of option allows you to expand your laptop's universe and reconfigure your laptop's storage abilities.

✔ Not every laptop supports swappable storage options.

✔ One advantage to removable mass storage is that you can lighten the laptop's weight when you can make do without the device. But ensure that the laptop is designed to operate that way (and that nothing nasty sneaks into the empty hole).

✔ Be mindful that you remove storage devices by following the directions that come with your laptop. Sometimes, the devices can be removed in the way you would eject any media; at other times, you may need to turn off the laptop before swapping mass storage.

✔ See Chapter 9 for more information on using removable storage on your laptop.

The PC Card garage

The traditional way to expand a laptop is by using a PC Card. This tiny, credit-card-size gizmo can add features to your laptop's basic hardware configuration.

It plugs in, or *docks,* using a hole on the side of the laptop. A tiny "garage door" may cover the hole, or the hole might be hidden behind a panel.

The PC Card is inserted into the slot, "holy" end first. In fact, it fits in only one way. Push the card in all the way until it fully docks with the connectors deep inside the laptop.

To remove the card, locate the eject button alongside the slot, right next to the door, as illustrated in Figure 6-1. Press the eject button all the way in, and the card pops out a little. You can then pinch the card between your thumb and forefinger and pull it out the rest of the way.

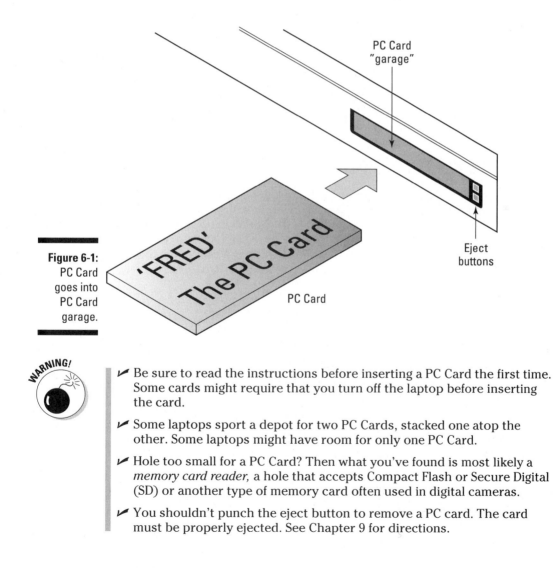

PC Card "garage"

Eject buttons

Figure 6-1: PC Card goes into PC Card garage.

'FRED' The PC Card

PC Card

WARNING!

✔ Be sure to read the instructions before inserting a PC Card the first time. Some cards might require that you turn off the laptop before inserting the card.

✔ Some laptops sport a depot for two PC Cards, stacked one atop the other. Some laptops might have room for only one PC Card.

✔ Hole too small for a PC Card? Then what you've found is most likely a *memory card reader,* a hole that accepts Compact Flash or Secure Digital (SD) or another type of memory card often used in digital cameras.

✔ You shouldn't punch the eject button to remove a PC card. The card must be properly ejected. See Chapter 9 for directions.

✔ Be aware of the PC Card eject button. It sometimes tends to stick out, beyond the edge of the laptop case. Ensure that you press the PC Card back into the laptop so that it doesn't snag on something and break off.

A place for the old ball-and-chain

Most laptops have a special "belt loop" through which you can snake a security cable. The belt loop's name is *Universal Security Slot*, or *USS*. A common icon for the USS is shown in the margin.

Another option is the Kensington Security Slot, or K-Slot. The slot looks like a tiny oval labeled with the padlock icon sporting a *K* in the middle.

✔ Note that the security cable must be attached to a solid and immovable item to prevent the laptop from being stolen. Simply threading a cable through the security hole doesn't do the trick.

✔ See Chapter 21 for more information on laptop security.

The thing's gotta breathe

As you conclude your hole-locating journey around your laptop, discover where its breathing slots are. They might not be obvious; they might not even be there. If they are, note their locations and try to keep the vents clear.

Always set a laptop down on a hard surface. Never block the vents, or else the laptop becomes too hot and malfunctions in various amusing yet annoying ways.

Not a hole, but an eye

Something you might find on the laptop's lid, monitor side, top center, is the laptop's webcam. No, it's not a hole.

The *webcam* is your laptop's eyeball, used to capture still images or video. Special software that comes with the laptop activates and uses the webcam, allowing you to video-chat, snap pictures, or compose video messages for e-mail. See Chapter 22 for more information on using your laptop's webcam.

✔ Not every laptop comes with a webcam. If yours doesn't, you can buy a USB webcam that squats atop the laptop's lid.

✔ The webcam is on only when you want it to be; the computer doesn't spy on you.

Those Pluggable-Innable Holes

Yes, laptops are supposed to be light and portable. Then again, laptops are also computers, and computers are notorious for having lots of things plugging into them. These things plug into various holes on the computer using various cables with various ends, variously. Laptops also sport those holes, suitable for plugging in things in much the same manner as you do on desktop computers.

Table 6-1 lists the official name, configuration, symbol, color, and description of the various holes you might find located around your laptop. The table should give you an idea of what the hole is used for and what you might eventually want to plug into it.

Table 6-1	Laptop Ports and Their Symbols, Designs, and Colors			
Port Name	**Configuration**	**Symbol**	**Color**	**What You Can Do with It**
Digital Video			White	Connect an external digital (LCD) monitor or HDTV
eSATA		**eSATA**	Black	Connect an external hard drive.
HDMI		**HDMI**	Black	Connect to an HDMI TV or monitor
Headphone			Forest green	Plug in headphones, which automatically disables the laptop's speakers
IEEE (or 1394 or FireWire port)			None	Connect high-speed peripherals
Line In			Gray	Plug in an external audio device
Line Out			Lime	Send sound to the Audio Out jack or speakers
Mic			Pink	Connect a microphone

(continued)

Table 6-1 *(continued)*

Port Name	Configuration	Symbol	Color	What You Can Do with It
Modem/ phone			None	Attach a modem for online communica-tions, or send or receive faxes
Monitor			Blue	Connect an external monitor or a video display for presentations
Power			Yellow	Plug the laptop into an AC power socket
RJ-45/ Ethernet			None	Add your laptop to an Ethernet net-work, or connect to the Internet
S-Video Out			None	Attach a desktop video projector, or attach the laptop to a TV or VCR
USB			None	Add a variety of components to the laptop, including printers and disk drives

As usual, keep in mind that not every laptop sports all these items. Smaller laptops and netbooks have only a few of the essentials: headphone, modem, monitor, power, Ethernet, and USB.

✔ Those holes are officially known as *ports*.

✔ Keyboards and external mice are attached to your laptop using the USB port. When you need more USB ports, you attach a portable USB hub to your laptop. See Chapter 12 for more information about USB.

✔ The RJ-45/Ethernet port might also have the icon shown in the margin labeling its trapezoidal crack.

✔ By the way, that Ethernet port and the modem port look awfully similar. Happily, one (the Ethernet port) is larger than the other (the modem port).

✔ The power jack might look different from its description in Table 6-1. Be sure that you don't plug the power cable into a microphone port!

  ✔ The IEEE symbol might be different on some laptops. Apparently, the Y type of symbol isn't universal.

  ✔ If your laptop has S-Video Out, note that the S-Video connection is video only, not sound.

  ✔ Check out Chapter 8 for some specific items to look for on a Tablet PC.

Look at the Pretty Lights!

What would a computer be if it weren't for all the blinking lights? Even before real computers were popular, these monster computers of science fiction came equipped with banks and banks of blinking lights. Although I'm certain that a modern laptop could easily replace all the Batcomputers in TV Batman's Batcave, it just wouldn't be visually impressive — or believable, to a 1960s television audience.

Your laptop most likely has many more lights than the typical desktop computer. I'm trying to think of a reason, but it honestly baffles me. Suffice it to say that Table 6-2 lists common lights, lamps, and bright, blinking things that you might find on your laptop and describes what they do or why they're necessary.

Table 6-2	Pretty Laptop Lights
Symbol	*What It Could Possibly Mean*
☾	The laptop is in Sleep mode.
🔋	The laptop is running on battery power. This lamp can change color when the laptop is charging.
🔌	The laptop is plugged in.
⏻	The laptop is on.
⛁	The hard drive is being accessed.
Ⓐ A	The Caps Lock state is on. You might also see a light on the Caps Lock key.

(continued)

Table 6-2 *(continued)*

Symbol	*What It Could Possibly Mean*
⌂ 1	The Num Lock state is on. You might also see a light on the Num Lock key.
((•))	Wireless networking activity is taking place.
✳	Bluetooth wireless activity is taking place.

Other pretty lights doubtless exist, such as the bright light that may appear next to the webcam when you're recording video or taking a picture. Still, there are lights that are specific to your laptop's manufacturer. Thanks to the International Symbol Law, most symbols are pretty common. In fact, consider checking Table 6-2 to see whether any of these symbols appears on the laptop's pretty light strip as well.

✔ Some lights can blink or change color. For example, the battery indicator might change from green to amber to red as the battery drains. The hard drive or wireless lights might flicker when the drive is being accessed.

✔ When the laptop is off, or even in Hibernation mode, none of the lights are lit. (See Chapter 5 for hibernation information.)

✔ The plugged-in lamp and the battery lamp (refer to Table 6-2) may be lit when the laptop is plugged in whether the laptop is turned on or not. That's normal for some laptops.

✔ Some netbooks don't have any lamps on them — not enough room, I suppose.

This Isn't Your Daddy's Keyboard

The standard computer keyboard has 105 keys, not counting any special "web" keys, media keys, or other fancy knobs. That's a lot of buttons. You just can't sport that many keys on a laptop and keep it portable, let alone keep the keyboard on one side of the thing. Oh, sure, some of those laptops the size of aircraft carriers — the models with the 18-inch displays — can sport a full-size PC keyboard. But most laptops opt for portability over the need to use your laptop as a surfboard.

This section mulls over the laptop's keyboard.

The general keyboard layout

Figure 6-2 illustrates a typical laptop keyboard layout. The standard typewriter keys are a normal size, but the many other keys have been miniaturized and clustered around the standard keys in a confusing and arbitrary manner. Observing your own laptop's keyboard easily confirms it.

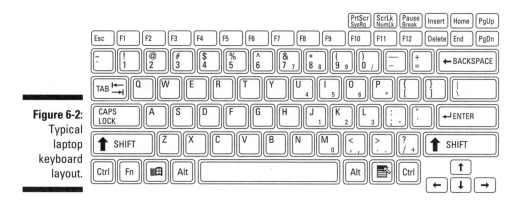

Figure 6-2:
Typical laptop keyboard layout.

As with a desktop keyboard, you should be able to identify these basic items on your laptop keyboard:

- ✔ **Alphanumeric, or "typewriter," keys:** These are the basic typing keys, each of which is labeled with a character (a letter, number, or punctuation symbol). When you're typing on the computer, pressing a key produces its character on the screen.

- ✔ **Shift keys:** The keyboard sports various shift keys used either alone or in combination with other keys. These include Shift, Alt, Ctrl, Fn, and the special Windows keys Win and Menu. The Win key appears in the bottom row between the Fn and Alt keys shown in Figure 6-2; the Menu key appears between Alt and Ctrl.

- ✔ **Function keys:** These keys, labeled F1 through F12, are on the top row of the keyboard, right above the number keys.

- ✔ **Cursor-control keys:** These keys can be anywhere around the keyboard. In Figure 6-2, they're split: arrow keys in the lower-right corner and other cursor keys (Home, End, PgUp, PgDn, Insert, Delete) in the upper-right corner.

- ✔ **Numeric keypad:** This area is covered in the next section.

The alphanumeric keys are approximately the same size and have the same *travel,* or feel, as on a desktop computer keyboard. An exception is found on some Ultrabooks and netbooks, where the alphanumeric keys are slightly smaller.

The text on certain keys is color coded. The colors tell you which keys are used in conjunction with each other. For example, if the Alt key is green and the Num Lock key is green, the Alt+Num Lock key combination is required in order to use Num Lock. (See the later section "The Fn key is the Fun key!")

The cursor-control keys are used to move the text cursor when you're editing text in Windows. They can also be used to help navigate the web. The keys can take on other functions in other programs as well.

Some keys are labeled with images or icons rather than with text. For example, I've seen the Caps Lock key labeled with the letter *A* and the padlock symbol.

European laptops often sport the AltGr key — the Alt (or Alternative) Graphic key. It's used to help produce the many diacritical marks and special characters that are part of various European languages.

European laptops also have the euro symbol, €, on the keyboard. Likewise, laptops in the United Kingdom feature the £ symbol on the 3 key, where the # symbol is found on keyboards in the United States.

Your keyboard might have more or fewer keys than those shown in Figure 6-2, and the arrangement might be different.

Where did the numeric keypad go?

The first thing the laptop designers decided to sacrifice to the Size Gods was the keyboard's numeric keypad. Rather than just saw off that end of the keyboard, laptops since the RadioShack Model 100 have used a combination of numeric keypad and alphabetic keyboard.

Most laptops combine the main keyboard with the numeric keypad: Examine the 7, 8, and 9 keys. These three keys are also the top three keys on a numeric keypad. Because of this similarity, a shadow keypad can be created by using the right side of the alphabetic keyboard, as illustrated in Figure 6-3. The trick, of course, is knowing how to turn the thing on and off.

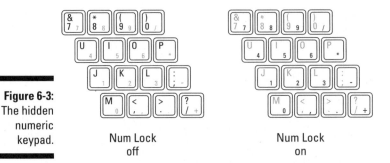

Figure 6-3:
The hidden numeric keypad.

Num Lock off

Num Lock on

The following steps help to train you in the proper use of the hidden numeric keypad on the laptop:

1. **Open a program you can type in, such as Notepad or your word processor.**

   A cinchy way to open Notepad is to press Win+R on your laptop's keyboard. Type **notepad** into the Run dialog box, and then click the OK button to summon the Notepad program.

2. **Type** I just love Kimmy.

   You discover in a few steps why you adore Kimmy.

3. **Find the Num Lock light on your laptop's strip of lights.**

   The light is your confirmation that your keyboard is in Num Lock mode and that you can use the embedded numeric keypad. (Refer to Table 6-2.)

4. **Find the Num Lock key on your laptop's keyboard.**

   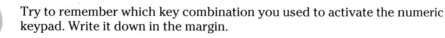 Somewhere on your keyboard is the Num Lock key. It might be labeled *NumLock* or *NumLk* or *Num,* or it might even be labeled with a symbol, as shown in the margin. Locate the key.

5. **Attempt to activate Num Lock.**

   Press the Num Lock key. If nothing happens, try Shift+Num Lock.

   If the text *Num Lock* is shown in a different color, find the matching-color key, such as Alt or Fn. Then press that key in combination with Num Lock.

   You're successful when the Num Lock light comes on. At this point, the keyboard has switched into Numeric Keypad mode.

6. **Try to type** I just love Kimmy **again.**

   It doesn't work. You see something like `14st 36ve 500y`. That's because most keys on the right side of the keyboard now have their numeric keypad abilities activated, which is helpful for entering numbers or working a spreadsheet but rather frustrating at other times.

7. **Deactivate Num Lock.**

   Press whichever key combination you used to turn it on.

8. **Close Notepad or whichever program you opened.**

   There's no need to save the document.

 Try to remember which key combination you used to activate the numeric keypad. Write it down in the margin.

Some netbooks don't feature this numeric keypad trick. In that case, you're stuck using the number keys across the top of the keyboard, or you can purchase an external, USB numeric keypad for your laptop.

The Fn key is the Fun key!

To make up for a lack of keys, many laptops came with a special function key, the Fn key. It's used in combination with other keys, like a Shift key, giving those keys multiple purposes.

Having an Fn key is an old, old laptop trick, dating back to the prehistoric days of portable computing. In those days, the Fn key was used to help produce keystrokes not available on a laptop's limited keyboard. The Fn key is now used in combination with other keys to activate special laptop features. Here's a list of things the Fn key may do in combination with other keys on your laptop's keyboard:

- Turn the laptop's internal speaker volume up and down
- Mute the laptop's internal speaker
- Increase or decrease the monitor's brightness or contrast
- Activate an external monitor for giving a presentation
- Activate Sleep mode
- Hibernate the laptop
- Eject an optical disc
- Enable or disable the wireless networking adapter
- Play, stop, pause, rewind, and advance media playing
- Lock the laptop
- Perform other special and specific tricks I can't think of right now

Take a moment to peruse your laptop and look over its available Fn keys. The Fn key and its companion keys are color coded and flagged with various icons.

Some Fn keys can be rather fun. For example, on one of my laptops, Fn+PgUp activates a tiny keyboard light in the laptop's lid.

I've seen the Fn key used to temporarily activate the numeric keypad on the laptop: Press the Fn key and then type on the keypad to produce numbers.

Sadly, there's no standard for naming or assigning the various Fn keys and their functions.

Mind these specific keys

In addition to the standard keyboard, or perhaps right along with it, your laptop may have some custom keys or buttons next to the keyboard. They're totally specific to the manufacturer, and you might never end up using them. But they're keys nonetheless.

The most common location for these keys is above the keyboard, although I've seen them on the left and right sides. Some keys can be used to pick up e-mail, browse the web, connect to a digital camera, or contact a vendor for technical support. I've also seen keys that control the display or speaker volume.

Use these keys if you will, but keep in mind that their functions are specific to your laptop. Don't expect to find similar keys on a desktop computer or even on a laptop from another manufacturer.

The special keys are controlled using specific software that must be loaded into Windows. If a problem occurs with this software, if you upgrade Windows, or if you end up using another operating system, don't be surprised when the special keys no longer function.

This Isn't Your Momma's Mouse

The marriage of mouse and laptop is an old idea. Even back before graphical operating systems such as Windows existed, laptop users were aware of how handy a computer mouse could be. Yet it took some time before the desktop mouse was properly transformed into the laptop mouse, which isn't really a mouse but rather a *touch pad*. This section explains how it works.

The touch pad

Your laptop most likely features a *touch pad* pointing device, though everyone calls it "the mouse." Like a desktop computer mouse, the touch pad is used to manipulate the pointing device on the display, which lets you fully enjoy the graphical goodness of the Windows operating system.

The typical laptop touch pad is shown in Figure 6-4. On either side, or below (as illustrated in the figure), you find buttons the same as the left and right buttons on a traditional computer mouse.

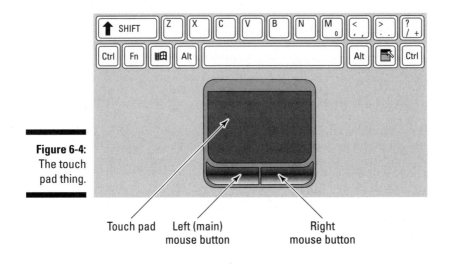

Figure 6-4:
The touch
pad thing.

Touch pad   Left (main)   Right
             mouse button   mouse button

There's an art to using the touch pad:

✔ Using your forefinger to move the mouse pointer is helpful. Use your thumb to click the left and right buttons on the bottom of the touch pad.

✔ A light touch is all that's required.

✔ You must be careful not to touch the pad in more than one spot. If you do, the pointer on the screen jumps about in an erratic and annoying manner.

✔ The most difficult mouse operation is the *drag*. That's where you have to hold down a button while moving the pointer. With practice, it can be done — but you must practice! (It's another excuse to play FreeCell.)

✔ Try to avoid accidentally hitting the right mouse button when you mean to hit the left one. Doing so causes context menus to pop up in Windows — very frustrating. Press the Esc key on the keyboard to back your way out of that horror.

✔ On some touch pads, you can tap the pad to simulate a mouse click.

The latest rage in the laptop touch pad is its ability to interpret finger strokes. The touch pad typically features a scrolling area on the left or bottom edge, or both, where you can drag your finger to scroll a window or pan the contents of a web page.

Some laptops might employ a multi-touch pad to compensate for the lack of a touchscreen. In this case, the touch pad allows you to use as many as five fingers at a time, which helps you work with Windows 8 while not actually having a multi-touch monitor on your laptop.

Where is the wheel button?

The traditional computer mouse often features a *wheel button*. The button sits between the mouse's left and right buttons and is used to scroll, pan, or click for various effects. People love the wheel button, and, obviously, they want it on their laptops. Well, *tough!*

Sadly, the common laptop mouse pad has no standard wheel-button replacement. I've seen Lenovo laptops featuring a middle touch pad button that can be used like a wheel button. Some laptop touch pads let you scroll by dragging your finger off to the side of the touch pad, perhaps on the far right side, where a symbol or row of dots lives. Not every laptop offers these features, however.

The bottom-line alternative: Get your laptop an external mouse. See the section "Get a real mouse," at the end of this chapter.

The "happy stick" keyboard mouse

Some Lenovo laptops feature a joystick-like mouse that looks like a pencil eraser jammed between the keyboard's G, H, and B keys. It's officially named the TrackPoint, though I prefer to call it the *happy stick*. Regardless, the gizmo is quite handy to use.

The idea behind the happy stick is that you can manipulate it by using the index finger of either hand. You can then use your thumb (on either hand) to click the left or right "mouse" buttons, as shown in Figure 6-5.

- ✔ As with the touch pad, using the happy stick takes some training and getting used to.
- ✔ Some laptop models come with both a happy stick and a touch pad. You can use either one.

Get a real mouse!

The best type of input device you can use on your laptop is . . . *a real mouse.* No, not the furry rodent kind. Silly. A desktop computer mouse.

Now you can readily use a desktop computer mouse on your laptop instead of, or along with, the touch pad. Yes, it's one more thing to carry. But because desktop computer mice are familiar and people are used to them, it often makes sense for the laptop to have a "big computer" mouse.

Figure 6-5:
The
TrackPoint.

Rather than use the same, full-size (and wired) computer mouse with your laptop, consider buying a portable mouse — specifically, a wireless mouse. This type of mouse uses a tiny USB connector that wirelessly transmits movement from the mouse into the laptop. It's light, portable, and tiny, which makes it easy to use on an airplane or on your thigh, when an airplane isn't available.

✔ Buy your laptop a nice, wireless mouse with a wheel. That way, you'll never again moan about your laptop missing a wheel button.

✔ Be careful when you install the software for your external mouse. Sometimes, doing so disables the software controlling the laptop's touch pad. Follow the installation advice that comes with the external mouse.

Chapter 7

Your Laptop and Windows

Someone has to be in charge. On a ship you'll find the captain, on the playground is the bully, and in the Milky Way galaxy it's the Yaxkoz Empire, which is right now hurtling a billion stellar battle cruisers toward Planet Earth. Before they arrive, you should know that the kingpin in charge of all the software in your laptop is Windows, which is your laptop's *operating system,* or the main program in charge of everything.

You're probably familiar with Windows if you've used a computer. Using Windows on a laptop works similarly to using Windows on any computer. But along with the disappointment and frustration that everyone experiences with Windows, you find a few laptop-specific issues you should know about. This chapter uses a smoothly paced, informative style to present these issues, which you have plenty of time to read about before the Yaxkoz Empire invades.

The Big Windows Picture

Windows is easy to use, but not simple. I could prattle on about the reasons, but this isn't a Windows book. Instead, you should know a few key things about Windows, starting with the first things you see after you log in to Windows. Those things are covered in this section.

The Start screen

In Windows 8, the first thing you see after logging in is the Start screen. It's the place you go to start programs in Windows. You can also start *apps*, which are programs represented by tiles on the Start screen. Click or touch a tile to start its associated app or program.

✔ Figure 4-4, in Chapter 4, illustrates a sample Start screen.

✔ You can return to the Start screen at any time by pressing the Win (Windows) key on your laptop's keyboard. You can also display the Start screen by clicking the mouse in the lower-left corner of the screen.

✔ Traditional Windows programs are run at the desktop, covered in the next section.

✔ Earlier versions of Windows use the Start button to run programs. See the later section "The Start button and Start button menu."

The desktop

The *desktop* is the main thing you see when you use Windows 7, Windows Vista, or Windows XP. It contains icons, the taskbar, the Start button, the Sidebar (optional), and other elements. Review Figure 4-5, over in Chapter 4, to see what's what.

Windows 8 has a desktop as well, included mostly for nostalgic reasons. Unlike the desktop from earlier versions of Windows, the Windows 8 desktop lacks a Start button and Start button menu. To start new programs (or apps), you must use the Start screen in Windows 8.

To quickly view the desktop, press the Win+D key combination.

The Start button and Start button menu

The most important thing you can use on the desktop in Windows 7, Windows Vista, and Windows XP is the Start button, found on the left end of the taskbar (at the bottom of the screen). Clicking the Start button, or pressing the Win key on the keyboard, displays the Start button menu, shown in Figure 7-1. It's a fun slab-o-stuff that includes a list of programs, fun places to visit in Windows, and other things to start.

Recently used programs area   Fun Windows places

Pin area   Account image

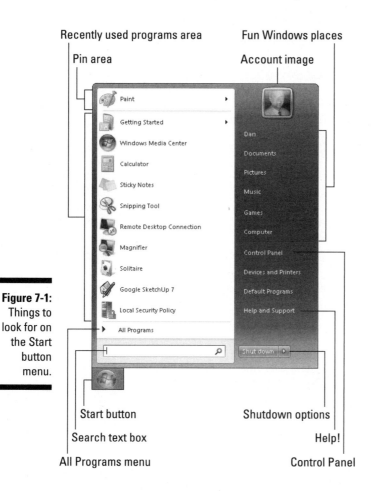

Figure 7-1:
Things to
look for on
the Start
button
menu.

Start button   Shutdown options

Search text box   Help!

All Programs menu   Control Panel

Take a few hours to find the following goodies on the important left side of
the Start-thing menu:

✔ **The pin area:** The upper-left half of the slab contains programs permanently attached, or *pinned,* to the Start menu.

✔ **Recently Used Programs area:** Just below the pin-on area, on the left
   side of the Start menu, you find the names and icons of programs you've
   used recently.

✔ **Recently opened files menu:** Click triangles next to programs to display
   a menu of documents you've recently opened or created. Choose a
   recently opened document to quickly open it.

✔ **Search text box:** In this box you can type the names of programs, files,
   or tidbits-o-text to find. When the text you're searching for is found on

your laptop, it appears on the Start menu, listed where the programs appear in Figure 7-1.

✔ **The All Programs menu:** Below the Recently Used Programs area is the All Programs link. Clicking this item displays a list of programs installed on your computer, all shoved into various menus and submenus. Choose a program from the list to run that program.

Find these items lurking on the right side of the Start menu panel:

✔ **Fun Windows places to visit:** The items on the right side of the Start menu represent places to go in Windows, where you can carry out interesting (or not) tasks and play or dawdle. These items include locations where you find the stuff you create as well as general computer and networking thingies.

✔ **The Control Panel:** One of the most important places to visit is the Control Panel, accessed by choosing the Control Panel item from the right side of the Start menu's palette. You visit the Control Panel often as you set up various options for your laptop. (See the section "The Control Panel," later in this chapter.)

✔ **Help:** Yes, there it is. Nestled in the lower-right area of the Start button menu is the place where you can start the Windows Help system. Don't get excited, however: The "help" is merely what you would have found printed in the Windows manual had Microsoft bothered to print it all.

✔ **Shutdown options:** Finally, in the lower-right area of the Start button menu, at the bottom, you find the Shut Down button as well as the Shut Down menu button.

Knowing where things are on the Start menu is important. Knowing how those things work is covered elsewhere in this chapter and throughout this book.

✔ The Start menu is customizable. What you see may differ from what's shown in Figure 7-1 and from what's listed in this section.

✔ You can make the Start menu go away by clicking the mouse on the desktop or pressing the Esc key on the keyboard. You can also make the Start menu go away by upgrading to Windows 8, though I don't recommend upgrading your laptop's operating system.

✔ Refer to Chapter 5 for information on using the various Shutdown options.

Goodies in the notification area

The *notification area* is located on the far right end of the taskbar, where it was banished ages ago because of a tribal spat with the Start button. The notification area is shown in Figure 7-2.

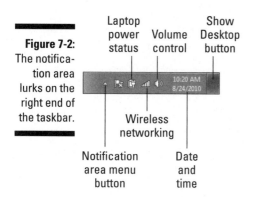

Figure 7-2:
The notifica-
tion area
lurks on the
right end of
the taskbar.

The icons in the notification area serve two purposes. First, they can notify you with pop-up bubbles. Or you can simply point the mouse at an icon to view status information, such as whether the network is connected or how much battery juice remains. Second, the icons provide instant access to some common features, such as networking, antivirus, volume control, and other things to keep handy.

The notification area is customizable, not only because each laptop is different and different items can be installed but also because you can control what appears and what doesn't. To see hidden items, click the menu button on the right end of the notification area. (Refer to Figure 7-2.) You can also choose the Customize command from the pop-up menu that appears, to determine which icons to show or hide in the notification area.

The Charms bar

Windows 8 has a special slide-in bar on the right side of the screen. It's the *Charms bar,* and the icons you see there are *charms*. It's about the only charming thing I've found in Windows 8. Figure 7-3 illustrates the Charms bar.

Figure 7-3:
The Charms
bar.

To summon the Charms bar, point the mouse at the upper-right corner of the screen. You don't need to click — just point. Then move the mouse down the right side of the screen to choose a charm.

- ✔ The keyboard shortcut to summon the Charms bar is Win+C.

- ✔ The Charms bar is cute, but not as direct as the Windows 8 shortcut menu. See the next section.

- ✔ Wouldn't it be nifty if you could buy a Charms bar candy bar? It would have to be packed with those candy marshmallows from Lucky Charms cereal.

The Windows 8 shortcut menu

The fastest way to get around in Windows 8 is to use the shortcut menu that dwells in the lower-left corner of the screen. Right-click the mouse in that corner of the screen. Up pops a handy menu full of popular places to go in Windows. This book makes good use of that menu.

- ✔ To quickly access the Windows 8 shortcut menu, press the Win+X key combination.

- ✔ Also see the later section, "The Windows Mobility Center," which uses the Win+X key combination in older versions of Windows.

Windows and Mass Storage Devices

One key part of any computer system is *information storage*. Storage is important because that's where all your stuff is kept on the laptop. Yes, the stuff is "inside there, somewhere." All the programs, the Windows operating system, and all the files you create must be put somewhere inside the laptop.

In Windows, you can view the gamut of storage devices available to your laptop in a single, handy place. It's the Computer window, shown in Figure 7-4.

To open the Computer window in Windows 8, right-click the mouse in the lower-left corner of the screen. Choose the Windows Explorer command from the shortcut menu. The Computer window should appear. If not, choose Computer from the left side of the window.

In older versions of Windows, either choose the Computer command from the Start button menu (refer to Figure 7-1) or open the Computer icon on the desktop (if it exists).

Libraries

Popular storage locations

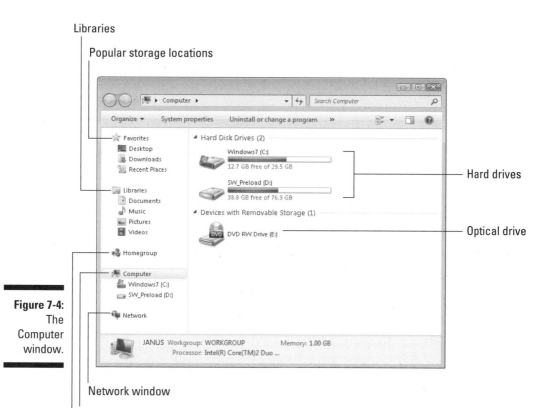

Figure 7-4:
The
Computer
window.

Network window

Even more popular storage locations

HomeGroup

Hard drives

Optical drive

The Computer window lists all storage devices available to your computer, including the hard drive or main storage device, removable media drives, available network drives you may have access to, and media devices. In Figure 7-4, you can see the standard laptop hard drive, `Windows7 C:`, plus a second hard drive and an optical drive.

✔ The Computer window is your gateway to the laptop's storage devices. When you're told to "examine drive C," for example, you open the Computer window, where you behold the drive C icon.

✔ A quick shortcut to open the Computer window is to press the Win+E combination on the keyboard.

✔ For more information on the various types of available disk drives, as well as to gain good background computer knowledge, refer to my book *PCs For Dummies* (Wiley), available at fine bookstores on Planet Earth.

✔ The icon for the optical drive may change, depending on whether you have a disc in the drive and the type of media on the disc.

A Place for Your Stuff

Your laptop uses various storage devices to keep your stuff organized. By *stuff,* I mean the files you create, the music you steal (er, download), videos, stuff from the Internet, pictures — all that junk has to dwell somewhere. By *organized,* I mean that you use folders on the storage devices in your laptop.

Under Windows, the location set aside for all your junk is the *User Profile* folder. It's the place for your stuff, and it's discussed in this section.

- ✔ A *folder* is a storage container for files.

- ✔ *Files* are those things you create using your software: documents and graphics, for example. Files live in folders.

- ✔ The concept of files and folders is all basic Computer Knowledge, stuff you probably ignored in school or assumed that you knew already.

- ✔ Your programs *do not* reside in your User Profile folder. No, they go in the *Program Files* folder. See the section "Where the Programs Lurk," later in this chapter.

Accessing your User Profile folder

In Windows, the User Profile folder is given the same name as the account name you use to log in to the computer. So, if your login ID is Sponge Bob, the folder is named Sponge Bob. On my laptop, the folder name is Dan Gookin, which is also my human name (not my cartoon name).

To open your User Profile folder, press the Win+E key combination on the keyboard, or summon the Computer window as described in the earlier section "Windows and Mass Storage Devices." Once there, choose your account name from the menu, as shown in Figure 7-5.

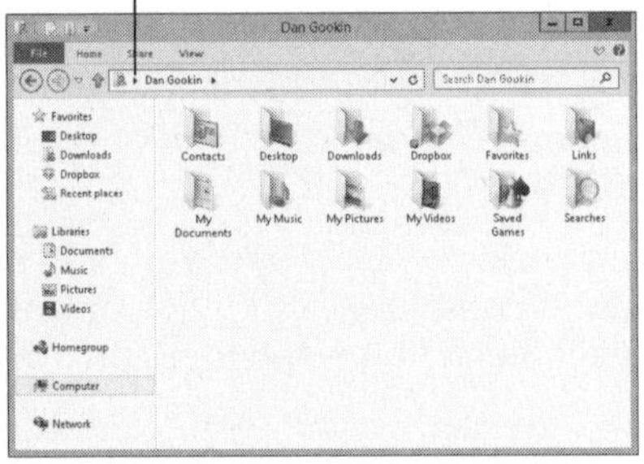

Click triangle to display menu.

Figure 7-5:
User Profile
folder.

The home folder on my laptop is shown in Figure 7-5. The window shows other folders for storing things (described in the later section "Special folders for your stuff") — plus, it may contain icons representing files. It's all my stuff — mine, I tell you!

To close the User Profile folder window, click the X Close box in the window's upper-right corner.

In Windows 7, Windows Vista, and Windows XP, you can quickly open your User Profile folder by choosing it from the Start button menu.

Special folders for your stuff

The key to not losing your sanity in Windows is to organize your stuff. You get a head-start on this task because Windows comes out of the box with certain folders designated to hold certain types of files. These folders include

My Documents: The main place where you store documents and other random files.

My Music: A place to store all audio files, especially songs downloaded from the Internet or ripped from your friends' mix CDs.

My Pictures: The folder where your graphics live. Most graphical applications automatically store your images in this folder.

My Videos: A special folder for storing digital video on your computer.

You have even more custom folders: Contacts, Desktop, Downloads, Favorites, Links, Saved Games, and Searches. Each of these folders is used somehow by one or another program in Windows or by Windows itself. You're also free to create and use your own folders or to create *subfolders* within the folders that are pre-created for you.

In Windows Vista, the four key folders are named without the *My* prefix.

Sharing files with Libraries

The preferred location for saving your stuff in Windows 8 and Windows 7 is the Library. The *Library* combines and stores — in one place — the contents of two or more folders on your laptop, plus maybe some folders out on the network.

Windows features four predefined libraries (refer to Figure 7-4): Documents, Music, Pictures, and Videos. These libraries contain your stuff, but also stuff from other folders on the laptop and, potentially, folders on other computers. Whether you use the Libraries is up to you, but they present another way to find documents and such that are stored on your laptop.

Placing the User Profile folder on the desktop

A handy way to access your User Profile folder is to place its icon on the desktop. When the icon appears on the desktop, you simply open it (double-click) to quickly see your stuff. If the icon doesn't appear on the desktop, you can obey these steps to put it there:

1. **Summon the desktop.**

   Specific directions are found earlier in this chapter.

2. **Right-click the desktop and choose the command New⇨Shortcut.**

   The Create Shortcut dialog box shows up.

3. **Click the Browse button.**

4. **Choose your account name from the list of folders.**

   On my computer, I choose the folder named Dan Gookin. Click the folder once to select it.

5. **Click the OK button.**

6. **Click the Next button.**

7. **Click the Finish button.**

You should then see your account folder's icon on the desktop, given the same name as your account.

Where the Programs Lurk

As with your own stuff, the computer stores all your programs, software, and applications on the laptop's mass storage system. If you don't believe me, you can read this section to discover where those things lurk.

"Where is Windows?"

Windows installs itself on your laptop's hard drive in a folder named Windows or WinNT. The folder name depends on which version of Windows you're using and whether you've upgraded from an older version of Windows. To view the folder, follow these simple steps:

1. **Summon the Computer window.**

   Refer to the earlier section "Windows and Mass Storage Devices" for information about the Computer window. The keyboard shortcut to display the window is Win+E.

2. **In the Computer window, open the icon for drive C, the laptop's primary hard drive.**

   In the Drive C window, you see several folders that represent the main branches of information stored on the hard drive. One folder is named `Windows` or `WinNT`.

3. **Point at the Windows folder and say, "There you are!"**

4. **Close the Computer window.**

Do not poke around the Windows folder. It's the same with any piece of fine art: Don't touch! Don't delete! Don't tell!

"Where are the programs and other software?"

Windows places the programs and other software you install on the laptop into a folder named `Program Files`. As with the `Windows` folder, you find this folder by opening the C disk drive from the Computer window. If you desire, repeat the steps from the preceding section, but in Step 3 point at the `Program Files` folder and say, "There you are, too!"

As with the `Windows` folder, do not modify or add to the `Program Files` folder. Installing and removing software are done in a specific way in Windows, as described in Chapter 9. Do not manually delete programs!

Out on the Network

When your laptop is connected to a network, it can access other computers on that network, including any resources (folders or printers, for example) shared by those computers. This section shows you some network places.

Visiting the Network window

The place to go for networking action is the Network window.

To display the folder full o' networking goodness, choose the Network item from the left side of the Computer window. You can also choose the Network command from the Start menu (which isn't found in Windows 8). Or if you see the Network icon on the desktop, open the icon. The Network window opens, as depicted in Figure 7-6.

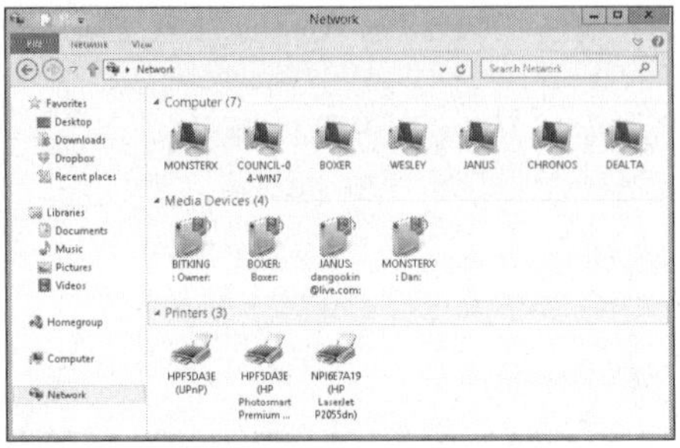

Figure 7-6: Things you're connected to on the network.

Each icon in the Network window represents a computer or network resource available elsewhere on the network. In Figure 7-6, you see the Network windows organized by resource type: computers, media players, and printers.

Instructions for using the Network window, and general networking information, are offered in Chapter 13.

Close the Network window when you tire of its presence.

Perusing the HomeGroup

In Windows 8 and Windows 7, you can easily access and share information with other Windows 8 and Windows 7 users on the network by joining a *HomeGroup*. The HomeGroup makes sharing stuff on a network easier than the folder-sharing method used by older versions of Windows.

To access the HomeGroup, choose the HomeGroup item on the left side of any folder window, such as the Network window. (Refer to Figure 7-6.) When your PC has already joined a HomeGroup, you see shared Libraries from that HomeGroup appear in the window. Otherwise, you're given the opportunity to create or join a HomeGroup. See Chapter 13 for more information.

The PC Settings Screen

Windows 8 places several popular and useful controls in two unique locations: the Settings charm or the PC Settings screen.

The Settings charm is accessed from the Charms bar. To get there, point the mouse at the upper-right corner of the screen, and then choose the Settings charm. (Refer to the earlier section "The Charms bar.")

The Settings charm lists several quick settings at the bottom, as shown in Figure 7-7. Also listed are other popular locations in Windows 8, as illustrated in the figure. The PC Settings screen is accessed by choosing the Change PC Settings item, found at the bottom of the Settings charm.

Popular places

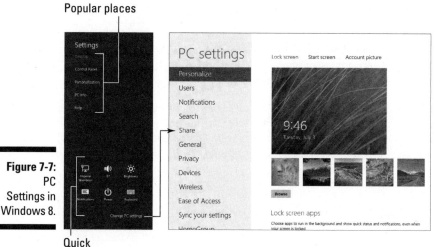

Figure 7-7:
PC
Settings in
Windows 8.

Quick
settings

The PC Settings screen is designed as a simple interface, almost like Microsoft believes that you're using a cell phone and not a laptop computer. For the true dirty work, you use the traditional Control Panel, as covered in the next section.

You can quickly access the Settings charm by pressing the Win+I keyboard shortcut.

The Control Panel

One of the main jobs of any operating system is to control the computer's hardware. In Windows, this control takes place in a spot aptly named the Control Panel. Anytime you want to adjust the various pieces and parts of your laptop, you visit the Control Panel.

Opening the Control Panel

In Windows 8, you can open the Control Panel window by using the Windows shortcut menu: Right-click the mouse in the lower-left corner of the screen and choose the Control Panel item.

In earlier versions of Windows, the easiest way to open the Control Panel window is to choose the Control Panel item from the Start button menu: Click the Start button and choose Control Panel from the right side of the menu. (Refer to Figure 7-1.) The Control Panel window appears, as shown in Figure 7-8.

In the figure, you see the Control Panel in Category view. The things you can control are listed by category and subcategory. Click a link to see more choices. Eventually, you click on a link that opens a window where you get to make adjustments to the laptop's hardware.

The Control Panel also features Icon view, where all the various activity windows are listed by icon. Some folks find Icon view more efficient than Category view. To use Icon view, choose either Large Icons or Small Icons from the View By menu in the upper-right corner of the Control Panel window. (Refer to Figure 7-8.)

Figure 7-8:
The Control
Panel.

✔ In this book, and in the Windows Help system, Category view is used.

✔ In Windows Vista, the Control Panel Home option, on the left side of the Control Panel window, switches to Category view; choosing the item Classic View displays only icons.

✔ Your laptop manufacturer or dealer may have put additional items in the Control Panel, items that don't appear in Figure 7-8. Those items control specific aspects of your laptop's hardware, such as a custom pointing device (mouse), a webcam, or special security software.

Visiting laptoppy places in the Control Panel

Certain places in the Control Panel are most useful to a laptop computer owner. They include the places in the following sections.

The Windows Mobility Center

A collection of laptop, Tablet PC, and mobile computing options is kept in the Windows Mobility Center, shown in Figure 7-9. You may even see in the window additional, customized options specific to your brand of laptop.

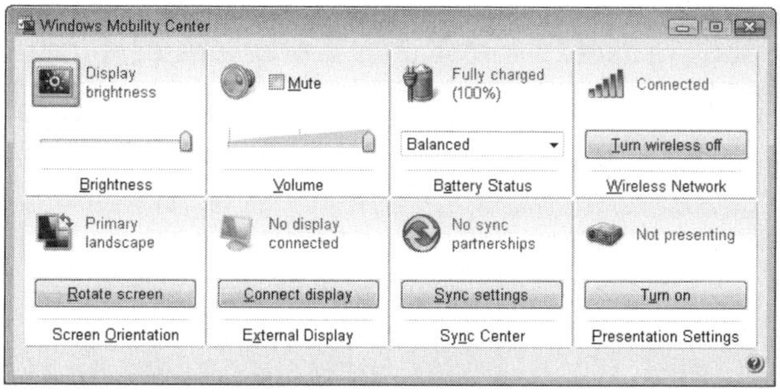

Figure 7-9: The Control Panel's Windows Mobility Center window.

The Windows Mobility Center is accessed by clicking the Adjust Commonly Used Mobility Settings link, found beneath the Hardware and Sound heading. (Refer to Figure 7-8.)

In Windows 7, Windows Vista, and Windows XP, the keyboard shortcut to open the Windows Mobility Center is Win+X.

Tablet PC settings

Unique to the Tablet PC is its ability to use a digital pen as an input device. To set up all that pen-input stuff, choose the Hardware and Sound category, and on the next screen, choose the options you want from the Tablet PC Settings category.

You find additional Tablet PC settings on the Control Panel's Hardware and Sound category page: Pen and Touch, Pen Tablet Properties, as well as other settings.

Biometric devices

Choosing the Hardware and Sound category in the Control Panel displays a list of hardware goodies available on your laptop. Some items there are used to control a fingerprint reader, if your laptop sports one of them. Look for the Biometric Devices category as well as custom categories for your laptop. For example, Lenovo laptops feature the Fingerprint Reader category.

Personalization and display settings

To mess with the screen, to control the way Windows looks as well as the way your laptop's monitor is configured, you visit the Personalization window. That's where options such as the desktop background, screen saver, and display settings are controlled.

To see the Personalization window, choose Appearance and Personalization from the main Control Panel window, and then choose Personalization. Or you can choose any of the links beneath the Personalization heading to do specific things, such as change the screen resolution, change the desktop background, or add a screen saver.

More information on configuring the laptop's display can be found in Chapter 9.

Networking things

The Network window, covered earlier in this chapter, shows network connections. But if you want to set up and configure the network, the Network and Sharing Center window is used. To open the window, you use the Control Panel.

To display the Network and Sharing Center window, click the View Network Status and Tasks link found under the Network and Internet heading. You see in Chapter 13 a sample of what this window looks like as well as what's useful and how it works.

Power management options

To control how your laptop manages power, and conserves battery life, you use the Power Options window. To display it, open the Control Panel and choose Hardware and Sound, and then choose the Power Options heading. Details for using the Power Options window are covered in Chapter 10.

Phone and modem options

Your laptop's modem options are set using the Phone and Modem window. To display the window, you switch the Control Panel to Icon view. Follow these steps:

1. **Open the Control Panel window.**

2. **Choose Large Icons from the View By menu in the upper-right corner of the Control Panel window.**

   Refer to Figure 7-8.

3. **Open the Phone and Modem icon.**

   You may have to scroll down in the list to locate the icon.

   If you've never used the Phone and Modem window, you're first asked to configure the modem for your location. More information on this task can be found in Chapter 16.

4. **When you're done, close the Phone and Modem window and the Control Panel window.**

Before you close the Control Panel window, you might consider switching it back to Category view, if you're comfortable with it.

Printer, fax, and other hardware settings

Both Windows 8 and Windows 7 keep all your laptop's hardware settings in one central location: the Devices and Printers window. You can open this window from the Control Panel by choosing the View Devices and Printers link found beneath the main Hardware and Sound heading.

In Windows Vista, you open the Printers window to work with and configure printers for your laptop to use: Choose the Printer link found beneath the Hardware and Sound heading. In Windows XP, simply open the Printer icon in the Control Panel.

Also see Chapter 11 for information on printing and faxing from your laptop.

User account stuff

To modify your account, login picture, and password, as well as to manage others who use your laptop (not recommended), choose the User Accounts and Family Safety category in the Control Panel. (It's called User Accounts in Windows Vista.) Then choose the item User Accounts.

In Windows 7, Windows Vista, and Windows XP, you can use a handy shortcut to quickly access your user account information: Click your account icon's picture in the upper-right corner of the Start button menu. This one-click shortcut instantly opens the User Accounts window, which displays information about your own account. Simple.

More information on customizing your account is in Chapter 9.

Chapter 8

The Tablet PC

The Tablet PC may be a miraculous improvement over the traditional laptop, but it's nothing new. Two thousand years ago, the Romans called it a *tabulae ceratea,* a wax writing tablet. Back then, it was *the* high-tech recording device: The wax was black, and you wrote on it using a sharp, metal stick, or *stylus.* You wrote with the pointy end of the stylus, and the wider, flat end served as an eraser. The *tabulae* was used for all kinds of writing, including important documents. And I'm certain that more than one Roman schoolkid used the excuse, "I left my homework in the sun" once too often.

Fast-forward 2,000 years and you can have, in your lap, a Tablet PC that does all that the *tabulae ceratea* could do — and more! You use a digital stylus to write on a computer screen rather than use an iron stylus to write on beeswax. Such a marvel seems like a must-have extension to the whole laptop concept, and therefore this chapter covers the Tablet PC.

 ✔ Don't confuse the Tablet PC with the mobile devices also called *tablets.* A Tablet PC is a convertible laptop, which is nothing like the iPad or the Windows Surface device.

 ✔ A common variation on the *tabulae ceratea* was the trifold version (three tablets tied together). Medieval scholars referred to it as a *triptych.*

 ✔ By the way, you didn't do math on a *tabulea ceratea*. Roman schoolboys learned to do math on the abacus. (Roman girls did not go to school.)

Types of Tablet PCs

There are three types of Tablet PCs, as shown in Figure 8-1: convertible, slate, and hybrid.

The *convertible,* the most common Tablet PC model, is basically a laptop with a hinged, swiveling lid. When the screen is up and facing the keyboard, the computer looks like a laptop. If you rotate the screen and fold it over the keyboard, the PC becomes a tablet. This model also has the bonus feature of allowing you to write on the screen no matter which configuration is used.

The *slate* model is the traditional type of tablet computer. It's basically a thick laptop screen without a keyboard. Often, it has buttons or options around the screen, but the slate model distinguishes itself by doing away with any type of keyboard. This model is rapidly disappearing as tablets such as the iPad, Samsung Galaxy Tab, and Windows Surface prove more versatile for the mobile computing market.

The *hybrid* model is the rarest of the bunch. It's basically a slate model that features a detachable or retractable keyboard.

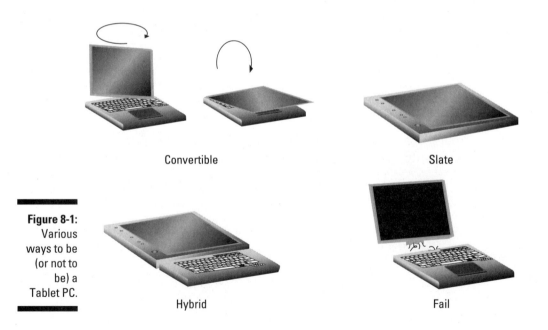

Convertible

Slate

Figure 8-1:
Various
ways to be
(or not to
be) a
Tablet PC.

Hybrid

Fail

- Tablet PCs are rare. By some estimates, Tablet PCs capture just over 1 percent of the entire laptop computer market.

- The biggest disadvantage of a Tablet PC is cost: It's more expensive than its laptop cousins because of its digitizer screen.

- Long before Windows 8 reinvigorated tablet computing, a special version of Windows, Pen Windows, was introduced in 1991. It was rereleased as Windows for Pen Computing in 1992. In 2002, Microsoft released Windows XP Tablet PC Edition. In Windows Vista, Windows 7, and Windows 8, Tablet PC support is provided in all releases and versions.

- The germination of the Tablet PC had to be the Xerox Dynabook concept, back in the 1960s. The Dynabook never appeared, but other attempts have been made to bring tablet computing to the masses.

The Tablet PC Tour

If you squint really hard, you'll be casually fooled into believing that a Tablet PC is basically a fancy laptop computer. It's not, of course. Although my portable computing advice that applies to laptops also applies to Tablet PCs, many things make your tablet computer special.

Looking at special tablet hardware

Everything you know about a standard laptop PC also applies to a Tablet PC. In addition, you should note three main physical characteristics about a tablet computer.

First, if you have a convertible Tablet PC, examine how the screen turns and folds to transform between Laptop and Tablet modes. Note that the screen probably twists only one way. Practice converting the computer between Laptop and Tablet modes.

Check to see whether you can find a way to secure the screen when the computer is in Tablet mode. You need to use the laptop's lid-catch release to release the screen whether the laptop is closed or open in Tablet mode.

Second, peruse the screen part of your Tablet PC. Figure 8-2 illustrates some features you might find on or around the screen.

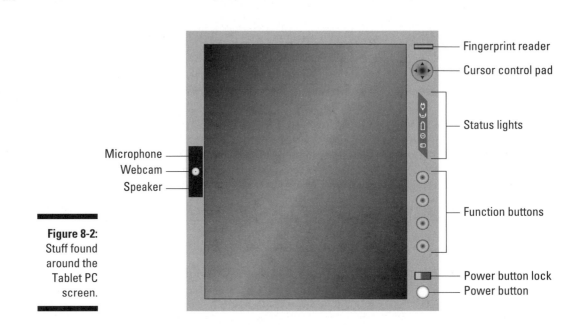

Microphone
Webcam
Speaker

Fingerprint reader
Cursor control pad
Status lights
Function buttons
Power button lock
Power button

Figure 8-2:
Stuff found
around the
Tablet PC
screen.

Here's a smattering:

Power button: This button is often a duplicate of a convertible laptop's main power button.

Power button lock: The lock allows you to keep the laptop turned on or off by disabling the power button's function. That way, the tablet doesn't accidentally turn itself on when it's jostled in its case.

Fingerprint, or *biometric,* reader: This feature is standard on many laptops, but it's found on the lid of a Tablet PC for obvious reasons.

Cursor-control pad: Some Tablet PCs offer this feature as an alternative way to control the mouse pointer, which is helpful if the stylus goes missing. You might also be able to press the control pad to simulate the mouse click.

Speaker/microphone: These features provide audio input and output in Tablet mode.

Webcam: This common laptop feature lets you capture video or still images using a teensy, built-in camera.

Status lights: Status lights on the keyboard do no good in Tablet mode, so when you don't find them there, look on the lid.

Various function buttons: These include buttons that control certain features that might be handy or otherwise necessary but that are out of reach when the keyboard is unavailable: the Esc key; an onscreen menu button; a button to control the screen orientation; a multifunction or menu button; a button to access security features; a button to lock Windows; a button to quickly access the Windows Mobility Center; a button to contact the manufacturer for support; programmable buttons; and others.

Other standard controls: Examples of these controls are for volume control, screen brightness, external monitor activation, and wireless networking.

Finally, a Tablet PC uses a special digitizer pen that I call a *stylus,* as depicted in Figure 8-3.

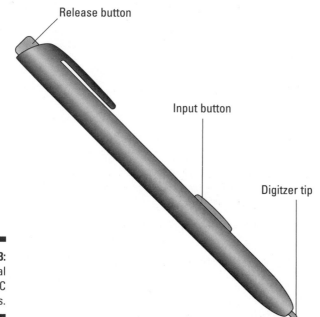

Release button

Input button

Digitzer tip

Figure 8-3:
A typical
Tablet PC
stylus.

Find the stylus. It most likely snaps or slides into a compartment somewhere on the tablet's case. Practice removing and inserting the stylus. For styluses inserted into the case, press in the stylus a little. That should pop it out so that you can grab it. The stylus is returned to its cave by inserting it all the way until it clicks.

The stylus works by touching the tablet's screen, which is a *digitizer.* In Windows, the stylus's touch is interpreted just like mouse movement. (See the section "Training the pen," later in this chapter, for tips on using the stylus.)

You may find one or more buttons on the stylus. The button might be used as a mouse click or right-click, or its function may be programmable.

It's important to note that the stylus is *not* a stick. Although you may be able to use your finger to work the tablet computer or you may find that a capped pen works sometimes, you truly need the stylus. Do not lose it!

✔ On convertible tablets, the lid sports features commonly found on the keyboard part of a traditional laptop. Obviously, you cannot access those necessary features when the laptop is in Tablet Configuration mode.

✔ You can still use the stylus on the screen of a convertible Tablet PC when it's in a standard laptop configuration.

✔ A convertible Tablet PC lets you lock down the lid in both Laptop and Tablet modes. Don't forget to use the lid catch to release the screen in either orientation.

✔ Buttons and controls for the tablet's screen might be hidden behind a panel.

✔ When your Tablet PC lacks buttons or controls on the screen, you can often access these same features by using software. Refer to the next section.

✔ Your Tablet PC probably comes with a spare stylus, or perhaps replacement parts for the stylus. Do not lose them!

✔ Some Tablet PCs feature a *pen tether,* a place where you can attach the stylus to the tablet by using a nylon cord. The tether comes in handy for all of us pen-droppers, who loathe the awkwardness of searching underneath an airline seat for *anything.*

✔ The stylus is far more accurate than your fingertip.

✔ If your Tablet PC features a multi-touch monitor, you have to use your fingers (rather than the stylus) to manipulate objects on the screen.

Finding Tablet PC settings in the Control Panel

Two special places in the Control Panel allow you to configure the Tablet PC. They're the aptly named Tablet PC Settings dialog box and the Pen and Input Devices dialog box. To visit these places, open the Control Panel window as described in Chapter 7.

Tablet PC Settings: To open the Tablet PC Settings dialog box, choose Hardware and Sound from the Control Panel window, and then choose Tablet PC Settings. The purpose of the Tablet PC Settings dialog box is to adjust or control settings specific to your tablet computer, some of which are covered later in this chapter.

Pen and Touch: The second Tablet PC–specific place to visit in the Control Panel is the Pen and Touch dialog box. To open it from the Control Panel main window, choose Hardware and Sound, and then choose Pen and Input Devices. You use the Pen and Touch dialog box to specifically deal with the Tablet PC stylus. There, you can set up the stylus-mouse equivalent actions (double-click and right-click, for example), set up feedback options, configure other stylus options, and set up the tablet for finger input.

> ✔ In Windows Vista, the Pen and Touch dialog box is named Pen and Input Devices, which is also the name of the link you click.
>
> ✔ Performing finger input is covered later in this chapter.
>
> ✔ Your Tablet PC may feature additional items in the Control Panel for setup and configuration, including an entire Tablet PC category in the main Control Panel window.

> ✔ An option to rotate the Tablet PC screen might be found in the Windows Mobility Center. See Chapter 7 for more information on the Windows Mobility Center.

The Pen Is Mightier Than the Mouse

Not the keyboard. Not the mouse. The Tablet PC's main input device is a *digitizer pen,* which I call a *stylus*. It's used just like you use a computer mouse, though it's pressed directly against the screen. Yes, ignore what you learned about not touching an LCD screen — a Tablet PC's screen is designed to be touched by the stylus.

Using the stylus is easy, and Windows offers a host of features that may make you soon forget the keyboard. (Well, not for long.) This section explains how to use the stylus on your Tablet PC. These instructions are different from those for using a multi-touch monitor with Windows 8.

Training the pen

You don't need to train the stylus, but you probably need to train yourself how to use it, to understand its quirks. Follow these simple steps for basic stylus orientation:

1. **Remove the stylus from the tablet's clutches.**

2. **Bring the stylus near the screen, but don't touch the screen yet.**

   You should see the mouse pointer change to a target-like thing, as shown in the margin. (Some programs may display the mouse pointer as an insertion bar. To see the target-like thing, display the desktop.) That's the *pen cursor,* and it appears instead of the mouse pointer (or mouse cursor) when you use the stylus on your tablet.

3. **Hover the stylus around the screen (but not touching the screen).**

   The pen cursor follows the movement. Don't move too far away with the pen, or else the signal gets lost.

4. **Tap (touch and release) the stylus on an icon.**

   For example, tap the Internet Explorer icon on the taskbar.

   Touching an icon with the stylus works like clicking it with the mouse.

5. **If the icon didn't open, tap the icon twice to open it.**

   The icon opens a window on the screen. If the window appears in full-screen mode, tap the Restore button, as shown in the margin.

6. **Use the stylus to drag the window around the desktop.**

   Touch the top part of the window and, keeping the stylus on the screen, drag the window around.

   To move the pen cursor without dragging, just point the stylus at the screen. To drag items on the screen, touch the stylus to the screen.

7. **Press and hold the stylus on the screen.**

   As you hold down the stylus, you see the pen pointer grow a halo, forming in a clockwise direction.

8. **Release the stylus after the circle appears.**

   The press-hold-release operation is a "right-click." The circle is your visual clue that the "right-click" was successful. Well, also, the shortcut menu for the icon appears when you've done a proper press-hold-release.

9. **Tap the desktop to dismiss the shortcut menu.**

10. **Practice your tapping skills to close the window.**

11. **Put the stylus back into its garage for now.**

Table 8-1 quickly lists pen and mouse equivalents.

Table 8-1	Pen and Mouse Actions
Mouse Activity	*Pen Equivalent*
Point	Point the stylus at the screen. (Don't touch!)
Click	Tap the stylus on the screen.
Double-click	Tap the stylus twice on the same spot.
Drag	Touch the stylus to the screen and move the stylus a little.
Right-click	Touch the stylus to the screen, pause, and then lift the stylus. Alternatively, touch the stylus while pressing its button.
Right-drag	Press and hold the stylus button while keeping the stylus touching the screen.

If the stylus sports a button, it can be used to quickly emulate a right-click. Essentially, pressing the button is the same as a right-click or right-drag operation, depending on what you're doing with the stylus.

For more help in using the stylus, you can use the Tablet PC Pen Training program. The program is available only in Windows 7 and Windows Vista: From the Start menu in Windows 7, choose All Programs⇨Pen Tablet⇨Tablet PC Pen Training. In Windows Vista, the Pen Training program is found on the Tablet PC submenu. Work through the program by following the directions onscreen.

✔ You can use the Control Panel's Pen and Touch dialog box to customize the way the stylus interacts with Windows.

✔ In Windows Vista, the Pen and Touch dialog box is named Pen and Input Devices.

✔ Don't be too slow on the press-hold-release right-click action. If you wait too long before lifting the stylus, the operation fails and you have to try again.

✔ I find using the stylus button easier than the press-hold-release method for emulating a right mouse-click.

✔ In some cases, the top of the stylus can be used as an input device; for example, to erase parts of an image in a graphics program. The availability of this feature depends on custom software that might have come with your Tablet PC.

✔ The stylus actions are independent of what you can do by touching the monitor with your finger in Windows 8. If your laptop has a multi-touch monitor compatible with Windows 8, it probably didn't come with a stylus, anyway.

Accessing the onscreen keyboard

To make up for the absence of a keyboard, your Tablet PC comes with an onscreen keyboard. The keyboard type varies, depending on which version of Windows you have.

The Windows 8 touch keyboard

 In Windows 8, the onscreen keyboard is summoned by touching (or clicking) the Touch Screen Keyboard icon — shown in the margin — on the taskbar. When you do, you see the Touch Screen keyboard displayed, as shown in Figure 8-4. The Touch Screen keyboard might also appear whenever you type text and a physical keyboard is unavailable.

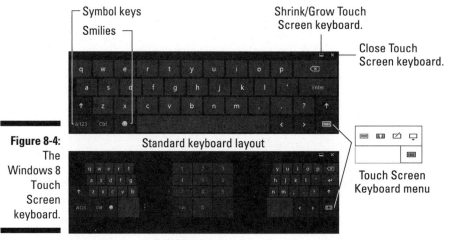

Figure 8-4:
The
Windows 8
Touch
Screen
keyboard.

Symbol keys
Smilies
Shrink/Grow Touch Screen keyboard.
Close Touch Screen keyboard.
Standard keyboard layout
Touch Screen Keyboard menu
Split keyboard layout

Windows 8 sports three Touch Screen keyboard styles: standard, split, and handwriting. You switch styles by touching the menu key, shown in Figure 8-4.

Though the Touch Screen keyboard can be used on any Windows 8 laptop by clicking the mouse, it's designed for a multi-touch monitor. For a convertible laptop, however, it gives you keyboard access while the screen is folded down over the keyboard.

The input panel

In Windows 7 and Windows Vista, you can use the input panel as an on-the-fly gizmo to either scribble in text or use as a small, onscreen keyboard for those desperate situations when typing is required.

The input panel lurks on the right or left edge of the screen, looking like a window that has gone astray. Touching the input panel with the stylus pops out the panel a bit more, as shown in Figure 8-5. Touch the input panel again to summon it in its full-blown glory, also shown in Figure 8-5.

The input panel lurks on the side of the desktop.

Tap the input panel with the stylus to pop it out a bit.

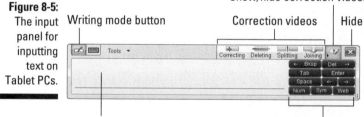

Show/hide correction videos.

Figure 8-5:
The input
panel for
inputting
text on
Tablet PCs.

Writing mode button   Correction videos   Hide

Write text here.   Edit text buttons

Figure 8-6 shows the input panel in Keyboard mode. To switch to that mode, click the keyboard icon in the upper-left part of the Input Tablet window, shown in the figure.

Keyboard   Tools
mode button   menu button   Hide

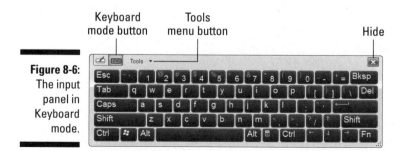

Figure 8-6:
The input
panel in
Keyboard
mode.

To use the input panel in Keyboard mode, simply point the stylus at the key you want to "press." To use the input panel to write on the screen, refer to the next section.

To control how the input panel appears, as well as configure its settings, you use the Options dialog box. The quick way to open it is to point the stylus at the Tools menu button (refer to Figure 8-6) and choose Options from the Tools menu.

For example, you can use the Options dialog box to specify whether the input panel appears on the left or right side of the desktop or is permanently docked at the top or bottom of the desktop.

Writing text on the screen

What's the point of having a touchscreen laptop if you can't use your finger to quickly jot down text? Keyboards? Why, they're so 20th century, after all.

You can use the text-input part of the onscreen keyboard to actually write on the screen. You can type short bursts, such as for filling in a text box on a web page, or type longer stretches. Here's how it works:

1. **Click the mouse or touch the screen where you want the text to appear.**

2. **Summon the input panel.**

   Refer to the preceding sections. You want to summon the part of the onscreen keyboard that's used to scribble text.

3. **Type or print the text you want to type.**

   As you write, Windows interprets your scrawl. Sometimes, it's amazingly accurate. Sometimes, the text needs work. Figure 8-7 shows the Windows 7 version of the text input panel; the Windows 8 panel looks similar.

Figure 8-7:
Using the
input panel
Handwriting
mode to
input text.

Type text here.

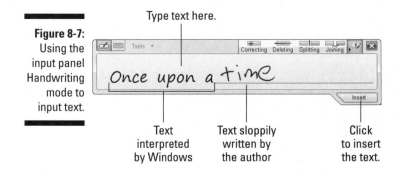

Text
interpreted
by Windows

Text sloppily
written by
the author

Click
to insert
the text.

4. **If you make a mistake, tap the stylus on the incorrect word.**

   The word you tap is spread out, allowing you to retype or erase certain characters, as shown in Figure 8-8.

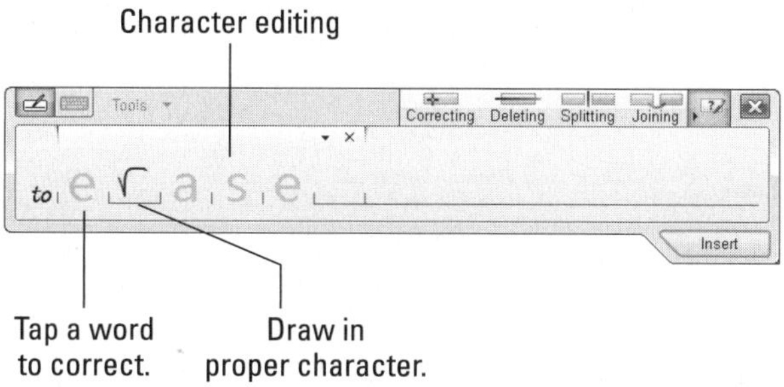

Character editing

Figure 8-8:
Using the
input panel
Character
mode to
input text.

Tap a word   Draw in
to correct.   proper character.

   To erase a character, drag the stylus horizontally across it from right to left.

   When you're correcting, a series of word suggestions appears above the word you're editing. Tap one of those words to choose it as a replacement.

5. **When you're done, click or tap the Insert button.**

   The text you've written appears on the screen as though you've input it from the keyboard.

The input panel expands as you write, so don't worry about running out of room.

The input panel can also be accessed anytime you click in a text box, such as in a dialog box or even on a web page. When you click in such an area, the Input Tablet icon appears, as shown in the margin. Tap the icon to summon the input tablet and quickly "type" what you need. This feature may not be available in all versions of Windows.

   ✔ Erase text by drawing a line back and forth over the text. This action "rubs out" whatever you wrote.

   ✔ The input panel in Windows Vista has a button that activates Character mode for writing text one character at a time.

   ✔ When all else fails, remember that you can convert some tablet computers into the standard laptop configuration and just use the keyboard.

Giving your laptop the finger

Some Windows 7 and Windows Vista Tablet PCs allow you to use your finger as an input device, just like your nose does! Although it's not as elegant a solution as the stylus, it may do in a pinch. Honestly, I've not gotten the hang of the finger thing (and it smudges the monitor). You might find it handy, however.

To use your finger, extend it from the rest of your hand. Any finger will do. (Yes, even that one.)

To have the laptop recognize finger input, use your extended finger to work these steps:

1. **Open the Pen and Touch dialog box.**

   Directions are offered earlier in this chapter.

   The dialog box is named Pen and Input Devices in Windows Vista.

2. **Click the Touch tab.**

   What? No Touch tab? Then your laptop doesn't have that ability. Oh, well.

3. **Place a check mark by the option Use Your Finger As an Input Device.**

4. **You can click the Settings button to make adjustments or to practice.**

   Click the OK button to close the Settings dialog box if you elect to go there.

5. **Put a check mark in the Touch Pointer area to activate that feature.**

6. **Click OK to close the Pen and Input Devices dialog box, and also close the Control Panel window if it displeases you.**

When you touch the screen with your finger, you see a tiny mouse icon appear, as shown in the margin. It's the *touch pointer,* which helps you with right-click and drag activities.

Special Tablet PC Software

You can do anything on a Tablet PC with a stylus that most people do on a laptop with a mouse. But you have an edge in certain areas. To help you exploit that edge, Windows comes with a slate of useful programs and tools available only to Tablet PC users. This section explains some highlights.

Windows Journal

Finally, it has come to this: Your pricey Tablet PC serves the same function as a cheap pad of ruled paper. In fact, the Windows Journal program, shown in Figure 8-9, follows this paradigm visually.

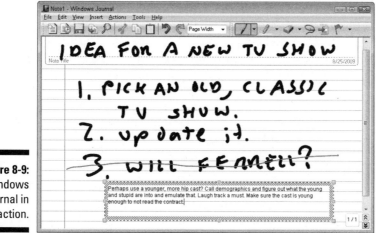

Figure 8-9:
Windows
Journal in
action.

In Windows 8, you can start the Windows Journal program by summoning the Search command on the Charms bar. Type **windows journal**, and then touch or click the Windows Journal button on the left side of the screen. (See Chapter 7 for more information on finding the Charms bar.)

In older versions of Windows, choose Windows Journal from the Start menu's All Programs menu: All Programs⇨Accessories⇨Tablet PC⇨Windows Journal.

After the program starts, scribble. If you need to write text, create a text box by choosing Insert⇨Text box, and then use the keyboard or input panel to write. Don't forget to save your work!

Sticky Notes

For taking quick notes, you can use the Sticky Notes program, shown in Figure 8-10. It's not quite a virtual Post-it Note, but the program comes close. It's simpler than using the full-blown Windows Journal, and it offers a way to take audio notes by using your computer's microphone.

Figure 8-10:
The Sticky
Notes
program.

In Windows 8, summon Sticky Notes by choosing the Search charm and typing **sticky notes**. Touch or click the Sticky Notes button on the left side of the screen.

In Windows 7 and Windows Vista, start Sticky Notes from the Start button menu: Choose All Programs⇨Accessories⇨Sticky Notes.

InkBall

What would life be like without computer games? Well, everyone would probably read more books. So when the urge to enrich your mind with a good book reaches its peak, you can play a game like InkBall instead.

InkBall was apparently too vapid to be included with Windows 8. So in earlier versions of Windows, you can start InkBall by choosing All Programs⇨ Games⇨InkBall from the Start menu. InkBall is an arcade game that should help you hone your stylus skills.

Part III
You and Your Laptop

The 5th Wave
By Rich Tennant

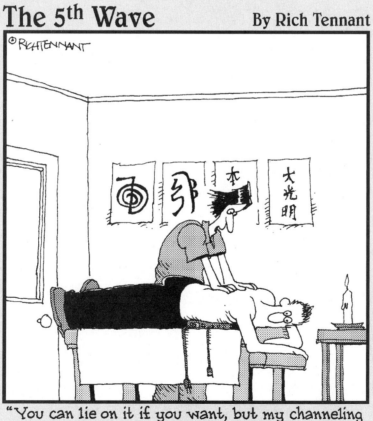

"You can lie on it if you want, but my channeling energy through your body's chakras isn't going to increase your laptop's battery life."

In this part . . .

Once upon a time, back in the early days of the computer era, there was a lawyer. This lawyer liked the way a computer looked on his desk. It was an imposing, scary piece of office machinery. Having that PC powerhouse on his desk was a status symbol; it impressed his clients and intimidated his foes. Of course, the lawyer didn't know how to use the computer. Heck, he never turned it on. It was a very expensive prop, as far as he was concerned.

Your laptop is more than a prop. It can become not only a tool you use to work and communicate but also an extension of yourself. This part of the book discusses how you can use your laptop and get the most from its portable features. Also touched upon are unique laptop issues, such as power management and using a printer.

Chapter 9

Using Your Laptop

I'm fond of saying that no two computers are alike. Sure, they may come from the same manufacturer or have the same case design or even the same internal components and software. But it's up to you to configure the laptop, customizing such things as the screen or your user account and truly making the computer your own.

Using your laptop involves a slew of typical boring, mundane tasks. Beyond these tasks lies a world of customization. It truly is *your* laptop. This chapter tells you how to make it so.

You, the Computer Operator

The computing power in your laptop is greater than the power of all computers on Planet Earth until the 1970s. That's a lot of power. Imagine all the brilliant scientists and engineers striving for decades to develop computer technology, and all their skill sets and education. Now think of what they'd give you to have, back in the 1960s, something as powerful as your laptop.

Okay, they'd probably just give you a lot of pizza, but that's not my point. My point is that your laptop is a complex machine, and you're in the driver's seat. To make the seat more comfortable, this section presents suggestions for personalizing your beloved portable gizmo.

Changing your user account picture

I would bet that your user account picture is a flower. Or a chess piece. Or a fish. The picture can change: You can set your account picture to anything. Likewise, you can change many things about your user account. Make it your own!

In Windows 8

In Windows 8, the quickest way to change your account picture is to follow these steps:

1. **Click your account picture, found on the Start screen.**

2. **Choose the Change Account Picture command.**

3. **If your laptop has a webcam, click the Camera button. Pose for the picture and click the Capture button.**

4. **When your laptop lacks a webcam, or when you'd rather use another image, click the Browse button. Plunge through your laptop's image library to select a suitable sketch.**

In older versions of Windows

To change your account image when your laptop has a webcam, act upon these steps:

1. **Click the Change Your Picture link.**

    It's Change My Picture in Windows XP. After you click the link, a slate of insipid images appears. Ignore them.

2. **If your laptop features a webcam, click the Get a Picture from a Camera or Scanner link. Click the Capture button when you like what you see. Click the Get Picture button, and then choose that picture from the list to set it as your account's picture.**

3. **When your laptop lacks a webcam, click the Browse for More Pictures link. Use the Browse dialog box to find an image. Click the Open button.**

Configuring your laptop's display

As on a desktop computer, you can set various options for how Windows displays information on the laptop's screen. Here are the items most people want to customize:

- Screen size (resolution)
- Desktop background
- Screen saver

Resolution: To set the monitor's resolution, right-click the desktop and then, depending on which operating system rules your laptop, do this:

- ✔ *In Windows 8 and Windows 7,* choose the Screen Resolution command.
- ✔ *In Windows Vista,* choose the Personalize command, and then click the Display Settings link.
- ✔ *In Windows XP,* choose the Properties command, and then click the Settings tab in the Display Properties dialog box.

Your laptop's display has certain modes and resolutions that work best — for example, 1280 x 800. These and other resolutions are known as *native* settings for the monitor. Although other resolutions might be possible, the results don't look good and can wreak havoc on the display.

Background: To set the desktop background, also known as *wallpaper,* do the following after right-clicking the desktop:

- ✔ *In Windows 8 and Windows 7,* choose the Personalize command.
- ✔ *In Windows Vista,* choose the Personalize command, and then click the Desktop Background link.
- ✔ *In Windows XP,* choose the Properties command, and then click the Desktop tab in the Display Properties dialog box.

You can choose a solid color or select from a raft of designs and images supplied with Windows.

Screen saver: The final toy, er, important display setting used by most folks is the screen saver. After right-clicking the desktop, choose the proper command, depending on which operating system is controlling your laptop:

- ✔ *In Windows 8 and Windows 7,* choose the Personalize command and then click the Screen Saver link in the lower-right corner of the Personalization window.
- ✔ *In Windows Vista,* choose the Personalize command, and then click the Screen Saver link.
- ✔ *In Windows XP,* choose the Properties command, and then click the Screen Saver tab in the Display Properties dialog box.

Choosing the proper screen saver is up to you — have fun with it. I recommend, however, that you place a check mark by the option On Resume, Display Logon Screen (or On Resume Password Protect) because it adds a level of security to your laptop.

✔ On Tablet PCs, you can also set the screen orientation — Landscape mode or Portrait mode. That's because the Tablet PC's monitor can be used vertically (landscape) or horizontally (portrait). A button on the monitor may also let you change the screen orientation.

✔ Notice that the resolution-setting window or dialog box often features two displays. The second display is the external monitor or video protector used to make presentations. See Chapter 22 for more information on setting up the display and for information about making presentations with your laptop.

✔ You can save a modicum of battery power by choosing a lower screen resolution. Choosing a solid background color also saves a sliver of battery life.

✔ See Chapter 21 for more information about laptop security.

✔ The screen saver time-out value should be less than the time-out value used to "sleep" the monitor. Refer to Chapter 10 for more information on setting a sleep timeout for the laptop's display.

✔ Avoid downloading screen savers from the Internet. Though many of them are legitimate, some are spyware or worse: They spew ads all over your screen, and the software is nearly impossible to remove.

Dealing with User Account Control (UAC) alerts

All recent versions of Windows (sorry, Windows XP) present laptop users with a heightened level of security, primarily in the form of User Account Control (UAC) warnings. These warnings are designed to alert you to situations where your computer's configuration, and therefore its security, might be compromised.

The UAC appears as a warning message in Windows 8 and Windows 7 primarily when you're using a standard-level account. In that case, you see the warning message appear, informing you that you must log in using an administrator account to complete the task.

In Windows Vista, the warnings appear for both standard- and administrator-level accounts: You're required to click the Continue button for an administrator account or type the administrator's password for a standard account.

UAC warnings are nothing to be concerned about — unless they happen unexpectedly. In Windows, you see the UAC warning whenever you click a link flagged by the shield icon, as shown in the margin. When you see this warning and you didn't click such a link, my strong advice is to choose Cancel to stop the operation.

✔ See Chapter 21 for more information on laptop security.

✔ When faced with the UAC, instantly ask yourself: "Did I summon this warning?" or "Does this warning make sense, given the software I've recently installed?" If not, cancel the UAC warning.

The Ins and Outs of Removable Storage

As the Lord High User of your laptop, it's your job to manage the laptop's storage media. The main media is the mass storage inside the laptop, either the traditional hard drive or the SSD (the solid-state drive). This gizmo is held snugly in the laptop's digital bosom. It's fixed and cannot be removed. Other media, however, can pop in or out. These media include digital media cards, optical discs, and a plethora of devices such as thumb drives and the like. All these gizmos must be properly added or removed from the laptop, lest you incur the imperious wrath of Windows.

This section explains how to properly add media to, and remove it from, your laptop as well as how to avoid Windows' wrath.

Adding a drive

There's a difference between a *drive* and the *media* inside the drive. Basically, it's the media that stores the information. The drive is simply the container that holds the media and allows the computer to access the information on the media.

When you add a drive to your laptop, you're connecting something that can read media. An example is a media card reader or some kind of adapter that accepts media cards. A more common example is an optical drive, which reads optical discs (the media).

When adding an external hard drive, a media card, or a thumb drive, you're adding both the media and the drive at the same time; the media cannot be removed from the drive.

Basically, to add the drive to your laptop, simply connect it: Plug in the USB cable. After Windows contemplates the situation for a few seconds, the drive is ready to use. Well, it is unless you need to turn on the drive; some external hard drives have power buttons or switches on the back. Turn the thing on, and *then* it's ready to use.

✔ External drives that you add to your laptop show up as storage icons in the Computer window. See Chapter 7.

✔ External media and drives must be properly removed when you're done with them; don't just unplug them! See the section "Removing an external drive," later in this chapter.

Inserting media

Media is a general word for "the stuff on which you store computer information." Traditional computer media are the disk drive, the hard disk, and the optical disc. Newer media include what I call *media cards,* also known as *memory cards.* These removable wafers and sticks store computer information, and they're also used in digital cameras and cell phones to store stuff.

To use a media card, or an optical disc, on your laptop, insert the media into its proper hole. (Refer to Chapter 6 for identifying proper holes on your laptop.) What happens next is that you'll most likely see an AutoPlay notice or dialog box, similar to the one shown in Figure 9-1.

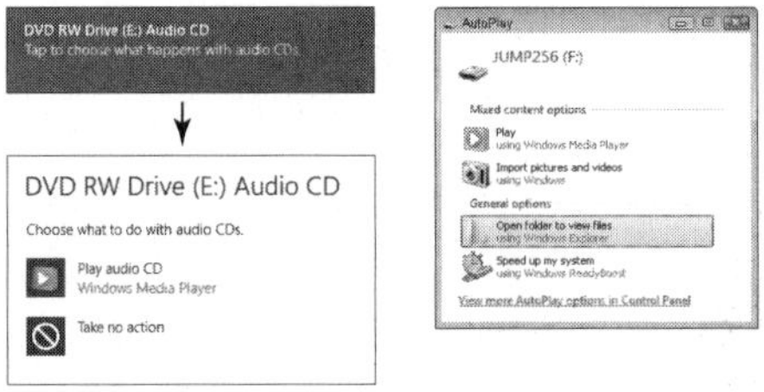

Figure 9-1: Options for reading freshly inserted media.

Windows 8   Windows 7 (and earlier)

The details of the AutoPlay notice depend on a guess that Windows makes about the media's content. You're free to choose an option, as shown in Figure 9-1, or you can dismiss the AutoPlay warning: In Windows 8, click or touch anywhere outside the warning; in older versions of Windows, close the AutoPlay dialog box.

An icon representing the media is found in the Computer window; refer to Figure 7-4, in Chapter 7, for more information on the Computer window.

To access files stored on removable media, simply access it as you would any folder in Windows. Start at the Computer window. (See Chapter 7.) Open the media's icon. Then you can see the files stored on the media.

- ✔ In Windows 8, you must tap the initial AutoPlay warning (refer to the top of Figure 9-1) to see more details.

- ✔ When you choose the option Take No Action in Windows 8, you're dismissing the AutoPlay dialog from appearing again whenever the same type of media is inserted. To override this selection, open the Computer window and right-click the icon representing the media you've inserted. From the pop-up menu, choose the AutoPlay command. In fact:

✔ Anytime you want to see the AutoPlay notice or dialog box for removable media, open the Computer window and right-click the media. Choose AutoPlay from the shortcut menu. (Press the Win+E keyboard shortcut to quickly access the Computer window.)

✔ You can leave the removable media attached to your laptop as long as you like. But be careful when you remove it! See the next section.

✔ Be mindful of USB gizmos, like thumb drives, that stick out from your laptop. You can knock them off or even damage them when you put the laptop back into the case. Always remove the drive when you're done using it; refer to the next section.

✔ See Chapter 12 for more information about USB and the USB port and about adding USB devices to your laptop's hardware repertoire.

Removing media from the laptop

Media must be properly removed from your laptop. Not only does Windows get all moody when you forget that rule, but you can also lose data or damage the media. Nope — obey the rule and follow these steps to remove media being used by your laptop:

1. **Open the Computer window.**

   The easiest way to do this is to press Win+E on the keyboard.

2. **Right-click the media's icon.**

   For example, in Figure 9-2, the removable USB drive uses drive letter E. That's the icon to right-click.

3. **Choose Eject.**

   If the Eject command isn't on the shortcut menu, look for the Eject button on the window's toolbar.

4. **Remove the media from the drive.**

   For example, take an optical disc from an optical drive, or take a media card from a media card reader.

These steps remove only the media, not the drive. If you need to remove or detach the drive, such as a USB optical drive, an external hard drive, or a media card reader, follow the steps in the next section instead (or after removing the media).

Removable optical drive

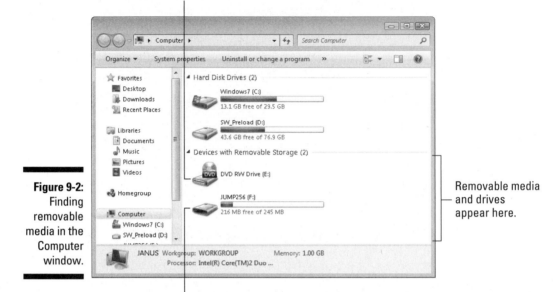

Removable media
and drives
appear here.

Figure 9-2:
Finding
removable
media in the
Computer
window.

USB thumb drive

✔ If you see a warning that the media cannot be removed, click the OK button. Locate whichever programs have open data files on the drive, save the files, and then close the programs. That should allow the drive to be removed.

✔ Refer to Chapter 7 for more information about the Computer window and the notification area.

✔ In Figure 9-2, the media available to the computer is grouped by storage type. To organize the Computer window that way, press F10 if you need to see the menu, and then choose View➪Sort By➪Type from the menu. In some versions of Windows, the command is Group By➪Type.

Removing an external drive

There's a difference between removing media and detaching the *drive* that contains the media. As with any media, you really shouldn't just unplug the drive, especially an external hard drive. Such things must be done properly.

The easiest way to remove an external drive is to turn off the laptop. After it's off (not hibernating or sleeping), you can detach any external storage device.

To remove an external drive when the laptop is on, you use the Safely Remove Hardware icon, which dwells in the notification area. (Its icon is shown in the margin, and you may need to click the Show More button to see the icon.) Click the icon to display a pop-up menu of removable drives. Choose from the list the drive you want to remove. Remove the drive.

When you only want to remove the media from the drive, such as a media card or an optical disc, use the Eject command as described in the preceding section.

The Software Side

In the realm of computers, all hardware requires software to make it go. Your laptop is no different, and it most likely came with lots of software pre-installed. Windows is software, after all. You may also have Microsoft Office installed, plus other software: security, antivirus, financial, and lots o' junk. You may even add more software. And you probably want to remove the junk. This section explains the details.

Adding new software

To expand your laptop's abilities, or to provide support for new hardware, you add new software to your laptop's repertoire. Installing new programs is one of the basic computer-operator duties.

Software can be installed from two sources:

- ✔ An optical disc
- ✔ The Internet

The standard and easiest way to install new programs on your laptop is to stick the software's optical disc into your laptop's optical drive. After inserting the disc, just sit back and watch as the installation program runs. Follow the directions on the screen. The operation may take a while, and it may require decisions and choices on your part. Don't fret: Eat a snack and watch. Soon, you're done.

To install a program from the Internet, the program must first be downloaded into your laptop. This is a common and safe way to add programs. Follow these general steps:

1. **In the web browser, click the link to download the software.**

   Choose the EXE, or *executable,* link. Avoid GZ, RAR, SRC, TAR, ZIP, and other links because they involve more setup steps, require programs you don't have, or contain information you don't need.

   A warning might appear in the web browser window. It says something like, "To help protect your security, Internet Explorer blocked this site from downloading files to your computer. Click here for options."

2. **Choose the option that lets you download or save the file.**

   If a problem occurs and the download doesn't start, look on the page for a link like Click Here to Download Directly. Clicking this link should start the download.

   The File Download security warning appears, as shown in Figure 9-3.

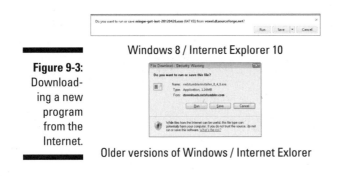

Windows 8 / Internet Explorer 10

Figure 9-3:
Download-
ing a new
program
from the
Internet.

Older versions of Windows / Internet Exlorer

3. **Click the Save button.**

   I recommend saving the file so that you have a copy on your laptop. The copy makes it easier to reinstall the file later, if the need arises.

   In some web browsers, the Save As dialog box appears. It has the Downloads folder selected for you, which is the disk location in which I recommend saving downloaded files. Click the Save button to proceed with the download.

   Wait while the file is downloaded. Well, actually, you can go do something else if the download is lengthy; Windows continues to retrieve the file as you work on other tasks.

   When the download is complete, you see a message telling you that the download is complete.

4. **Click the Run button to install the program.**

   You're done with the download, but not with the security warnings.

5. **Click the Yes (or Run) button.**

   This last step confirms that you trust the software developer and that you're certain you haven't downloaded something nefarious.

At this point, installing the program works the same as though you were setting things up from an optical disc: Read and obey the directions on the screen.

✔ If the program doesn't automatically install after you insert the optical disc, open the Computer window and right-click the optical drive's icon. From the shortcut menu, choose the Play, AutoPlay, or Install menu item.

✔ You need to attach an external (USB) optical drive to install software from an optical disc on an Ultrabook or a netbook that lacks an optical drive.

✔ Install software from the Internet that comes from a reliable source. If you question the source, use Google to search for the software name or for the software developer's name. When the software is questionable, you can find many links that explain why or that answer questions about potential dangers.

✔ Some programs require that you restart Windows before the installation is complete.

✔ The reason you occasionally have to quit all other running programs is that some programs, such as antivirus and security software, may interfere with the installation process. Also, if the computer automatically restarts when the installation is over, you can lose unsaved data in any running program.

✔ EXE is the filename extension for programs in Windows. ZIP is the filename extension for Compressed Folders. When you download such a file, you must first *extract* the compressed files from the folder and then install, which is a pain. The filename extensions GZ, RAR, and TAR represent archives, like ZIP does, but require special software to extract their contents. The SRC filename extension is given to downloads that also contain the programming source code.

Removing software

Back in the days when you needed permission from the electric company to start your computer, you could easily uninstall or remove computer software: You simply deleted the program. Despite the fact that those days have been over for about 20 years, some people out there still believe — and spread the word — that you remove software by playing duck hunter. Not true!

To rid yourself of unwanted software, obey these steps:

1. **Open the Control Panel window.**

   Refer to Chapter 7 for help with locating the Control Panel, if you haven't yet been there.

2. **Click the Uninstall a Program link found beneath the Programs heading.**

   If you're using Icon view, open the Programs and Features icon. In Windows XP, open the Add or Remove Programs icon.

What did they preinstall this time?

Most laptops come with a bloat of software preinstalled. Don't feel compelled to use it. In fact, if the software annoys you, uninstall it. There's no point in keeping anything on your laptop's hard drive that you don't plan to use. Don't want AOL or NetZero? Bye! Don't plan to use Disk Doctor? Buh-bye! *Remember:* It's *your* laptop!

3. **Click to select the program you want to remove.**

4. **Click the Uninstall or Uninstall/Change button that appears on the toolbar.**

   In Windows XP, click the Remove button that appears to the right of the program name.

5. **If you see the User Account Control warning, click the Continue button.**

   What happens next depends on the software you installed. Each program has its own uninstall procedure, and most are easy to follow.

6. **Close the Programs and Features window when you're done.**

Some applications, such as Microsoft Office, run a special program that lets you change or repair the installation as well as remove programs. My advice: Read the screen directions *carefully*.

- Uninstalling a program erases its files from the laptop's hard drive.

- Not every uninstall operation is successful. Sometimes, pieces of the program, or its files, remain behind. This situation is normal, sadly, and there's little you can do about it.

- You can't undo the uninstall action, though you can always reinstall the program — as long as you have the original installation file or optical disc.

- Removing a program *does not* remove the data files it created. For example, removing a graphics program doesn't delete all the graphics images you created with that program. After all, you created and own those files, and only you can remove them.

- Removing programs frees up space on your hard drive.

- Occasionally, you can find the Uninstall command on the All Programs menu (from the Start thing in non-Windows 8 versions of Windows). The command sits on the same menu as the program itself — very handy.

Chapter 10

Portable Power

· ·

In This Chapter

▶ Knowing various types of batteries

▶ Locating your laptop's battery

▶ Monitoring battery use

▶ Setting low-battery warnings

▶ Charging the battery

▶ Using a spare battery

▶ Saving power

▶ Creating your own power plan

· ·

> *L* aptop manufacturers seem to have solved the issues of size and weight
> quite effectively over the past few decades. One issue that remains on
> hold, however, is that of battery power. For all laptop users, the question
> remains: How long you can you use the thing without having to scramble
> desperately for a wall socket somewhere? Honestly, today's laptop batteries
> should last for days, not hours.

If the laptop's processor is the muscle, and software the brain, the battery is
its heart. As long as that sucker keeps beating, you can use your laptop anywhere. This chapter covers the basics of laptop batteries and how to make
the power last longer.

The Battery Will Get a Charge Out of This!

It's simple. The laptop's battery is what separates the laptop from the wall.
Portable computers are portable only when they lack power cords. So, in a
way, having a battery-powered computer gives you freedom. Lots of folks know
that, but few truly know or appreciate what goes into a laptop's battery. This
section explains it.

The dreaded memory effect

In the old days of the NiCad, and even NiMH, batteries, the mantra was that you had to fully discharge the battery, all the way down to empty, before you even considered recharging the thing. This principle was true and necessary: If you didn't fully drain the battery, it began to lose its potency over time.

What happened, especially with the NiCad battery, was that the battery would "remember" how long it was used. So, if the battery held one hour of power when it was fully charged and you recharged it after only 30 minutes of use, the former one-hour battery would become a 30-minute battery. That's *the dreaded memory effect*.

Today's lithium-ion batteries don't suffer from the dreaded memory effect. They're smart. You can use them for a minute and then recharge them, and the battery is still as good as it was when you bought it. So boldly use your battery without fear. And the next time someone mentions the dreaded memory effect, giggle with a smug laugh of confidence, secure in the knowledge that you're safe from the power problems of the past.

What's a battery?

When you think of a battery, the image that probably comes to mind is that of the standard cylinder battery, used in flashlights and toys. Then there are those boxy car batteries, full of lead and acid — nasty things, intimidating. Only people who are comfortable with jumper cables bother with the car's battery.

Basically, a *battery* is a gizmo that stores electricity. The electricity is stored chemically, and it stays in the battery for a time before it gradually dissipates. When the charge is gone from a standard flashlight battery, the battery is done. Batteries found in computers and other high-tech devices can be recharged, allowing you to use them over and over.

Bottom line: The battery is used to supply electricity to your portable gizmos.

- ✔ Batteries were developed in the 1700s, originally from a Leyden jar, which was a device used to store static electricity. Benjamin Franklin used Leyden jars arranged in a series like an artillery battery, which is where the term *battery* comes from.

- ✔ By the way, those cylinder batteries we use in our flashlights (and in many netbook computers) were developed in the 1890s.

Types of batteries

All batteries store electricity. How they store electricity depends on the chemicals inside the battery. Those chemicals determine which type of battery is being used. Here are some popular battery types:

Alkaline: This type of battery is the most common, used in flashlights, portable radios, remote controls, smoke alarms, and kids' toys. It's standard but not rechargeable, which makes it a poor choice for a laptop.

Lead acid: If ever two words could make an environmentalist blanch, they're *lead* and *acid.* Yet those two chemicals supply the robust power of a car battery. The batteries are durable, long lasting, and rechargeable, but they're also heavy and caustic for use in a portable computer.

NiCad: Nickel-cadmium batteries were some of the first consumer batteries that could be recharged. Sadly, they suffered from a malady known as the *memory effect*, which you can read about in the nearby sidebar "The dreaded memory effect."

NiMH: The nickel-metal-hydride battery proved to be longer lasting than the NiCad, but it too suffered from the memory effect.

Lithium-ion: This type of battery is the one you most likely have in your laptop. Lithium-ion, or *Li-ion,* batteries are lightweight and perform better than other types of batteries, and they don't suffer from the memory effect. Their power can be managed by using the computer, and they can be rapidly recharged. Finally, this type of battery is more environmentally friendly than the other types; plus, it has a cool *Star Trek*–sounding name.

✔ Always dispose of old batteries properly; never just throw a battery in the trash. Most communities have special recycling or disposal bins for batteries. Use them.

✔ You can confirm which type of battery your laptop has by looking at its label. See the next section.

✔ Your laptop might have *two* additional batteries inside. A secondary, alkaline battery inside is used to power the laptop's internal clock. An optional third battery keeps things powered for the minute or so that it takes you to swap out a spent main battery with a fresh one. See the section "Using a second battery," later in this chapter.

✔ Using unapproved batteries in your laptop may lead to bad situations, such as, oh, the laptop catching fire and exploding. If you doubt me, search for *exploding laptop* on YouTube: www.youtube.com.

Fuel cells

The future of the battery looks weak. I could say *drained.* That's because electronic gizmos in a few short years will start using fuel cells rather than batteries.

Fuel cells use a magical combination of chemistry and physics that provides power for much longer periods than typical batteries do. Although a fuel cell drains like a battery does, you can refill it — add fuel similar to filling a gas tank — and keep the fuel cell power going until it needs refilling again.

Fuel cells are available today, but they're a bit too bulky to be used with laptop computers. The estimated time schedule given by scientists and engineers states that "real soon now" mankind will have small, light, compact fuel cells for use in laptop computers. When that time comes, power management on your laptop becomes a different creature, and battery-saving tips and techniques become a thing of the past.

Locate the laptop's battery

Take a moment to locate your laptop's battery. Odds are good that it loads into the bottom of the laptop, though a few laptop models have their batteries inserted through a hole or door in the side.

All laptop batteries are labeled, though you may have to remove the battery to see the label. The label contains information about the battery type. It also has disposal information, plus various stickers and tattoos from safety organizations, national and international.

- Some Ultrabooks and netbooks lack removable batteries. Battery information might appear on the laptop's bottom or might not even appear.

- A few netbooks operate using standard alkaline batteries.

- Know where your battery is stored in your laptop. You may need to remove or replace it in the future.

- Most laptops use a few sliding locks or clips to help keep the battery in place. The locks may be numbered when you have to follow a sequence to release the battery. Don't force a battery into or out of your laptop.

- Batteries get warm as they're being used. That's simply their nature. However:

- Watch out if the battery gets too hot! For example, the battery can become too hot to touch or hold for more than a few seconds. The heat can be a sign of a malfunctioning battery, and such a thing is *dangerous.* Phone your dealer or laptop manufacturer immediately if you suspect that the battery is running hot.

Monitor the battery

The laptop's battery drains as you use it, which is to be expected. You should plan for at least two or three hours of active computer use under battery power. The rate of drain varies, however, depending on what you're doing with the laptop. And, naturally, depending on what you're doing, the time may pass rather quickly.

You can monitor the battery in several ways, some of them useful.

In Windows 8, you can summon the Charms bar to see the battery status icon. Press the keyboard shortcut Win+C to see the Charms bar. Refer to Figure 7-3, in Chapter 7, to see an illustration.

The most popular way to check the laptop battery status is by viewing the tiny battery icon in the notification area on the taskbar. The icon graphically shows how much power remains; the icon's color "drains" out as you use the laptop.

When the notification area's battery icon is too tiny for you to see properly, you can point the mouse at the icon. A pop-up bubble appears, explaining how much juice is left, similar to the one shown in Figure 10-1.

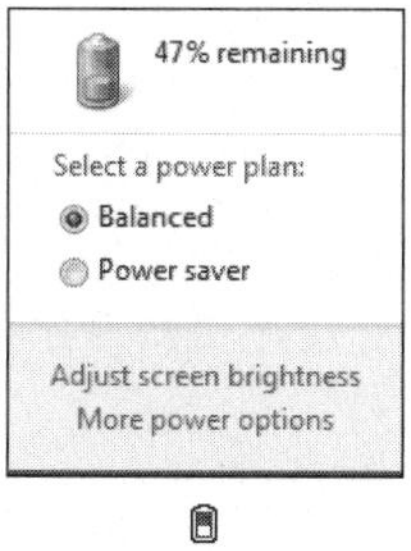

Figure 10-1:
Less
than half
the juice
remains.

47% remaining

Select a power plan:
- Balanced
- Power saver

Adjust screen brightness
More power options

Older versions of Windows displayed specific time "guesstimates" for battery life, as shown in Windows Vista in Figure 10-2.

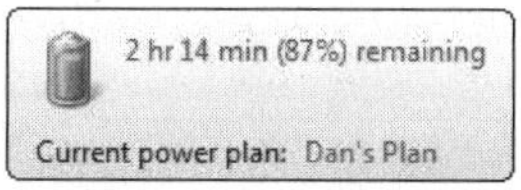

Figure 10-2:
Windows
Vista battery
status.

2 hr 14 min (87%) remaining

Current power plan: Dan's Plan

In addition to the power information displayed by Windows in the notification area, your laptop may have come with specific battery-monitoring hardware, which might display more detailed (and accurate) information.

The Battery Status area in the Windows Mobility Center displays both time remaining and percentage values for your laptop's battery. Refer to Chapter 7 for details on accessing the Windows Mobility Center.

- Your laptop may feature a battery light on its case. The light may change color as the laptop drains. Or the battery light may be a fancy display that accurately tracks battery power. See Chapter 6 for more information on the pretty lights that festoon your laptop.

- Some laptops feature custom battery displays. For example, my laptop has a battery icon on the 3 key. Pressing Fn+3 on my laptop displays the battery status on the screen.

- Gadgets are available for monitoring battery life. In Windows 8 and Windows 7, right-click the desktop and choose the Gadgets command to start your battery-monitoring gadget search. In Windows Vista, use the Windows Sidebar to find a battery-monitoring gadget.

- When the battery is plugged in, the icon in the notification area changes, and the laptop's battery begins to recharge.

- Smart-battery technology is responsible for the ability of Windows to determine how much power remains in the battery. Be aware, however, that such a thing is an *estimate*. Different factors can affect battery life, so don't bet real money on how much longer your laptop can survive on battery power.

Should you keep the battery in the laptop when you use AC power all the time?

Quite a few folks use laptops as their primary computers. If that's you, and your laptop is plugged in all the time, there's really no need for the battery to be in the laptop.

In situations where you never use the laptop's battery, such as when the laptop is more or less permanently docked, consider removing the battery. The laptop should run just fine without it, and by removing it, you keep the battery in good condition for when you do need it.

To store the battery when it's not in use, place it in a nonmetallic (or nonconducting) container. Keep it in a cool, dry place. Over time, the battery drains. That's just the way nature works. When the battery has been in storage a while, don't be surprised if it's dead when you retrieve it. You can recharge it by inserting it into your laptop and charging it as described earlier in this chapter.

RIP, battery

Eventually, your laptop's battery will die. It's inevitable. Just as humans are subject to death and taxes, batteries are subject to death. (Fortunately, the government hasn't figured out how to plunder tax money from a battery. Yet.)

You can tell when your battery is about to die by observing one unique trait: It suddenly becomes useless. It no longer holds a charge, and the charge it does hold is quick and unreliable.

✔ Don't mourn a dead battery! Dispose of it at once!

✔ Never chuck an old computer battery into the trash. Batteries are considered toxic waste in most communities. You must properly dispose of or recycle dead computer batteries according to the rules of your jurisdiction.

✔ A dead battery doesn't mean a dead laptop. Get a new battery! Replacements are sold online, locally, or from the manufacturer.

When the Power Gets Low

Thanks to smart-battery technology, your laptop computer gives you a whit of warning before the battery poops out. Don't panic! You have enough time to finish what you're working on, save it, close programs, and properly shut down the computer. This section explains how it all works.

Receiving low-battery warnings

To prepare for the inevitable, you receive a series of warnings.

It starts with the various battery icons and lights changing color. The battery light on the laptop's case may go from green to yellow or red. The battery icons on the desktop do the same. This type of warning happens gradually as you use the laptop.

As battery life passes below the 25 percent available mark, the battery icon in the notification area may grow one of those international warning triangles: yellow with an exclamation point in the middle. Humans grow the same thing after they turn 75, though only angels and little kids can see it.

You may hear an audible warning as the battery's life grows shorter and shorter. See the next section for particulars.

When you see the low-battery warning bubble on the notification area's teensy battery icon, similar to the one shown in Figure 10-3, you can be sure that time is just about to expire. At that point, save your stuff and shut down (or hibernate) the laptop. I'm serious, because the last thing that happens when the power gets low is that the laptop shuts itself off. The screen goes dark. You're done.

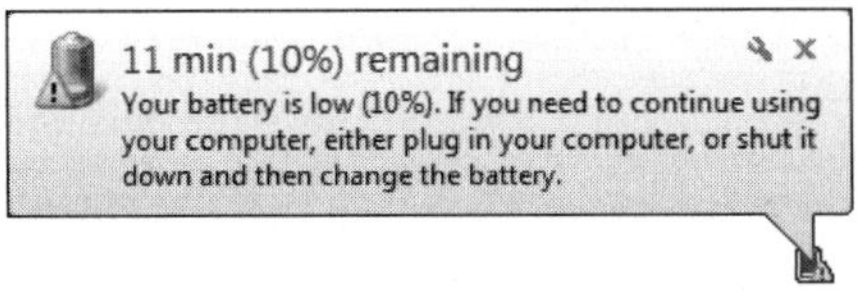

Figure 10-3:
Oops!
Quittin'
time!

> 11 min (10%) remaining
> Your battery is low (10%). If you need to continue using your computer, either plug in your computer, or shut it down and then change the battery.

Adjusting low-battery warnings

You have control over when the warnings are displayed as the battery drains. You can set the percentage at which the low and critical warnings kick in, and you can specify what happens when they do. Here's how:

1. **Open the Control Panel.**

   Choose the Control Panel item from the Start button menu.

2. **Choose the Hardware and Sound link.**

3. **Choose the Power Options link.**

4. **By the selected power-plan setting, click the Change Plan Settings link.**

5. **Locate and click the link that says Change Advanced Power Settings.**

   Finally, the Power Options dialog box shows up. It's *the* happening place for all things having to do with power management in Windows.

6. **Scroll the list, and locate the item labeled Battery.**

   As you would expect, it's the last item in the list.

7. **Click the plus sign (+) by Battery to display various battery notification and action options.**

   Each item has two subitems — one for settings when the laptop is on battery power and a second for when the laptop is plugged in.

In chronological order, here are the items you can set:

a. *Low battery notification:* Sets a warning for a low-battery level, before the situation becomes critical. Values are *On* to set the low warning and *Off* to ignore it.

b. *Low battery level:* Determines what exactly is the low-battery level as a percentage of battery power. This value should be generous, well above the critical level. (See paragraph D.)

c. *Low battery action:* Tells the laptop what to do when the battery charge reaches the low-battery level. Your options are Do Nothing, Sleep, Hibernate, and Shut Down.

d. *Critical battery level:* Sets the battery power level at which the crucial action takes place. This is the last-gasp thing Windows can do for your laptop just before the power goes out. The level is set as a percentage of battery power, and it should be less than the low-battery level (item B).

e. *Critical battery action:* Directs the laptop to sleep, hibernate, or shut down when the critical battery level is reached.

Other items may appear in the list, depending on your laptop's power management hardware.

8. Set each item according to your needs.

To see a pop-up menu, click the colored text next to either the On Battery item or the Plugged In item. Choose the setting you want from the pop-up menu.

I set the low-battery action to Do Nothing and the critical-battery action to Hibernate.

9. Click OK to confirm your settings; close the remaining dialog boxes and windows.

The battery-warning settings have no visual effect; the low-battery icon in the notification area continues to drain and appears in yellow with a warning flag, and then the pop-up message appears (refer to Figure 10-3) at the low-warning point.

✔ When the low-battery notice sounds or appears and you're blessed with a second battery for your laptop, pop it in and keep working! See the section "Using a second battery," later in this chapter.

✔ That critical-battery notice is serious. Computer time is over! You see no warning; the laptop simply hibernates or turns itself off — whichever option is set.

✔ The best thing to do when power gets low: Plug in! This is why I take my power cable with my laptop wherever I go.

Charging the battery

This task is easy to do: Plug the laptop into a wall socket, and the battery begins to charge. Nothing could be simpler. Well, dropping your new laptop on hard concrete and having it break is simpler, but not recommended.

✔ You can recharge your laptop's battery whether the battery is fully drained or not.

✔ I leave my laptop plugged into the wall whenever I can.

✔ There's no need to fully drain your laptop's lithium-ion battery every time you use it.

✔ The battery continues to charge even when the laptop is turned off (as long as it's plugged in).

✔ It doesn't take longer to recharge the battery if you use the laptop while recharging.

✔ Never short a battery to fully drain it. By *short,* I mean that you connect the two terminals (positive and negative) directly so that the battery simply drains. This is a bad and stupid thing to do. It can cause a fire. Don't do it.

Using a second battery

An option that you probably ignored when you bought your laptop was a second battery. Having a spare battery is a must for anyone seriously on the road or in a remote location, where a long time is spent away from the power socket.

Before you use a spare battery, ensure that it's fully charged. Either charge it in the laptop or use an external charger (if available). Put the fully charged spare battery in your laptop case or in any nonconducting (nonmetallic) container. Then head out on the road.

Most laptops support some type of quick-swapping ability. When the power gets low, you can eject your laptop's original, spent battery and quickly insert the spare battery. But be sure that your laptop can survive such a heart transplant before you attempt it! Perform a test swap in a noncritical situation, just to be sure.

✔ Save your stuff before you attempt any battery swap.

✔ If your laptop doesn't have the ability to hot-swap batteries, simply turn off (or hibernate) the laptop when the original battery is nearly spent. Remove the old battery, insert the fresh one, and then turn on the laptop again.

✔ I recommend labeling batteries with a Sharpie so that you don't confuse the two (or more) and accidentally insert a dead battery.

✔ You can buy a spare battery from your dealer or from stores that sell extra batteries, such as Batteries.com (`www.batteries.com`).

✔ Be wary of generic batteries! Always try to buy a manufacturer's (or manufacturer-approved) battery for your laptop. Get anything less and you run the risk of setting your laptop ablaze! It has happened!

Managing Your Laptop's Power

The battery will drain. It's a matter of when. You may not have control over the physics, but you have control over the things that go on in your laptop. By using the computer's power management software, plus a few deft moves that I'm about to share, you can squeeze every ion of electricity from your laptop's battery.

Power-saving tricks and tips

Your laptop was built to consume less power than a desktop computer does. The laptop uses a special processor that draws less power and produces less heat. Everything inside the laptop case is geared toward battery savings. Even so, they do draw power.

Here's the short list of items that consume the most power in your laptop:

✔ The hard drive

✔ The optical drive

✔ The audio system (speakers)

✔ The modem

✔ The wireless network or Bluetooth adapter

✔ The (wired) network interface

✔ The display

Each of these devices consumes power when it's in use. I don't even mention the things you plug in that use power! Unless that external gizmo has its own batteries or plugs into the wall, it too adds to the battery drain.

By not using these devices, or by rationing their use, you can save power.

Some laptops come with the ability to quickly disable things you're not using. For example, on some laptops you can disable the optical drive when the laptop is battery-powered. Or you can dim the display to save juice.

One common trick I use is to mute the speaker when I'm on the road. (And, no, using headphones still draws power and doesn't save battery life.)

Disabling the wireless networking adapter or Bluetooth connection saves the battery.

Using a laptop cooling pad helps keep the laptop from overheating, which keeps the laptop's internal fans from spinning fast and consuming more power. See Chapter 26 for more information about a laptop cooling pad. To be most efficient, the cooling pad should use its own power source.

Further battery savings are possible by using your laptop's power management techniques, covered in the next section.

Creating a power management plan

The real power-saving power comes not from the trivial energy-saving crumbs you toss the battery but rather from the power management hardware built into the laptop. To control the hardware, you must create a power management plan. Here's how:

1. **Open the Control Panel.**
2. **Choose Hardware and Sound.**
3. **Choose the Power Options heading.**

   The Power Options window appears.
4. **From the list of links on the left side of the window, choose Create a Power Plan.**

   The Create a Power Plan window appears, listing the three standard PC power plans. Each plan is rated by battery life and computer performance.
5. **Choose an existing power plan.**

   You'll base your new power plan on the existing plan. I chose the Balanced plan.
6. **Type a name for your new plan in the Plan Name text box.**

   I named mine Dan's Power Plan, which has nothing to do with global domination.

7. Click the Next button.

In the next window, shown in Figure 10-4, you set the various time-outs and screen-brightness levels for your power plan. The time-outs and brightness settings for my plan are shown in the figure.

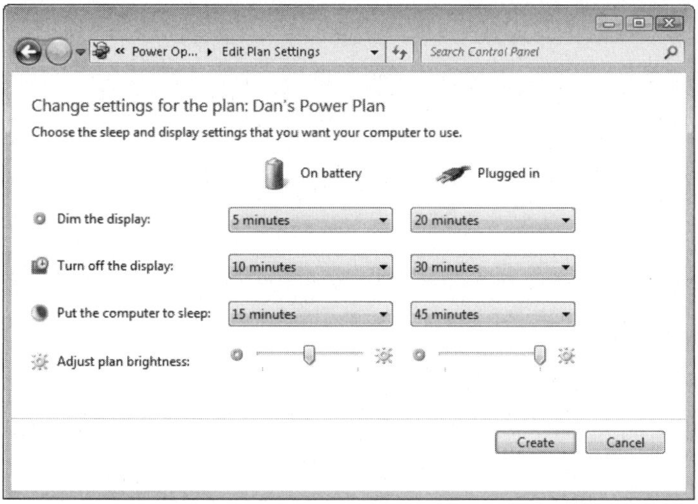

Figure 10-4:
Creating
your own
power man-
agement
plan.

8. Set the time-out and brightness values for the items present in the Edit Plan Settings window.

9. Click the Create button to create your plan.

The plan you just created is selected and shown in the Power Options window.

10. Close the Power Options window.

You can follow these steps to update an existing plan: In Step 4, click the Change Plan Settings link by the plan you want to modify. Make the modifications, and then click the Save Changes button.

The screen may go blank before its time if you have set up a screen saver time-out that's less than the Turn Off Display time-out. Likewise, if you set the screen saver time-out to a value greater than the Turn Off Display time-out, you never see your screen saver kick in.

If you've modified the battery time-out values (see the section "Adjusting low-battery warnings," earlier in this chapter), you must re-enter that information for your new power management plan.

Chapter 11

The Laptop, the Printer, and the Fax

*L*aptop computers can use printers just like desktop computers can use printers. The biggest difference is that laptops are portable. If you try too closely to emulate a desktop computer with a laptop, you'll lug around a lot of stuff, which kind of defeats the purpose of portability. Even so, you can use a printer with your laptops. You can even find portable printers that help sate your urge for printing on the road. This chapter covers printing with your laptop; plus, it covers sending faxes, which is just like printing, albeit remotely.

A Portable Printer for Your Laptop

When Adam Osborne originally proposed the portable computer, portable printing wasn't part of the big picture. He was right! How many times have you been in a café or at the airport and seen someone printing from a laptop? Never! That's because printing is a task that can be done later. To print, you wait until your laptop is back home.

There are portable printers, of course. They can be small and light, though they're often more expensive and slower than desktop printers. Most portable printers run on standard flashlight batteries, so you can print literally anywhere.

I must confess that I don't use a portable printer with any of my laptops. Once upon a time, I had a Canon Bubble Jet portable printer. It was a good printer, but too much to take with me for the few times I used it.

- ✔ The laptop and the printer don't need a physical connection between them. Wi-Fi and Bluetooth portable printers let you print stuff without having extra wires to carry around.

- ✔ If you plan to use the portable printer in your car, get a model that features a *car adapter* — a thing you can plug into the car's 12-volt adapter (previously known as a cigarette lighter).

- ✔ When the printer features rechargeable batteries, remember to fully charge the printer before you venture out on the road.

- ✔ Printers need paper! If you take a printer with you on the road, you also need to take some paper.

- ✔ Printing can always wait. It's not necessary to use a printer with a laptop computer, especially when you can attach a printer later or access a printer on a network. Later sections in this chapter tell you how.

- ✔ You can also send a fax as a way to print a document when a printer isn't available. Businesses and hotels feature a fax machine to which you can send stuff that needs printing. See the section "The Fax Printer," later in this chapter.

Laptop Printer Setup

Using a laptop with a printer works just like using a desktop with a printer: Connection issues, setup issues, and other frustrations await you, just like always. This section clears things up.

Finding printers in Windows

Any printers that have been configured for use with your laptop appear in one location in Windows. In Windows 8 and Windows 7, that location is the Devices and Printers window, shown in Figure 11-1. In addition to various gizmos available to your laptop, you find printers in that window, as shown in the figure.

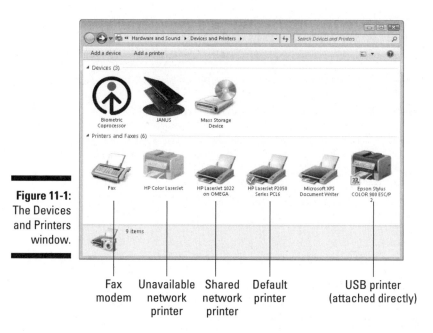

Figure 11-1:
The Devices
and Printers
window.

Fax
modem

Unavailable
network
printer

Shared
network
printer

Default
printer

USB printer
(attached directly)

To view the Devices and Printers window, click the View Devices and Printers link found in the Hardware and Sound category in the Control Panel. In Windows 7, you can also choose Devices and Printers from the Start button menu.

The Devices and Printers window lets you add and manage printers, the details of which are covered throughout this chapter. And because faxing is similar to printing, you also find the Fax "printer" located in the Devices and Printers window.

- ✔ In Windows Vista, printers show up in the Printers window. To view this window, and to see which printers are available to your laptop, choose the Printers command from the Start button menu.

- ✔ Windows XP lists printers in the Printers and Faxes window; choose Printers and Faxes from the Start button menu.

- ✔ In addition to listing printers, you can manage what's printing from the Devices and Printers window (as well as its ancestor windows in older versions of Windows). To see what's printing, double-click to open a printer icon.

- ✔ The Microsoft XPS Document Writer icon represents a printer used to print to a document, like a PDF file but not a PDF file because it's Microsoft and not Adobe. See the later section "Printing when you don't have a printer."

Adding a printer directly to your laptop

Hooking up a printer to your laptop works just like connecting a printer to a desktop computer. It's relatively simple. It all starts with buying a USB cable.

True, your laptop didn't come with a USB cable, and neither did the printer. Go back to the store and buy one now. Also consider boning up on the whole USB issue by reading Chapter 12 on your way to the store. Better yet, be safe and bring someone else along to read Chapter 12 to you while you drive to the store to buy a USB cable.

The next step is to read the directions that came with the printer. This step is important because some printers can simply be plugged into the laptop's USB port and — *voilà!* — they're ready to use. Other printers require you to run a software setup program before they're connected. You need to know which is which, lest you screw up printer installation.

Installation works like this:

1. **Connect the USB cable to the printer and to your laptop.**

2. **Turn on the printer.**

Or like this:

1. **Install the printer's software.**

2. **Connect the USB cable to the printer and to your laptop.**

3. **Turn on the printer.**

If you doubt the amazingly simple process by which you add a printer to your laptop's peripheral armada, simply confirm that an icon representing the printer dwells in the Devices and Printers window for Windows 8 and Windows 7, or in the Printers window for more ancient versions of Windows.

- ✔ Refer to Chapter 12 for more information on what *USB* means and how it works.

- ✔ You set up the printer only once. Then you can simply attach the printer to your laptop and use it for printing stuff.

- ✔ Feel free to add as many printers to your laptop as you might end up using.

- ✔ See the earlier section "Finding printers in Windows" for information on opening the Devices and Printers window.

- ✔ You can disconnect the printer when you don't need it. Reconnecting the printer simply reactivates its support in Windows.

Adding a network or wireless printer

Most network printers or wireless printers don't need additional setup. Windows is smart enough to find those printers (as long as the printers are turned on) and install the network or wireless printer for you.

When a network or wireless printer isn't automatically installed, you need to do the setup yourself. It involves installing the printer's software on your computer: Insert the optical disc into the laptop's optical drive, and follow the directions on the screen.

For network or wireless printers that don't automatically configure themselves, you need to open the Devices and Printers window and click the Add a Printer button to set up manually. Follow the directions on the screen. My advice: If the network or wireless printer doesn't show up, consider getting someone else to help you.

✔ You can use an external, USB optical drive on laptops that lack an internal optical drive.

✔ Windows refers to any printer directly connected to your laptop as a *local* printer. Network, wireless, and Bluetooth printers fall into the *nonlocal* category.

✔ Both Windows 8 and Windows 7 automatically select and let you use network printers. In Windows Vista, you can browse the network to look for shared printers: Open the Network window, and then open a computer icon to find a shared printer. After you find it, right-click the shared printer's icon, and choose the Connect command from the pop-up menu.

✔ The key things you need to know for setting up a network printer are its IP address and its manufacturer's name and model number. When Windows doesn't list the printer model number, click the Windows Update button to see a more complete list, or use the optical disc that came with the printer.

"What is the default printer?"

Your laptop can print documents to only one printer at a time. You can choose the printer when you print (refer to the later section "Printing something in Windows"), or when you don't specify a printer, Windows uses the *default* printer.

You can determine which printer is the default by looking in the Devices and Printers window. (Refer to Figure 11-1.) You see a green circle with a white check mark flagging the default printer. In Figure 11-1, the default printer is the HP LaserJet P2050 Series PCL6. (It's a long name for a rather modest printer.)

One printer must always be chosen as the default. To change the default, right-click any printer icon in the Devices and Printers window and choose the command Set As Default Printer from the pop-up menu.

Print Something

There's no point in having a printer for your laptop unless you're going to print something. Then again, you might not be near a printer when you need to print something. This section covers both situations.

Printing something in Windows

Printing in Windows is done from within the application that's showing the document you want to print. The Print command's location can vary, depending on the program you're using. Here are some places in which to look:

- ✔ On newer programs, check the File tab on the ribbon. Choose Print⇨Print.

- ✔ Traditionally, the Print command dwells on the File menu.

- ✔ Also look for the Print toolbar button.

- ✔ When all else fails, the common keyboard shortcut to summon the Print dialog box is Ctrl+P.

No matter how you get there, eventually you see the Print dialog box, shown in Figure 11-2. It's the location where you control the printing of your documents. It's also where you choose which printer to use for printing that document.

Clicking the Print button in the Print dialog box instantly (more or less) prints your document. Or you can set options that allow you to change the number of copies or choose a range of pages to print. (Refer to Figure 11-2.)

- ✔ Watch out! Using the Print toolbar button often prints the document instantly, without visiting the Print dialog box. That's why it's called the Quick Print shortcut.

- ✔ You choose the paper size and set margins by using the Page Setup dialog box. Summon this dialog box by choosing the Page Setup command from an application's File tab on the ribbon or from the File menu.

- ✔ Sometimes, the Page Setup dialog box is found on a Print submenu.

Default printer   Other available printers

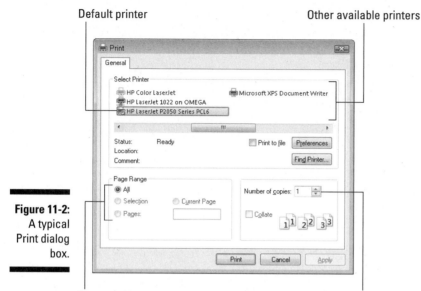

Figure 11-2:
A typical
Print dialog
box.

Choose which pages to print.   Set the number of copies to print.

Stopping a printer run amok

One of the most common printing issues, aside from a paper jam, is when the printer spews out page after page and you want it to stop. The correct solution for this situation varies, so I present several, from easiest to most drastic.

First, look on the printer for the Cancel button. It's probably red and shaped like a stop sign or maybe a circle with an X in the middle. Punching this button cancels the printing, though a modicum of text — or a page or two — might still print. That's okay.

Second, you can cancel printing in Windows. Open the printer's icon, which is found in the Devices and Printers window. When the icon opens, you see a list of *jobs* waiting to print, one of which is actively printing. To cancel a job, choose it from the list and press the Delete key on the keyboard. Click the Yes button to confirm that you want to cancel the print job.

Third, and most drastically, you can turn off the printer. That works. It may screw things up because turning off the printer may leave a page stuck, or jammed, in the printer. You can deal with that problem later. Additionally, after turning off the printer, heed the directions I give for the second option (in the preceding paragraph) to delete the print job from the printer's window.

- A quick way to summon a printer's window is to look for the printer icon in the notification area on the taskbar. Clicking the wee printer icon instantly pops up the printer's window, displaying the queue from which you can cancel a print job.

- A wee bit of text may continue to print after you cancel a print job. That's okay. Eventually, the printer will stop.

- In Windows Vista, printer icons are found in the Printers window. In Windows XP, it's the Printers and Faxes window — same place, different names.

- Things that are printed are *jobs*. The list of jobs in a printer's window is the *queue*. The process of printing while you're doing other things in Windows is *spooling*.

Printing when you don't have a printer

The urge to print is seldom immediate. When printing can wait, let it wait: Save a document. Then open the document again, and print when your laptop is connected to the printer. Otherwise, I offer these nonprinter printing suggestions:

- Decent hotels and airports have business centers, where you can temporarily connect to a printer and put your stuff on paper.

- Some office supply stores offer printing services. Print shops and places such as FedEx Kinko's also have printers available for rent by the hour or by the sheet.

- Fax machines are printers. If you know of a fax machine nearby, just send your document as a fax. Note that plain-paper faxes are preferred; avoid wax-paper faxes, if possible. Note that faxes don't print in color. See the next section for more information about faxing from your laptop.

- You can create PDF (Adobe Acrobat) files, which can be displayed and printed on any computer that has the Acrobat Reader software installed. You must, however, buy the Acrobat Writer software to create PDF files.

- The Microsoft XPS Document Writer can be used when you don't have a printer. When you choose this printer and click the Print button, you see the Save As dialog box. The document is then saved as an XPS document, which can be viewed by using the XPS Viewer program in Windows. Yeah, it's similar to a PDF file, but not as admired.

The Fax Printer

It's true: A fax machine is like a printer. In fact, a fax machine *is* a printer — a printer that connects to your laptop with a modem instead of with a printer cable or over the network (or wirelessly). Using a fax machine like a printer is yet another option for printing, but it's also an option for sending the traditional fax. This section explains how it works.

- ✔ Your laptop doesn't have a fax machine per se. It's the laptop's modem that can be used for sending faxes. See Chapter 16 for more information on using a modem with your laptop.
- ✔ Technically, the laptop's modem is a *fax/modem*.
- ✔ When your laptop lacks a modem, it cannot be used to send or receive faxes. Duh.
- ✔ The following sections describe how to use the faxing facility inside Windows. Other faxing programs are available that you might find easier to use and manage than the one Windows offers. Visit your local Software-o-Rama to see the variety.

- ✔ You can also use various web-based fax services.
- ✔ Not every edition of Windows comes with faxing software.
- ✔ Faxes are a bit antique when you think about it. The e-mail attachment has supplanted the fax as the standard way documents are sent these days. Even so, I recognize that the legal and medical communities continue to use faxes. So, it's obvious that I can't just wiggle out of writing about this stuff.

Sending a fax

Faxing works just like printing, so sending a fax starts with the standard printing operation. Do this:

1. **Connect the laptop's modem to a working phone line.**

   The fax is sent over the phone line. The line must be connected before you can send a fax.

2. **Prepare the document that you want to fax.**

   You can fax from any application that has a Print command on its File menu.

3. **Choose File⇨Print, or use whichever command prints a document in your application.**

Do not click the Print button on the toolbar! That action often just prints the document on whichever default printer you selected. If the default printer is the fax machine, that's fine.

4. **Choose the fax modem as your printer.**

5. **Make any other selections as needed in the Print dialog box.**

For example, specify which pages to print, the number of copies, and other options as they're available in the dialog box.

6. **Click the Print button.**

Windows may require some setup before you proceed with the next step. You may be asked to choose between a fax modem and a fax server. To use the laptop's modem to send a fax, choose the Fax Modem option, and continue to work the setup steps on the screen.

The New Fax window appears, as shown in Figure 11-3. Yes, it looks a lot like a new e-mail message window.

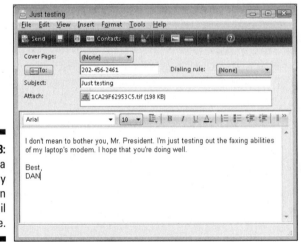

Figure 11-3:
Sending a fax the way you send an e-mail message.

7. **Use the To button to select a recipient from the Windows Contacts folder, or just type a phone number for the receiving fax.**

8. **(Optional) Fill in the rest of the fields.**

9. **Click the Send button.**

At this point, the fax goes into the *queue,* which means that it sits and waits for the fax modem to do its job and send the fax. The fax-status window holds you in suspenseful agony while the modem does its thing.

To confirm that the fax has been sent, you must visit a place that I call Fax Central. Refer to the next section.

Visiting Fax Central

To observe all the fast-paced, thrilling fax action as it happens (or even after the fact), visit Fax Central in Windows. Because faxing in Windows works like sending an e-mail, the Fax Central window greatly resembles an e-mail program. Know e-mail, and you can work the Fax Central window.

To get to Fax Central, open the Fax icon in the Devices and Printers window. (Refer to Figure 11-1.) Yes, the real name of the place is Windows Fax and Scan. I call it Fax Central.

Fax Central is also where you can cancel a fax, if you have a modem or connection problem. Simply locate the fax by opening the Outbox folder. Click to select the fax, and press the Delete key on your laptop's keyboard. This task is necessary because simply unplugging the phone cord from the fax modem merely delays sending the fax.

Receiving a fax

When you're aware of a thundering fax speeding your way, summon the Windows Fax and Scan window (I call it Fax Central), as described in the preceding section. Then follow these steps:

1. **Ensure that the laptop's modem is connected to a phone line.**
2. **Wait for the ring (if you have another phone attached to the incoming line).**
3. **From the window's toolbar, click the Receive a Fax Now button.**
4. **Sit and wait.**

   Doh-dee-doh-do.

After the fax has been received, a pop-up bubble may appear, or you may notice the little Pending Fax Guy in the notification area. It's your clue that a fax has come in.

Any fax that's received appears in the window's inbox — just like e-mail does. To view the fax, double-click its icon, or select the fax and then click the View button on the toolbar. The fax is displayed in a special window, from which you can print, save, or mess with the fax.

Faxes are received as *image* files. Specifically, they're TIFF images. You cannot edit the files as text documents. Faxes are *images*.

Chapter 12

Expanding Your Laptop's Universe

* *

In This Chapter

▶ Understanding USB

▶ Connecting a USB device

▶ Using a USB storage gizmo

▶ Expanding your USB universe

▶ Working with PC Cards

▶ Adding an extra keyboard or mouse

▶ Connecting an external monitor

▶ Using the laptop with the lid closed

* *

*I*t's weird. Your laptop has pretty much the same external expansion options as a desktop computer. It kind of flies in the face of the portable, carefree, untethered, and wireless existence that laptop computing promises. Oh, well. So be it: When you want to, you can expand upon your laptop's hardware universe by adding all sorts of peripherals. You might end up adding so many gizmos and gadgets that you need a second case just to haul them around. Oh, and batteries! Don't forget all the batteries for those gizmos. This chapter describes the possibilities for laptop hardware expansion.

USB Expansion Options

The main way you add bonus goodies to your laptop is by using the laptop's USB port. This section tells you how it all works.

That USB thing

Your laptop may have one or more USB ports on its sides or rear. They may look like square holes to you, perfect for inserting a Sucrets, but they're USB ports.

A *port* is a "hole" in the computer's case into which you plug something. The port is also the "smarts" that make useful whichever device you plug into the laptop. For a USB port, you plug in USB devices.

A USB device can be plugged directly into a USB port, such as a thumb drive. Mostly, however, a USB device is connected by using a USB cable, such as an external hard drive, scanner, printer, or full-size keyboard.

The beauty of USB is that you can plug stuff in and take stuff out without having to turn the laptop off or on or having to complete a complex setup or configuration. That's why USB is so popular and why you use it to expand upon your laptop's hardware abilities.

✔ Please don't stick a Sucrets lozenge into a USB port.

✔ USB stands for Universal Serial Bus. The key word is *Universal,* like the movie studio, but in this case it means that the USB standard supports a vast array of gizmos.

✔ All USB devices, even the cables and the spot where the USB port lives on your laptop, sport the USB symbol, shown in the margin.

✔ The newest USB standard is USB 3.0. It uses a similar-looking port and logo as the currently popular USB 2.0 standard. Only laptops running Windows 8 are able to use USB 3.0 devices.

The USB cable

Most USB gizmos attach to your laptop by using a cable. Like all cables in this universe, USB cables have *two* ends. One is the A end, and the other is the B end, as illustrated in Figure 12-1. This A-B end-thing was done so that you can never plug a USB cable in backward, upside down, or sideways.

The A connector is rectangular. It plugs into the computer. It's often called the *upstream* end.

Figure 12-1:
The A and
B ends of a
USB cable.

The A end   The B end

The B connector has a D shape. This type of hole and cable connector are fitted on USB devices. It's the *downstream* end.

For example, to connect a USB printer, you plug the A end of the cable into your laptop and the B end into the printer. That's it.

✔ Some USB devices (thumb drives, for example) attach directly to the laptop, which means that you don't need a USB cable.

✔ Not every USB device comes with its own USB cable. USB printers are notorious for not including USB cables in the box. You must buy a separate USB cable. Computer stores, as well as most office supply stores, keep a variety of USB cables in stock.

✔ USB cables come in a variety of lengths, but they can be no longer than about 16 feet. Any longer and the computer believes the USB device to have been disconnected. Besides, who needs to use a laptop with a USB gizmo sitting 16 feet away?

✔ For your laptop, shorter cables are best.

✔ When you shop for a USB cable, find a USB A-to-B cable.

✔ If you want a USB *extension* cable, you want a USB A-to-A cable or one that's labeled as an extension.

✔ In addition to the standard A and B connectors are smaller connectors, dubbed *micro* and *mini.* Usually, a device that requires these special types of connectors comes with the proper USB cable. For example, my digital camera uses a cable with an A connector on one end and a micro B connector on the other. Most cell phones and smartphones feature micro USB connectors.

Plug in a USB gizmo

A USB device is a snap to connect — literally. You don't need to turn off your laptop, run a special program, or incant a spell in Latin. Just plug in the USB gadget and you're ready to roll.

Given that I said that, please read the directions that came with your USB gizmo before simply plugging in the thing. True, some USB devices are instantly recognized and configured when you attach them. But other USB devices require software to be installed on the laptop first.

- ✔ If the USB device has its own power switch, you must switch the thing on before the computer recognizes it.

- ✔ Be sure to read the manual that comes with the device to determine whether you need to install special software before plugging in the device or turning it on.

- ✔ The ability to plug and unplug USB devices without having to turn the computer off or on is known as *hot swapping*. It sounds risqué, but it's not.

USB-powered devices

Quite a few USB doohickeys are powered by the USB cable itself. That is, they draw the electricity they need from the laptop's USB port. The good news is that you don't need an extra cable, power supply, wall socket, or battery for the device. The bad news is that it sucks up the laptop's precious power juice even faster.

I believe that the good news outweighs the bad on using USB-powered devices. For me, when I need the device, I prefer not to lug around extra cables or forget about including the power cables or batteries required by non-USB-powered doohickeys. Anything that lightens your load is good.

- ✔ Most flash memory devices (thumb drives and memory cards) are USB powered.

- ✔ Those cooling fan pads you can get for your laptop can also be USB powered.

- ✔ Some laptops come with the option not to supply power to the USB ports — specifically, when the laptop is running on battery power. Be sure to check your laptop's power management system, or use the Power Options icon in the Control Panel (see Chapter 7) to determine whether it's an option.

Here a hub, there a hub

Expandability is one key to the USB port's popularity. It may not seem practical, but your laptop can have as many as 127 USB devices attached to it at any given time. Yes, all at once. Imagine dragging that chain of goodies through the airport. You'd win a medal. Well, after making it through security.

A USB *hub* is nothing more than a USB device with more USB ports on it. You plug the hub into your laptop's USB port. Then you can plug anywhere from two to four to eight USB devices into the hub.

✔ Some devices cannot be run from hubs, such as certain high-speed hard drives. In this case, the device must be plugged directly into the laptop's USB port. Don't fret: A warning message appears and instructs you when such a thing happens.

✔ Keep your eye out for *pass-through* USB devices. For example, a USB keyboard may sport more USB ports on its sides, so you can plug the USB device into your laptop and then plug more USB devices into the first device. That way, you don't run out of USB ports.

✔ There are two types of hubs: powered and unpowered. The powered hub must have its own power source. (It must be plugged into the wall.) Powered hubs are necessary in order to supply more power to certain USB devices.

✔ Note that smaller, more portable, laptop-size USB hubs are available. They're quaint — and more portable than the desktop, or full-size, USB hubs.

✔ One of the best ways to add more USB ports to your laptop is to get them on a PC Card. See the section "The PC Card," later in this chapter.

✔ Every USB port on your laptop is considered a *root port*. The 127-device limitation is per root port, so if your laptop has two USB root ports, it can access as many as 254 USB devices. Golly.

USB goodies galore

I just checked the online encyclopedia Wikipedia, and it lists officially *one gazillion* different USB devices you can attach to your laptop. Rather than lift them all from the web pages of Wikipedia, I decided to list the most common USB gizmos in Table 12-1. In Table 12-2, I listed some of the more unusual and uncommon USB gizmos — specifically, those that are beneficial to laptop computer owners.

Table 12-1	Typical, Plain, Boring Uses for the USB Port
Device	*Typical Boring Use*
Digital camera	Grab photos from the camera's memory card and store them on your laptop. You can also do this directly, by removing the camera's digital storage media, which is covered in Chapter 9.
External storage	Use external hard drives, optical drives, thumb drives, and media card readers for storage. See Chapter 9 for more information on external storage.
Headphones	Listen to your laptop all by yourself. Headphones with a microphone let you use digital voice communications on your laptop.
Network adapter	Add networking to your laptop, such as Digital Cellular, Wi-Fi, or Bluetooth.
Printer	Print stuff on paper. See Chapter 11 for printer information.

Table 12-2	More Unusual Ways to Use the USB Port
Device	*Unusual Thing You Can Do*
Legacy adapter	Connect *legacy* (antique) serial, parallel, joystick, or other devices to your laptop. You can use this adapter to continue to use antique computer hardware with your laptop.
Numeric keypad	Quickly enter values without having to toggle the main keyboard between numeric and alpha modes.
Sound hardware	Add high-quality sound hardware to your laptop. For example, add the Sound Blaster Audigy sound card by using the USB port to give your laptop full 5.1 Dolby surround sound. (No word on how best to lug around the five speakers and a subwoofer.)
Speakers	Hear sound. To go along with the USB sound expansion, you can get mini-USB-powered speakers for your laptop. Get the type with the handy tote strap.
Video camera or webcam	Handle all your on-the-road videoconferencing and self-voyeuristic needs when your laptop lacks a webcam.
Scanner	Do your document scanning in a portable manner, especially if you're a lawyer.
Little light	Imagine! Plug it in, and it's powered by the USB port. Furthermore, imagine it with a stiff-yet-twistable neck so that you can see the keyboard when you use your laptop in the dark.

Device	Unusual Thing You Can Do
Game controller	Control your little man, pilot your spaceship, or wield that sword of truth.
Laptop cooler	Set your laptop on it, which acts like a fancy pad. It contains a tiny, quiet fan that helps keep your laptop cool, and it runs from the power supplied by the USB port. (Also see Figure 26-1, over in Chapter 26.)
Mobile phone recharger	Transfer some of the laptop's power to your mobile phone.
Security device	Use the USB port to power an alarm on a cable lock, or plug in to the USB port and unlock (or unscramble) the laptop's data.

The PC Card

The most ancient and most laptoppy method for expanding your laptop's hardware is to use something called a PC Card. Honestly, with the advent and popularity of the USB port, the PC Card just isn't as popular as it once was. Ultrabooks and netbooks don't use PC Cards. Mac laptops don't use them. I suppose that PC laptops won't use them either, but that's down the road. For now, this section tells you how to use the PC Card.

Parking a PC Card in the PC garage

Parking a PC Card is cinchy: Stick the PC Card into the PC Card slot. It slides in only one way: The narrow edge with the holes goes in first. If the computer is on, Windows recognizes the card instantly, popping up a bubble from the notification area to alert you to the presence of new hardware. At this point, you can start using the card or whichever other features with which it has just blessed your laptop.

Some PC Cards may require extra software to make them go. It says so in the card's manual. Other cards, like many USB devices, can simply be plugged in and they're off and running.

Using the PC Card

After the PC Card is inserted and properly set up, you can use its features. In fact, you can keep the card inside your PC for as long as you need those features. The only thing you need to be careful about is removing the card when you're done using it. Refer to the next section.

✔ Some cards jut out from the PC Card slots. Some may have pop-out connectors. Be careful with them! They can get caught on things, so you might consider removing the PC Card before you put the laptop back into its case and potentially break off an expensive gizmo.

✔ Removable storage devices can be used after they're inserted and recognized by Windows. Be sure to properly remove the device, as covered in Chapter 9.

✔ Several types of PC Card exist: Type I, Type II, and Type III. Technical trivia aside, the main difference in card type is thickness. Type III cards are twice as thick as Type II. The only caveat here is that you should avoid buying a Type III PC Card unless your laptop's PC Card garage can accommodate it.

Backing a PC Card out of the PC garage

To remove a PC card, you either pinch the card and pull it out or use the handy Eject button, located to the side of the PC Card garage. Before doing so, ensure that you properly disable or unmount the card's hardware. Otherwise, you may anger Windows, and most people don't relish upsetting the computer's operating system.

Heed these steps to properly remove a PC Card:

1. **Click the Safely Remove Hardware icon in the notification area.**

   Use Figure 12-2 to locate this icon; it looks like a USB plug with a green check mark by it. In some cases, you may need to click the arrow button on the left end of the notification area to see the Safely Remove Hardware icon.

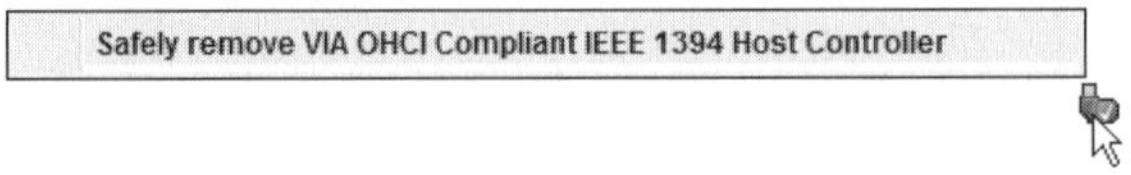

Figure 12-2:
Safely
removing a
PC Card.

Safely remove VIA OHCI Compliant IEEE 1394 Host Controller

2. **Choose from the pop-up menu the device you want to remove.**

    A message appears, telling you that the device can be safely removed.

3. **Pull the PC Card from its slot.**

4. **Click OK to dismiss the message box, or close the message bubble that appears in the notification area.**

Store the PC Card in a proper place, such as in your laptop bag or in a drawer or cubbyhole with the rest of your laptop gear. The idea is to keep the PC Card from being stepped on or crushed by a 20-ounce, ceramic coffee mug that says *Life Is a Beach.*

The Laptop Becomes a Desktop

If you plan to park your laptop in one place all the time, you probably want to upgrade its teensy portable features with more-robust desktop counterparts. Specifically, I speak of the keyboard, monitor, and mouse. Any of these desktop-size items can be added to and used with a laptop rather than with their feeble laptop counterparts. Use one. Use them all. It's quite easy.

Using a full-size keyboard and mouse

If you miss the full size and action of a real PC keyboard, get one! Ditto for a full-size computer mouse: Simply plug a keyboard or mouse into your laptop's USB port. You can start using the keyboard or mouse the second it's plugged in.

When you're done using the keyboard or mouse, simply unplug it. Once again, the laptop can roam free and untethered.

✔ Adding an external keyboard often doesn't disable the laptop's internal keyboard. Likewise, adding an external mouse might not disable the laptop's touch pad. You can use both! But you're probably not crazy enough to do that.

✔ If all you're yearning for is to have a separate numeric keypad, consider getting only that item. You can pick up a USB numeric keypad, which is only the keypad and not the entire keyboard, at most computer stores and office supply stores.

Using a second monitor

Your laptop is readily able to handle two monitors: the laptop's own LCD and an external monitor. That's because a monitor connector is a standard feature on all laptops. The reason is so that you can easily connect an external monitor or projector for making presentations. Even if you're not making a presentation, you can use the monitor connector to add a larger or second monitor to your laptop computer system.

To add the external monitor, locate the monitor connector on your laptop's back or side. Plug in the monitor, and you're ready to go.

You have three options for using a second monitor on your laptop:

✔ Use the second monitor to show the same information that appears on the laptop's monitor.

✔ Use the second monitor to extend the desktop, giving you one computer with two monitors.

✔ Use the second monitor exclusively, disabling the laptop's own monitor.

Some laptops may ask you how to set up the second monitor when you plug it in. Sometimes, you have to press an Fn (I pronounce it "eff enn") key combination to use the second monitor. Or you can use the Screen Resolution dialog box, shown in Figure 12-3, to configure an external monitor. Obey these steps:

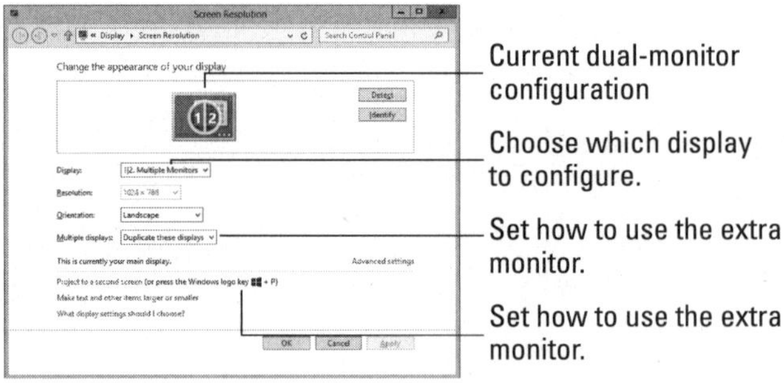

Current dual-monitor configuration

Choose which display to configure.

Set how to use the extra monitor.

Set how to use the extra monitor.

Figure 12-3: Behold the external monitor.

1. **Visit the desktop in Windows 8.**

   The keyboard shortcut is Win+D in Windows 8 to instantly display the desktop.

2. **Right-click the desktop background.**

3. **Choose the Screen Resolution command.**

   In Windows Vista, choose the Personalize command, and then choose Display Settings from the Personalization window.

4. **Work the dialog box to configure how the monitors are set up.**

   The options are displayed in the dialog box controls, as described earlier in this section. You can duplicate the displays, extend (use both displays at once), or choose which display to use primarily.

5. **Click the Apply button to temporarily confirm the setup.**

   If you're unhappy, repeat Step 4.

6. **Click OK to lock in any changes.**

If you don't need to use the laptop's screen while using an external monitor, you should configure the laptop to run with its lid closed. See the next section.

Running the laptop with its lid closed

When you plan to keep your laptop in one spot and you've attached an external keyboard, mouse, and monitor, you can get away with closing the laptop's lid and using only the full-size desktop computer gizmos. I've set up my laptop that way on many occasions, especially when it's been in only one spot for a long time.

To ensure that the laptop doesn't sleep or hibernate when you close the lid, you configure the system so that the laptop does nothing when the lid is closed. See the section in Chapter 5 about shutting the laptop's lid. Choose the Do Nothing option to close the lid.

Of course, you may have to open the laptop to turn it on, but after it's on, you can close the lid and use the keyboard, monitor, and mouse just like you do on a desktop computer.

Part IV
Laptop Communications

In this part . . .

The computer nerds enjoy using scary, intimidating terms. A word like *networking* isn't enough. No, they must say *Ethernet* and use complex numbers, such as 802.11, which is pronounced "eight-oh-two dot-eleven." There's the LAN. There's the modem. The whole topic can be a veritable salad of random letters and numbers, mixed up with a confusing goo they call *IP protocol*. Ick.

The real topic here is communications. The idea is to get your laptop to talk with other computers, to share information. It's a good thing, but thanks to the jargon and some oddball configuration options, it can be something most people dread. There's nothing for you to dread, of course, because you have this part of the book, which eases you into the realm of laptop communications.

Chapter 13

Basic Networking

· ·

· ·

*W*hen I think of networks, my mind goes right to ABC, CBS, NBC, and even Fox. These are television networks, of course, not computer networks. There are no computer networks on television, unless you count the one carried only by the cable company on channel 10011, which no one can *see,* let alone watch. But that's not what computer networking is all about.

Computer networking is about communications and sharing. It's friendly stuff. Well, it's friendly after you clear the hurdle of unfriendly jargon and get everything set up. Not to worry: This chapter explains the terms and helps you set up basic, wired networking in no time.

✔ Wireless networking, which is the most popular type of laptop computer networking, is covered in Chapter 14. I do, however, recommend reading about wired networking first, to help you better understand the whole networking thing.

✔ Using your laptop's networking goodness to connect to the Internet is covered in Chapter 15.

✔ In an office setting, please ensure that your networking administrator, or one of his minions, assists in setting up your laptop for networking.

Wired Networking Overview

Computer networking has hardware parts. Computer networking has software parts. You need them both in order to do the networking thing.

Network hardware

The hardware side of networking consists of three parts:

- A network interface card, or NIC
- Cables and wires to carry the signal
- A hub, switch, or router

Every laptop comes with a NIC, or network interface card. On the wired side of networking, the NIC is evident by the network hole, or RJ-45 *port,* found on the laptop's case. (See Chapter 6.) Every device on the network — computer, printer, modem, hard drive, and other network hardware — has a NIC.

The cables and wires are required in order to send information from, and to get information into, your laptop. The cables are how all devices on the network connect with each other.

Finally, all cables find themselves connected to a hub, switch, or router. These devices, in various degrees of sophistication, manage and monitor the information as it flies over the wires, to and from the various networked gizmos.

Figure 13-1 illustrates the entire networking hardware concept. Each computer in the figure has its own NIC. The NIC is connected to the central router, which also hosts a USB printer.

- Even though every laptop comes with a NIC, some Ultrabooks and netbooks may have only wireless networking abilities. Such laptops would lack the RJ-45 port.

- The cable you use to plug your laptop into the network is commonly called *Ethernet* cable. It's also known as Cat 5 or Cat 6 — some kind of cat, but not a housecat. You can buy this type of cable in assorted lengths, colors, and flavors. It's available at any computer or office supply store.

- *Ethernet* is the name of the computer networking hardware standard.

- A *hub* is simply a place where Ethernet cables from various network devices plug in. It's the simplest way to network several computers. It's also referred to as a *switch.*

✔ A *router* is a faster, smarter version of a switch. Routers can handle large amounts of network traffic and manage connections between networks. That's why routers are most often used with broadband Internet connections.

✔ Actually, a home network doesn't use a router — it has a *gateway*. You often see the word *gateway* used in Windows because it's a technically correct description, whereas *router* is not.

✔ The basic network setup can include both wireless and wired networking. It all depends on the basic components involved. Wireless networking is covered in Chapter 14.

Barbara's PC

Network printer

Router

Figure 13-1:
Typical
network
hardware
setup.

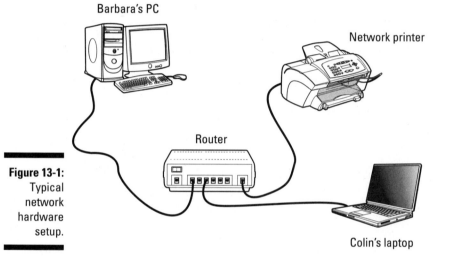

Colin's laptop

Network software

After several versions, Windows finally has this network software thing down pat. I remember, in the bad old days, when Windows 98 required you to manually configure every computer on the network. It was high-school-math painful. Since Windows 7, setting up a network on the software side is practically effortless.

Basically, after connecting your laptop to the network, your next step is to turn on the laptop. Or, well, you can connect to the network with the laptop turned off; it doesn't matter. Windows is smart enough to recognize the network and start using it right away.

After Windows finds the network connection, you're asked which type of network you're connecting to: Home Network, Work Network, or Public Network. Choose the appropriate location.

Always choose the Public Network option when you're using the laptop in a public location. The Public Network option is the most secure.

To confirm that the network is up and working, you open the Network and Sharing Center window, similar to the one shown in Figure 13-2. To display that window, open the Control Panel and click the link View Network Status and Tasks, found just beneath the Network and Internet heading.

Wireless network connection

How you're connected to the network and Internet

Windows 8   Windows 7

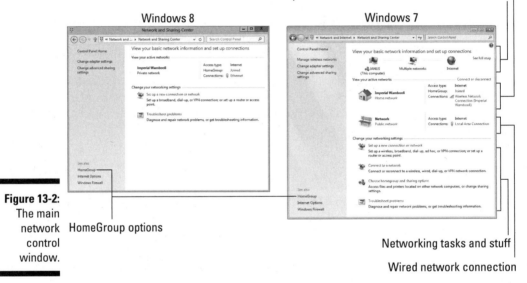

Figure 13-2:
The main network control window.

HomeGroup options

Networking tasks and stuff

Wired network connection

The Network and Sharing Center window is a place you visit in Windows for making network adjustments, troubleshooting, or just checking on things. Most of the time (and if the network gods are willing), everything should work fine after the initial setup.

✔ Refer to Chapter 7 for more information on the Control Panel.

✔ After the initial setup, you connect to any other network you've used by simply plugging the network cable into your laptop. That's it.

✔ To disconnect from a network, simply unplug the network cable. You can do this when the laptop is on, off, sleeping, or distracted by nearby fireworks.

Your Laptop Plays on the Network

After making the hardware and software connections, your laptop becomes part of a computer network. The network hardware and software provide the communications, allowing information to be sent and received between your laptop and other computers (and gizmos) on the network. That's when all the sharing happens.

Setting your laptop's network name

All devices attached to a computer network have their own names, or what the network nerds call *unique identification*. Your laptop is no exception.

To view your laptop's network name, visit the System window, shown in Figure 13-3. The quick shortcut to display this window is to press Win+Break on your laptop's keyboard.

Figure 13-3: The laptop's network name.

The System window shows you oodles of technical and boring information about your laptop, plus the laptop's network name, as pointed out in the figure. Four items are used to describe your computer:

Computer Name: The name of the computer as it appears on the network. Other computers see this name when they "browse the network."

Full Computer Name: The name given to the computer when you first set it up. It's probably your name or your company's name. It cannot be changed.

Computer Description: Optional text to describe your computer or what it does or, if you're feeling saucy, text that's rude and pithy.

Workgroup: The name of the local peer-to-peer network to which your computer belongs.

To set the network names, click the Change Settings link just to the right of where the names are found in the System window. Clicking the link displays the System Properties dialog box. You can type a computer description into a text box or click the Change button to change the computer name or workgroup.

If you elect to change the computer name or workgroup, keep in mind that the changes take place only after you restart the laptop.

- ✔ Workgroup names aren't that important. Most Windows laptops use the workgroup name WORKGROUP.

- ✔ Workgroups have been replaced by the HomeGroup concept in Windows 7. See the section "Creating a HomeGroup," later in this chapter.

- ✔ The Break key might also be labeled Pause on your laptop's keyboard.

- ✔ Win+Break is my favorite Windows key combination.

Finding other computers on the network

All computers on the local network can see each other. It's like being able to see everyone else who's sitting with you on the bus. And that weird guy over there, the one wearing the heavy coat in the middle of summer — what is that large plastic bag he's carrying? Is it leaking some kind of fluid? Wasn't he on the bus earlier and arguing with his girlfriend? Whatever happened to her? Networking is like that.

In Windows, you can view other computers and resources on the network by opening the Network window, as shown in Figure 13-4. The window lists computers on the same network you're using; plus, any media devices, hard drives, printers, and perhaps a router or gateway, as shown in the figure.

To see the Network window, choose the Network item from the left side of any Windows Explorer window; press Win+E to quickly summon such a window. In older versions of Windows, a Networking command is found on the Start menu. Or you can open the Network icon on the desktop.

- ✔ The icons you see in the Network window represent resources that can be shared on the network. The resources include shared computer storage (folders), printers, modems, media devices, hard drives, and other stuff.

- ✔ Computers that are sleeping or hibernating or that have been turned off do not appear in the Network window.

- ✔ Press the F5 key to refresh the Network window. That way, new computers that join the network will have their icons appear, and icons for computers that disconnect from the network will disappear.

- ✔ In Windows 7 and Windows Vista, you can see a graphical layout of the computers on the network: click the See Full Map link found in the upper-right corner of the Network and Sharing Center window. (Refer to Figure 13-2.)

✔ In Windows XP, the network window is named My Network Places.

✔ Seeing computers displayed in the workgroup window is a sure sign of success that the network is up, connected, and ready for action.

Figure 13-4: Computers sharing the same local network.

HomeGroup Sharing

One key thing you can do with a computer network is share resources. The key resource is probably a broadband modem, which you use to connect to the Internet. This topic is covered in Chapter 15. Sharing printers is covered in Chapter 11. Sharing files between computers on the network is covered in this section.

In Windows 8 and Windows 7, files are shared on a network by using the *HomeGroup* (or *Homegroup*, apparently, in Windows 8), which is a new concept in Windows. Older versions of Windows use the shared folder to allow computers to exchange files; see the section "Folder Sharing," later in this chapter.

Doing the HomeGroup thing

The way files are shared on a network in Windows 8 and Windows 7 is by using something called a *HomeGroup*. One computer on the network hosts the HomeGroup. The other computers then join that HomeGroup. That's how files and media are shared between computers.

Start your HomeGroup expedition by determining whether a HomeGroup is already available on the network. Obey these steps:

1. **Open the Control Panel.**

2. **Choose Network and Internet.**

3. **Choose HomeGroup.**

   If there's no HomeGroup item, you have an older version of Windows that doesn't support HomeGroups.

When no HomeGroup is available, you see a button in the window that says *Create a HomeGroup*. See the later section "Creating a HomeGroup" for how to set up a HomeGroup.

If a HomeGroup is already available, or if you've been invited to join one, you see an appropriate message displayed. To join a HomeGroup, click the Join Now button. For more details, see the section "Joining a HomeGroup," later in this chapter.

If you see the text *This Computer Belongs to a HomeGroup,* you're all set; your laptop already belongs to a HomeGroup. You can use the window to modify the HomeGroup settings. See the later section "Using the HomeGroup" to see what else you can do with a HomeGroup.

Creating a HomeGroup

When no HomeGroup exists on the network, you and your laptop can be the first to create one. Start by following the steps from the preceding section. Then continue here:

4. **Click the button Create a HomeGroup.**

5. **Click the Next button if the screen merely blathers on about what wholesome goodness a HomeGroup is.**

   The wholesome goodness screen appears only in Windows 8.

6. **Choose which types of files you want shared.**

In Windows 8, use the drop-down menus to choose whether a library or folder is shared or not shared. In Windows 7, place check marks by all the types of files you want to share.

All the items you choose will be available to other users on the network who join your HomeGroup. That way, you can share stuff easily between those network computers.

7. Click the Next button.

Windows creates a highly cryptic and deliberately confusing password for the HomeGroup. It's the password that other users on the network need to type so that they can join the HomeGroup.

I recommend printing the HomeGroup password now: Click the Print Password and Instructions link.

8. Click the Finish button and close the HomeGroup window.

You're done creating the HomeGroup.

Skip to the later section "Using the HomeGroup" to see how the HomeGroup works for sharing files.

✔ Only one HomeGroup needs to be created for the entire network. Even if you try, you cannot create a HomeGroup when one already exists.

✔ To kill off the HomeGroup, leave it: Follow Steps 1 through 3 in the previous section, and click the Leave the HomeGroup link. On the screen that appears, choose the option Leave the HomeGroup.

Joining a HomeGroup

When someone has already created a HomeGroup on the network, you can join it. These steps continue from the first three steps in the earlier section "Doing the HomeGroup thing":

4. Click the Join Now button.

5. In Windows 8, click the Next button.

6. Review which items you want to share with other computers using the same HomeGroup.

In Windows 8, use the menu by each item to choose whether it's shared or not shared. In Windows 7, select and deselect the option boxes. You must place a check mark by the Documents option if you want to share your laptop's documents with other computers on the network.

7. Click the Next button.

8. **Carefully type the HomeGroup password.**

   Obtain the HomeGroup password from the computer that's hosting the HomeGroup. Hopefully, that user read this book and printed a copy of the password, which they can give to you. If not, have the person follow these steps to print the password for you:

   a. Open the Control Panel.

   b. Choose Network and Internet.

   c. Choose HomeGroup.

   d. Click the View or Print the HomeGroup Password link.

   e. Buy my book.

9. **Click the Next button.**

   Congratulations! You've joined the HomeGroup.

10. **Click the Finish button, and close the HomeGroup window.**

You can resign from a HomeGroup by clicking the Leave the HomeGroup link from the HomeGroup window; follow the steps in the earlier section "Doing the HomeGroup thing" to open the HomeGroup window.

✔ See the next section for information on how to use the HomeGroup.

✔ You can join more than one HomeGroup. In fact, you can create as many HomeGroups as you like. I recommend, however, that you stick with only one HomeGroup on your computer network, especially if you're using your laptop in a home or small-office environment.

✔ The other computers in the HomeGroup must be turned on and not sleeping for you to access their resources.

Using the HomeGroup

All the resources shared by computers using the same HomeGroup can be found by browsing the HomeGroup. Follow these steps:

1. **Press Win+E to summon a folder window.**

   Or you can use any folder window.

2. **Choose HomeGroup from the list of places on the left side of the window.**

   The window displays a list of the HomeGroups your computer belongs to.

3. **Open the HomeGroup icon.**

   Or choose a HomeGroup icon to open when you have more than one.

   You see a list of shared Libraries: Documents (if available), Music, Pictures, Videos, and possibly more Libraries as set up on the network.

4. **Open a Library icon to peruse its contents.**

   For your Media Library (Music, Pictures, or Videos, for example), you see icons representing items you can hear or view; for document libraries, you see a list of files and folders, just like in any folder window.

5. **Open files, copy them — whatever.**

   At this point, using the HomeGroup Library works just like using a folder full of files on your computer.

You can also browse the HomeGroup, and access network files, from any Open or Save As dialog box.

Sharing a folder or Library with the HomeGroup

The easiest way to share stuff with a HomeGroup is to share an individual folder or a Library. It's cinchy:

1. **Right-click the folder or Library icon.**

2. **From the pop-up menu, choose the proper command from the Share With submenu.**

   To share files as read-only, choose the HomeGroup (view) or HomeGroup (Read) command.

   To share files with full access, choose Homegroup (view and edit) or HomeGroup (Read/Write).

Unlike in older versions of Windows, no icon appears on or beneath the folder or Library icon that indicates whether it's being shared.

To stop sharing a folder or Library, right-click its icon and choose either the Stop Sharing or Nobody command from the Share With submenu.

- ✔ A *read-only* folder means that others on the network can only read files. They cannot create new files or delete or modify existing files. Full access to a folder allows others on the network to do anything with a folder, including deleting files and engaging in other mayhem.

- ✔ Libraries allow you to group common files and folders into a single collection.

- ✔ To see the libraries available on your laptop, and to share them on the HomeGroup, choose Libraries from the list of locations found on the left side of any folder window.

- ✔ The Libraries you share are available immediately to all other users in the HomeGroup.

✔ The standard Libraries (Documents, Music, Pictures, and Videos) are shared when you first set up or configure the HomeGroup. See the sections "Creating a HomeGroup" and "Joining a HomeGroup" earlier in this chapter.

Folder Sharing

The traditional way to share the stuff stored on your computer with others on the network is to employ *folder sharing*. Basically, you flag a folder on your computer's storage system as shared. Other folks using the same computer network can then access that folder on your computer. Likewise, you can access shared folders on other computers on the network.

Finding a shared folder

To access storage shared by another network computer, open that computer's icon in the Network window. (Refer to Figure 13-4.) Opening the computer's icon reveals which storage resources are being shared, as shown in Figure 13-5. Or you may see a password dialog box prompting you for access.

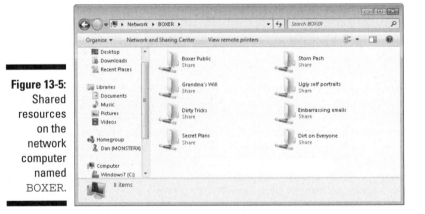

Figure 13-5: Shared resources on the network computer named BOXER.

To access a shared folder, double-click to open the folder. If the folder isn't password protected, you see its contents displayed in a window, just as though it were a folder on your laptop's storage system. If the folder is password protected, you need to enter a username and password before you can access the folder's contents.

Using a network folder works just like using any folder in Windows: You can open files or copy, rename, or edit them — within limitations, such as when a network folder is read-only.

Close the network folder when you're done using it.

> ✔ Folders are available for access on the network only when the computer owner volunteers to share the folders. This topic is covered in the next section.
>
> ✔ When a computer or folder is password protected, you're asked to provide a password for access. If you have an account on the computer, type your account name and password; otherwise, type the name and password you were given for access. Click OK.
>
> ✔ The password may allow you to view the folder contents and to copy files from that folder, or it may allow you full access (read, write, modify, and delete).
>
> ✔ Practice polite network etiquette: Close a network folder when you're done using it. If you forget and don't close the folder, an error message appears when the other computer disconnects from the network or the network goes down.

Sharing a folder from your laptop

Yes, you too can sacrifice one of your laptop's precious folders to the network gods. It's not necessary, but it does make sharing files between network computers easier. Here's how to go about that task:

1. **Right-click the icon for the folder you want to share.**

2. **Choose the Properties command from the pop-up menu.**

3. **In the Properties dialog box, click the Sharing tab.**

4. **Click the Advanced Sharing button.**

5. **If you're prompted with a UAC warning in Windows Vista, type the administrator password or click the Continue button.**

6. **Place a check mark by the item Share This Folder.**

7. **Click the OK button.**

8. **Click the Close button.**

   You can, optionally, close the folder window.

The folder is now available for others to use on the network.

- Folders shared from your laptop in Windows Vista sport icons with a little *sharing-buddies* flag superimposed. It's your visual clue that a folder has been shared.

- In Windows 8 and Windows 7, it's far easier to share stuff with the HomeGroup feature than to share individual folders. That is, unless you're used to the older, traditional method to share folders (described in this section). In that case, you can easily dispense with the HomeGroup nonsense.

- Sharing folders in Windows Vista works after you turn on Network Discovery in the Network and Sharing Center window: Open the Network and Sharing Center window as described earlier in this chapter, and ensure that the Network Discovery item and the File Sharing item are on.

- Also see Chapter 19 for more information on how to share files between your laptop and a desktop computer.

Unsharing a folder

To unshare a folder, repeat the steps from the preceding section, but in Step 6 remove the check mark by the Share This Folder option.

Chapter 14

The Wireless Life

*O*nce upon a time, wires were signs of progress. The modern home, well, it had wires, wires everywhere! Electric devices were festooned with power cords and, man, that was *modern*. Although television came in over the air, cable TV was better because it was on a wire! Oh, once upon a time, wires were good. Not any more.

The trend today is to make everything wireless: The fewer wires, the better, with no wires the best option. That's doubly important for a laptop — first, because the laptop cannot be attached to a power line, and second, because the laptop need not be tethered to a network, at least not physically. Wireless networking is where it's at. Indeed, wireless communications is the biggest boon to long-distance communications technology since the drum. This section explains what you need to know.

✔ Networking basics are covered in Chapter 13, which is all about wired networking.

✔ Also refer to Chapter 13 for information on sharing resources on the network. The same information applies whether the network is wireless or wired.

✔ Chapter 16 covers the digital cellular wireless standard, which allows your laptop to communicate wirelessly with the Internet without needing a Wi-Fi connection.

No More Wires

You'll never guess: Wireless networking works just like wired networking does, except that it uses no wires. Well, it uses no wires, but there are new **wireless hardware** and software goodies you need to know about. This section explains what's what.

Wireless networking hardware

As with wired networking, wireless networking requires hardware in order to work. Because cables are out of the question, that leaves only two hardware pieces for the wireless networking hardware list:

✔ A wireless networking adapter, or NIC

✔ A wireless base station, which serves as the wireless hub or router

The basic setup is illustrated in Figure 14-1.

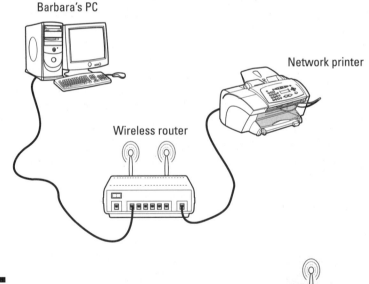

Barbara's PC

Network printer

Wireless router

Figure 14-1:
Typical
wireless
network
setup.

Colin's laptop

Your laptop came with wireless networking hardware. It's built in. You probably don't see the little antenna, but it's there. You also don't see the wireless signal traveling through the air, but it's there as well.

To complete the wireless network, you need a base station. The *base station* receives, relays, and transmits the wireless signals among all the wireless devices in the network. It may also feature wired-based networking options, such as a router. A typical base station is depicted in Figure 14-1.

✔ See Chapter 13 for information on the hardware requirements for wired networking. (***Hint:*** Wires are involved.)

✔ Many laptops feature a switch (hardware or software) that turns off the wireless antenna. Locate the switch on your laptop, if it exists, and ensure that wireless networking is activated for those times when you need it. Sometimes, the switch is an Fn key combination.

✔ Yes, sometimes you need to turn off wireless networking, such as when you travel by air or work in a hospital. See Chapter 20 for information on air travel with your laptop.

Wireless networking software

Windows comes with all the wireless networking software you need. In fact, it's the same software used for wired networking. It has a few differences, however, such as the requirement that you join or choose which wireless network you connect to. That subject is covered later in this chapter, in the section "Connecting to a wireless network."

Wireless networking protocols

Perhaps the most oddball thing about going wireless is the networking *protocol* — the nerd term for the rules and methods by which your laptop and the wireless network communicate. It's technical stuff but necessary to know, or at least necessary to know for now, so don't bother filling your long-term memory with this stuff.

The wireless networking protocol most commonly used on laptops is known as 802.11. It's pronounced "eight-oh-two dot eleven," or, to save time, you can omit the *dot:* "Eight-oh-two eleven."

To make things more confusing, the number 802.11 is followed by a letter. These days, the letters *g* and *n* are popular. The letters, which started with *a,* reflect the version of the 802.11 protocol being used. Here's the rundown:

802.11g: The formerly most common standard, and still common on many laptops. This standard can also be written as 802.11a/b/g, which means that it's compatible with the ancient 802.11a and 802.11b standards.

802.11n: The current popular standard, fully compatible with all previous standards. As you might suspect, the standard can also be written as 802.11a/b/g/n, though at this point that label is becoming ridiculous.

802.11ac: A proposed new standard that's bigger, faster, and stronger than the previous standards. You may see this protocol available on laptops in the near future.

Your laptop's wireless network adapter is most likely 802.11g or 802.11n. That's good.

- ✔ The newer standards offer more features and higher speeds than do the older standards.

- ✔ A laptop using an older standard cannot access wireless networks using a newer standard. Rather than confuse you, just keep in mind that as long as all computers on the wireless network use the same standard, you're okay.

- ✔ If your laptop sports an older 802.11 standard, you can buy a USB wireless network adapter that features a newer standard.

- ✔ The original 802.11 standard was 802.11a. It was followed by 802.11b. The higher the letter, the newer and better the standard. Also, higher letters (alphabetically) can communicate with the lower-letter standards, but not vice versa. For instance, a laptop with an 802.11b wireless network adapter cannot communicate with a wireless network using the 802.11g or 802.11n standard. The proposed 802.11ac standard kind of blows that logic out of the water, so just forget everything I wrote in this paragraph.

Hello, Wireless Network!

Unlike on a wired computer network, you cannot join a wireless network by simply plugging something in. Well, if you can figure out how to "plug into" air, my hat's off to you. Otherwise, you have to follow the formal steps and procedures outlined in this section.

Connecting to a wireless network

Accessing a wireless network works differently whether you're stuck with Windows 8 or are blessed with an earlier version of Windows.

Connect in Windows 8

Follow these steps to hook your Windows 8 laptop to an available wireless network:

1. **Summon the Charms bar.**

   The quickest way to summon the Charms bar is to press the Win+C key combination.

2. **Choose Settings.**

3. **Click or touch the Available icon.**

   The icon is shown in the margin.

4. **Choose a wireless network from the list.**

   Additional information about the network is displayed.

5. **Place a check mark in the Connect Automatically box if you want your laptop to always connect with the wireless network when it's in range.**

   The only time I don't put a check mark in the box is when it's a hotel or remote location that I don't plan to visit again.

6. **Click the Connect button.**

7. **If prompted, type the network's password.**

   Your laptop is now connected to the wireless network.

Skip to the section "After the connection is made" to read additional information about the wireless connection.

Connect with older, better versions of Windows

Obey these steps to hunt down and connect to a wireless network:

1. **Click the wireless networking icon found in the notification area.**

   Use Figure 14-2 as your guide. When you click the wireless networking icon, a list of available wireless networks appears, as illustrated in the figure.

   In Windows Vista, you choose the Connect To⇨Wireless Network item, found on the Start button menu.

   In Windows XP, you choose Connect To from the Start button menu.

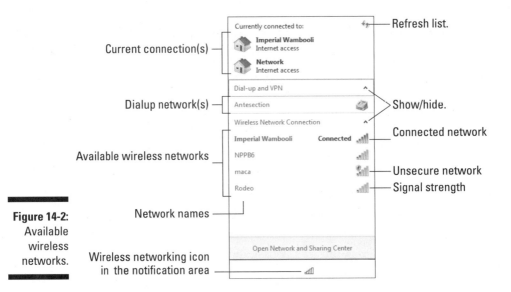

Refresh list.

Current connection(s)

Dialup network(s)

Show/hide.

Connected network

Available wireless networks

Unsecure network

Signal strength

Network names

Figure 14-2:
Available
wireless
networks.

Wireless networking icon
in the notification area

2. **Choose a network from the list.**

   The list shows the network name and its signal strength.

3. **Place a check mark by the Automatically Connect option if you plan to use the same wireless network in the future.**

   The Automatically Connect option doesn't appear for every network.

4. **Click the Connect button.**

   Windows attempts to "make friendly" with the wireless network.

   You may see a warning telling you that the network is unsecured. This message is common for certain free wireless networks that require no password for connection. Click the Connect Anyway option to proceed.

   If the network is familiar to your laptop (you've connected before and have elected to save the information), you're done. You can start using the network.

5. **Enter the network's password, if you're prompted to do so.**

At this point, you could be connected and ready to use the network, especially if it's a network you commonly use. Keep reading in the next section.

After the connection is made

At some point after connecting to the wireless network, Windows may ask you to tell it whether the network is public or private. The answer to this question is vital. A *public* network is one that's out in public, that others (strangers!) can also use. In this situation, you want to ensure that your laptop is locked down and not open to snooping. A home or work network is one that's in your home or office, available only to safe computers or folks you know. This type of network is more open than the public network.

- ✔ Sometimes, it pays to wait a few moments for the wireless connection to sync up (or something). Don't take the lack of an immediate "Connection made, yee-ha!" message as a sign of failure.

- ✔ When given a choice, pick the wireless network with the strongest signal. The signal graphic appears to the right of the wireless network's name.

- ✔ Avoid connecting to unknown networks in a public location. You're taking a security risk when you don't know exactly which network you're using.

- ✔ The best way to hunt down wireless networks is to use a third-party wireless network browser. Such a program may have come with your laptop's wireless adapter, or it can be found on the Internet.

- ✔ There's a distance-and-interference issue with wireless networking, and the picture isn't as rosy as the brochures claim. Basically, the best way to connect with a wireless network is to be in the same room with the wireless base station that's broadcasting the signal. Common items, such as walls, greatly reduce the potency of a wireless connection.

- ✔ A few wireless Internet locations offer their password-and-setup information on a USB flash drive. Simply insert the flash drive to connect to the network, or use the drive as indicated by the directions or when you're prompted to insert the drive when you connect to the network. Needless to say, a USB flash drive is a handy thing to have — much better than retyping those long password keys!

Connecting to a wireless network when you don't know the network's name

For security reasons, some wireless networks don't broadcast their network names (also known as SSIDs). Obviously, you cannot connect to a network if you don't know its name, mostly because the unnamed network doesn't even show up in the list of available networks. There's a reason for that: security.

To get the network name, you need to ask. The network manager or whichever human is in charge of the wireless network at your location should be able to divulge this information. After you know the network name, follow these steps in either Windows 7 or Windows Vista to connect to that network:

1. **Open the Control Panel.**

2. **From beneath the Network and Internet heading, click the View Network Status and Tasks link.**

   The Network and Sharing Center window appears.

3. **Choose the Set Up a New Connection or Network link.**

4. **Choose the Manually Connect to a Wireless Network option.**

5. **Click the Next button.**

   In the next window that's displayed, you input information that you've (hopefully) obtained about the network.

6. **Type the network name in the Network Name box.**

7. **Fill in the rest of the information as needed.**

   Check with the network administrator to see which other tidbits of information are required in order to complete the connection: security and encryption types and a security key or password.

8. **My best advice: Put a check mark in the box labeled Start This Connection Automatically.**

   This step saves you some time by preventing you from having to repeat these steps later.

9. **Click the Next button.**

   Hopefully, Windows goes out and finds the unnamed wireless network. If it doesn't, you probably goofed something up. Check with the network administrator or the settings on your wireless hub; otherwise, you're ready to connect.

10. **Choose the Connect To option.**

    Surprise! You thought you were connecting to the network, but you were merely setting things up. Go to the section "Connecting to a wireless network," earlier in this chapter, to complete the connection.

Windows XP works a bit differently to connect to an unnamed wireless network:

1. **Open the Network Connections icon in the Control Panel.**

2. **Right-click the wireless connection icon.**

3. **Choose Properties from the pop-up menu.**

4. **Click the Wireless Networks tab in the Properties dialog box.**

5. **Click the Add button.**

6. **Fill in the Wireless Networking Properties dialog box with the necessary information.**

7. **Click OK.**

After the wireless network is configured, it shows up in the list of available networks; see the earlier section "Connecting to a wireless network" to see what to do next.

- ✔ You can use various wireless networking tools to locate wireless networks that don't broadcast their network names. The networking software that comes with your laptop may even show unnamed wireless networks in the list.

- ✔ The technical term for a network name is *SSID*, which stands for Service Set IDentifier.

Getting the laptop's MAC address

Some wireless networks restrict access to only those computers they know. Not having eyeballs, a network needs another piece of identification to distinguish between computers it knows and utter strangers. That piece of ID is the wireless networking hardware's MAC address.

A *MAC address* is a unique number assigned to every networking adapter on Planet Earth and a few dozen networking adapters in orbit. No two numbers are identical, and the MAC address is very difficult to fake. By using the MAC address, a wireless network can restrict access to only those computers that are known and registered.

To find your laptop's MAC address, follow these simple steps:

1. **Open the Control Panel.**

2. **Click the View Network Status and Tasks link found beneath the Network and Internet heading.**

   The Network and Sharing Center window appears.

3. **Summon the wireless connections status dialog box.**

   In Windows 8, click the link that appears to the right of the Connections item. It should be the name of whatever wireless network you're connected to.

In Windows 7, click the Wireless Network Connection link.

In Windows Vista, click the View Status link.

 4. **In the Status dialog box, click the Details button.**

 Locate the item labeled Physical Address. That's the NIC's MAC address number. Write it down on a sheet of paper.

 5. **Close the various dialog boxes and windows.**

In Windows XP, follow these steps:

 1. **Open the Control Panel's Network Connections icon.**

 2. **Open the wireless network connection icon.**

 3. **Click the Support tab.**

 4. **Click the Details button.**

 The MAC address is listed as the physical address.

 5. **Close all open windows and dialog boxes.**

You can now use the MAC address or give it to a network administrator, who will help you set up the wireless network.

 ✔ Know that MAC stands for Media Access Control — as though that will make your day any brighter.

 ✔ The MAC address is 12 digits long, broken up into pairs, like this:

```
12:34:56:78:9A:BC
```

 ✔ The MAC address is a base 16 value (also called *hexadecimal*), so the letters *A* through *F* are also considered numbers.

Renewing your lease

To keep out goofballs, some networks let you use their services for only a given amount of time. The time allotted is referred to as the *lease*.

Your lease may expire, especially if you use a wireless network for a great length of time. To renew it, you need to disconnect from the network and then reconnect.

The instructions for disconnecting from a wireless network are offered later in this chapter. If you're not in a hurry, just restart Windows (see Chapter 5) to renew your lease.

Accessing a pay-service wireless network

Not everything is free. Some people out there have the gall to *charge* you for using their wireless services. Imagine! Darn those capitalists!

I've seen wireless access for pay work in different ways:

✔ You pay a cashier, and then he or she hands you a slip of paper with the network name and a password to use. Follow the steps in the earlier section "Connecting to a wireless network when you don't know the network's name" for instructions on connecting to the network.

✔ In the more devious way, the signal appears to be strong and available, and connection isn't a problem. But when you go to the Internet, the only web page you see is the sign-up page. Until you fork over your credit card number, you can't go anywhere else on the Internet or access any other service (such as e-mail).

✔ Well, some public websites, such as those in a library, may have you "register" by merely giving them your e-mail address. You still have to complete this task to use the network, but at least it doesn't require you to pay money.

Disconnecting from a wireless network

The main way I disconnect from a wireless connection is to close my laptop's lid. When I put the laptop into Sleep mode or Hibernate mode, the wireless network connection is broken automatically. Opening the laptop's lid (assuming that it's within range of the wireless hub) reestablishes the connection.

Likewise, you can also turn off the laptop to disconnect from the wireless network.

To disconnect without turning off your laptop, follow these steps in Windows 8:

1. **Summon the Charms bar.**

   Press the Win+C keyboard shortcut.

2. **Choose Settings.**

3. **Choose the wireless network icon.**

   It's the top left of the six icons at the bottom of the Settings panel. The wireless networking name (if available) appears beneath the icon.

4. **Choose the wireless network name from the list of networks.**

   Choose the name that has the bold text *Connected* to its right.

5. **Click the Disconnect button.**

In earlier versions of Windows, obey these steps to disconnect from a wireless network:

1. **Choose Connect To from the Start menu.**

   The Connect to a Network window appears. (Refer to Figure 14-2.)

2. **If the network you're connected to isn't chosen, click to select it.**

3. **Click the Disconnect button.**

4. **If a confirmation screen appears, click the big Disconnect button.**

5. **Click the Close button.**

If you've preconfigured the network to automatically connect when it's available, after completing Step 5, you find your laptop instantly reconnected to the network.

> ✔ Some laptops have a handy On–Off button associated with their wireless networking connections. You can press the button, slide the switch, or press the Fn key combination to instantly disconnect from the network by turning off the wireless networking adapter.

> ✔ This technique was just suggested to me: Start running in any direction. By the time you feel tired, you're probably far enough from the wireless hub that the connection is broken, although breaking a connection in this manner seems extraordinarily silly, especially when you're at a coffee shop and wearing a business suit.

That Bluetooth Thing

Bluetooth refers to a wireless standard for connecting computer peripherals, as well as other, noncomputer devices. As long as your laptop is equipped with Bluetooth technology, you can use various Bluetooth devices and gizmos with your laptop, including printers, keyboards, speakers, and input devices.

> ✔ The advantage of Bluetooth is that it lets you connect wirelessly to a variety of peripherals without having to use a separate wireless adapter for each peripheral.

> ✔ Bluetooth began its existence as a wireless replacement for the old serial (RS-232) interface, popular with computers in the 1980s and 1990s.

Checking for Bluetooth

Before you can get all excited about using Bluetooth, you need to ensure that your laptop has a wireless Bluetooth radio. Not every laptop does. The way to tell is to look for the Bluetooth logo (shown in the margin) on your laptop. All Bluetooth gizmos feature this logo.

If your laptop lacks a Bluetooth radio, you can easily add one: A Bluetooth gizmo easily plugs into a USB port. As a bonus, USB Bluetooth dongles are relatively inexpensive. They also install all their own software, so you don't have to set up anything.

When Bluetooth is available and configured, you see the Bluetooth logo appear as an icon in the desktop's notification area (on the right end of the taskbar). You use the pop-up menu from that icon to control Bluetooth gizmos from your laptop.

Pairing with a Bluetooth gizmo

There's a wee bit of a complicated dance required to connect a Bluetooth peripheral to your laptop. As an overview, here's how it works:

1. **You turn on the Bluetooth peripheral and make it "discoverable."**

   The gizmo has a button on it or some way to switch it into discoverable mode. In this mode, the device broadcasts a wireless signal saying that it's available.

2. **On your laptop, you choose the option to add a new device.**

   The laptop then scans for discoverable Bluetooth peripherals.

3. **Choose the Bluetooth device from the list.**

4. **Optionally, type a passcode to ensure that the proper device is being added.**

   The passcode is usually a four-digit number broadcast by the device. It's required because a Bluetooth peripheral can be paired with only one other device at a time.

Once paired, the Bluetooth peripheral can be used with your laptop. For example, I use a wireless Bluetooth mouse with my laptop. Because the mouse is paired with my laptop, it cannot be purloined by other Bluetooth-equipped computers.

✔ Make the Bluetooth peripheral discoverable before you pair it with your laptop. Directions for making the device discoverable come with the device itself.

✔ Bluetooth devices are discoverable for only a brief length of time, usually two minutes. If you fail to connect during that period, you need to make the device discoverable again.

✔ To connect to a Bluetooth device in Windows 8, click the Bluetooth icon in the desktop's notification area, and choose the Add a Bluetooth Device command. Choose the Bluetooth device from the Select a Device list that appears.

✔ In Windows 7, click the Bluetooth icon in the notification area, and choose the Add a Device command. Choose the Bluetooth device from the Add a Device window.

✔ Manage your laptop's Bluetooth connections by clicking the Bluetooth icon in the notification area and choosing the Show Bluetooth Devices command. In Windows 8, keep in mind that Bluetooth devices are listed along with all other devices in the computer — another shortcoming of Windows 8.

Chapter 15

Hello, Internet

. . . .

In This Chapter

▶ Arming yourself for the mobile Internet

▶ Using broadband Internet

▶ Configuring for a public network

▶ Accessing the Internet through a dialup connection

▶ Connecting with a dialup connection

▶ Disconnecting a dialup connection

▶ Working with dialup connections

. . . .

*T*he *Internet* is the part of your computer that isn't inside your computer. It's no longer optional. So, as a mobile computer user, you need to — often and with the regularity of an addict — connect to and use the Internet. It's such a necessity that I don't even need to explain why any more. Good for me!

Using the Internet with your laptop works just like using it on a desktop. Good for you! Using a laptop, of course, you can access the Internet from anywhere — that is, from anywhere the Internet is. Though the Internet is everywhere, it's not really *available* everywhere. So you must be flexible! To meet that flexibility, you have to be prepared to hop on the Internet in a variety of ways. This chapter covers those details.

Mobile Internet Connection Tips

Like a quality rash, the Internet is something you can find everywhere. That's not really the issue. The issue for a portable PC person is whether you can access the Internet from wherever you are. That means getting the information you need from anywhere. It means being able to access your e-mail while you're on the road. And for a dialup ISP, it means being able to access that ISP from a variety of locations.

Ask Professor Dan: What is the Internet?

Billy: What is the Internet?

Prof. Dan: I'm glad you asked, Billy. The Internet isn't a computer program. Nor is the Internet a single large computer somewhere. And no, the Internet isn't owned by Google.

Billy: You had better not tell the Google stockholders!

Prof. Dan: What they don't know won't hurt them.

Billy: So the Internet isn't located in Mountain View, California?

Prof. Dan: Don't be silly. The Internet isn't one computer — it's millions upon millions of computers, all connected. Information is stored on many of those computers, and the protocols and methods of the Internet allow your computer, or any other computer connected to the Internet, to access and use that information. Indeed, any computer connected to the Internet is the Internet.

Billy: That's cosmic! Like, the atoms that comprise our bodies were once deep inside stars! We are the universe because we *are* the universe! Wait. Why are you looking at me that way?

Prof. Dan: I'm just checking to see whether your pupils are dilated.

✔ *ISP* stands for *Internet service provider,* or the outfit that provides you with Internet access. Your ISP can be your company or your school or any of a number of national and local Internet providers.

✔ Just because you use dialup ISP access at home doesn't mean that you're limited to dialup access on the road.

✔ Using wireless networking, you can access the Internet at no cost when you find an open wireless connection. My local coffeehouse offers free wireless Internet access for the price of a cup of joe. (It would bother me to use the service and not buy something to drink or a cookie while I'm there.)

✔ Free Internet access is available in most community libraries.

✔ Many national ISPs — such as AOL, EarthLink, and NetZero — have access points all over. Before you go on the road, check to see whether your ISP has any local access numbers for your destination. That way, you can use your laptop's modem to connect with your ISP, just as you do at home.

✔ In addition to local access, a dialup ISP might offer a toll-free phone number to connect. Note that you may have to pay a surcharge for accessing this feature.

> ✔ Most ISPs offer a form of web-based e-mail. This system allows you to access your e-mail from any computer connected to the Internet. Simply navigate to your ISP's web e-mail page and log in as you normally would. You can then read your e-mail on the web rather than use an e-mail program.
>
> ✔ See Chapter 18 for more Internet, web browsing, and e-mail tips.

Broadband Internet Access

Getting on the Internet in the high-speed way is simple: Connect your laptop to any existing wired or wireless network that's already attached to the Internet. When that network is already on the Internet, so will your laptop, after it's connected.

Understanding broadband

The Internet is based on the same type of networking used to create a home or small-office network, which is discussed in Chapters 13 and 14. Having that type of network set up, even when your laptop is the only computer on the network, is how you get *broadband,* or high-speed, Internet access. Use Figure 15-1 as a guide for basic broadband Internet access setup.

Yes, the broadband Internet setup looks just like the basic network setup. In fact, they're nearly identical. That's not just because I recycle illustrations in this book. It shows that any time you're connected to a network, you're probably also connected to the Internet. The key is the broadband modem. (Refer to Figure 15-1.)

The broadband modem connects to the Internet by using cable, DSL, satellite Internet service, or a cellular modem. The broadband modem also connects to a router, or gateway. This device provides the bridge between the local network and the Internet. It performs all the magic for you.

The gateway (router) can be wire-based or wireless. In Figure 15-1, Peggy is connected to the Internet using a wireless connection. Bobby is using a wired connection. Both laptops have the same access to the Internet, thanks to the wired/wireless gateway.

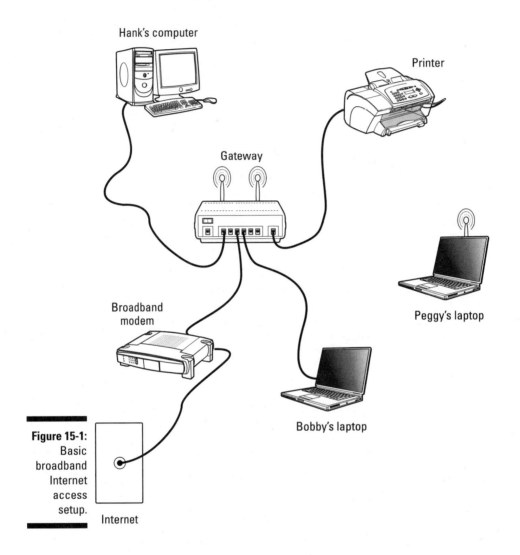

Hank's computer

Printer

Gateway

Broadband modem

Peggy's laptop

Bobby's laptop

Figure 15-1:
Basic
broadband
Internet
access
setup.

Internet

- Broadband means *high-speed*.

- Router rhymes with *chowder*. Do not pronounce it "ROO-ter."

- Yes, it's really a gateway, not a router. How can you tell? If you paid $600 for it, it's a router. If you paid about $100 for it, it's a gateway.

- See Chapter 16 for information on cellular modems.

- Broadband Internet access works the same way no matter where you are. Even for a public network, such as in a hotel or café, the access works the same.

✔ When your laptop is connected to the network, you're "on" the Internet. Just start your web browser, check e-mail — the whole nine yards.

✔ The number of computers on your network can be anything from one to as many computers as the gateway can handle. That's usually dozens of computers for a good router. By the way, if you have dozens of laptops, note that your laptop warranty requires you to buy one copy of this book for each laptop. Thank you.

✔ When you set up broadband access for yourself, you must configure the gateway. That's done by logging in to the gateway using your web browser. The gateway has an IP address, and you use web browser software, such as Internet Explorer, to connect to the gateway, log in, and configure the settings. Instructions for doing this come with the gateway. (For public networks, the gateway is configured by whichever outfit is hosting the network.)

Setting the network's location

After making the network connection, you may be prompted by Windows to set the network location. You have three choices: Home, Work, and Public.

Anytime you use a network in public — in a hotel, cybercafé, public library, or similar location — always choose the Public option. By designating a network as public, you're ensuring that Windows kicks in a few extra protections for your laptop.

When you're unsure about the network's location, you can confirm it by visiting the Network and Sharing Center window: Open the Control Panel, and click the View Network Status and Tasks link found beneath the Network and Internet heading. The Network and Sharing Center window lists the network location beneath the network name; in Figure 13-2 (over in Chapter 13), you can see a home network and public network listed.

To change the network location in Windows 7, click the link (titled Home Network, Work Network, or Public Network) found beneath the network name in the Network and Sharing Center window. In Windows Vista, click the Customize link found to the right of the network name.

Also see Chapter 17 for information on using a firewall.

Disconnecting from broadband access

There's no formal requirement for disconnecting from the broadband Internet. Unlike when you use a dialup modem, you don't need to worry about disconnecting officially or hanging up a modem.

✔ Your laptop is disconnected from the network when it's turned off, hibernating, or sleeping.

✔ See Chapter 13 for information on disconnecting from a wired network.

✔ See Chapter 14 for information on disconnecting from a wireless network.

✔ Disconnecting from a broadband Internet connection isn't a big deal. The only reason I mention it is that disconnecting from a dialup Internet connection *is* a big deal. That topic is covered later in this chapter.

Dialup Internet Access

Nothing beats the 1990s! Ho-boy! We were younger then. Had a booming economy. A lovable but morally questionable guy in the White House. Dialup Internet access as far as the eye could see. Those were the good, old, slow days.

Even if you prefer broadband, have it at home, and use it all over the world, there may still be those few times when you need to play *E.T.* and phone home to the Internet by using one of those annoying things developed by Antonio Meucci and properly stolen by Alexander Graham Bell. The telephone. Antique. Sluggish. Unreliable. Annoying. Your last hope. Good luck.

This section covers how to set up your laptop for creating a dialup connection. For general information on using a modem with your laptop, refer to Chapter 16.

Windows 8 pretty much requires a full-time Internet connection. Though it's possible to connect to the Internet using a dialup connection in Widows 8, it's no longer practical.

Creating a dialup connection

Setting up your laptop for a dialup Internet connection is a task you have to do manually. Unlike in the broadband method, you cannot just plug and go. Instead, you need to know this basic information:

✔ The ISP's name (used to identify the dialup connection)

✔ The connection's phone number

✔ The username for your ISP account

✔ The password for your ISP account

Your ISP, or whichever outfit is giving you Internet access, provides this information for you. You then use the information provided to configure the dialup connection:

1. **Open the Control Panel.**

2. **Beneath the heading Network and Internet, choose View Network Status and Tasks.**

   The Network and Sharing Center window appears.

3. **Click the Set Up a New Connection or Network link.**

   The word *New* may be missing from the link in certain versions of Windows.

4. **Select the item in the list labeled Set Up a Dial-Up Connection; or in Windows 8, choose the Connect to the Internet option.**

   If you don't see that item, your laptop lacks a dialup modem or Windows is unable to recognize it. You can purchase a USB dialup modem and add it to your laptop, which is the solution I recommend.

5. **In Windows 8, choose the Set Up a New Connection Anyway option, and then on the next screen, choose Dial-Up.**

   In some versions of Windows, you may need to choose the option Broadband (PPPoE) instead of Dial-Up.

6. **If necessary, click the Next button.**

7. **Fill in the information as given to you by your ISP: its phone number, your account name (username), and your password.**

   The username and password are used here to get into your ISP's account. They may be different from the username and password that are used to access your e-mail inbox, and the logon and password you use for Windows.

8. **Place a check mark by the Remember This Password option.**

9. **Type a name for the connection.**

   My ISP is named CompuSoft, so I type `CompuSoft` in the box.

10. **Ensure that your laptop is plugged into a phone cord and that the phone cord is plugged into a telephone jack.**

11. **Click the Connect button.**

    Windows uses your modem to test-dial the phone number you entered.

If all goes well, you should be connected to the Internet. To dial up the Internet by using the modem in the future, see the later section "Making the dialup connection."

✔ Connect the laptop's modem to a phone jack before you dial the Internet!

✔ You have more options for dialing a phone number with a modem than most people would dare to dream of. Don't fuss over the options now; read about the details in Chapter 13.

✔ When you're using more than one ISP, you need a dialup connection for each one.

✔ If your ISP requires special software to connect, use it to connect to the Internet.

Making the dialup connection

Dialup Internet works just like making a phone call — a nice, slow phone call over wires, not on a cell phone. You're connected to the Internet only when the modem is using the phone. And most importantly, you need to "hang up" the modem when you're done. You'll probably forget this advice more than once.

Before you do anything, ensure that your laptop is properly connected to the phone jack. The cord must plug into the modem hole on your laptop and into a phone jack on the wall or else piggyback on another telephonic device.

Do not plug your modem into a digital phone system! It will fry your modem's gizzard! Digital phone systems are common in hotels and medium- to large-size businesses. When in doubt, ask.

The easiest way to connect to the Internet is to simply open or use an Internet program. For example, start up Internet Explorer to browse the web or tell your e-mail program to fetch new mail. Either action forces the laptop to look for an Internet connection by either connecting automatically or presenting a list of connections for you to choose.

If starting up an Internet program doesn't work, you can manually connect. In Windows 7, choose the connection from the list of networks that's displayed when you click the wireless networking icon in the notification area; look for the connection under the heading Dial Up and VPN. (Refer to Figure 14-2, in Chapter 14.)

In Windows Vista, choose the Connect To item from the Start button menu, and choose the dialup connection from the list that's displayed. Click the Connect button.

Windows 8 provides no direct access to dialup connections, so a manual connection isn't possible.

After the connection has been made, a tiny "modem connected" icon appears in the notification area. It's your clue that you're connected to the Internet. You can then use any Internet software.

Disconnecting the dialup connection

A dialup connection must officially be disconnected when you're done using the Internet. You may forget do so, especially when you use dialup on the road and have broadband at home.

Disconnecting works like connecting does: Refer to the preceding section for information on how to access a dialup connection. (The method differs, depending on which version of Windows you're using.) Rather than click the Connect button, click Disconnect.

You can also disconnect the modem from the Internet by right-clicking the little modem icon in the notification area. Choose the Disconnect command from the context menu that pops up.

Managing dialup connections

Don't get frustrated trying to find where Windows hides the dialup connections. They're well hidden. You can edit, delete, or otherwise mangle the dialup connections you make using the Internet Properties dialog box. It's an odd location, but that's where you need to go.

To open the Internet Properties dialog box, follow these steps:

1. **Open the Control Panel.**
2. **Choose Network and Internet.**
3. **Choose Internet Options.**

   The Internet Properties dialog box appears.

4. **Click the Connections tab in the Internet Properties dialog box.**

   The top part of the dialog box lists the dialup connections you've made, as shown in Figure 15-2.

5. **Close the dialog box and then the Network and Internet window when you're done.**

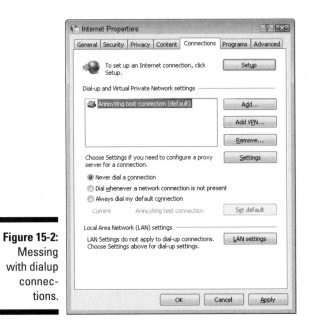

Figure 15-2:
Messing
with dialup
connec-
tions.

When the modem seems to dial at weird times, choose the option Never Dial a Connection in the Internet Properties dialog box (on the Connections tab). That way, the dialup modem connects only manually, not automatically. It's a useful setting, and it helps you avoid seeing the Connect dialog box at random times when you use your laptop.

Chapter 16

The Modem Lives

*I*n the early days of computing, few people had modems. The modem was an oddball, expensive, and technical peripheral. Then came the dawn of the Internet, and *everyone* had to get a modem. Modems used the phone system to communicate, and they were slow but popular. Then came the broadband era, where *modem* meant a cable, DSL, satellite, or cellular modem. So what exactly is a modem?

The modem thing is about communications. If you've read the preceding chapters in this book (against my wishes in the introduction), you know that part of the laptop computing paradigm is not only portability but also communications. Having a modem in, or available to, your laptop is a must.

About Mr. Modem

The word *modem* is formed by colliding the words *modulator* and *demodulator* at a speed of about 300 bits per second. The result of combining *mo*dulator-*dem*odulator is *modem.*

Originally, a modem was required in order to translate, or *modulate,* the digital signals from a computer into analog sounds that could travel over the phone system. The modem would also demodulate those analog sounds back into digital signals, which is how modems are used by computers to communicate over the phone lines.

The phone system today is all-digital. (Well, *almost* all-digital.) Therefore, the modulator-demodulator thing isn't necessary, but still the term *modem* has stuck. Today it's used to describe not only traditional dialup modems but also other types of computer communications devices. This section reviews the various modem types.

Broadband modems

The most common modem category is now the broadband modem. *Broadband* is simply a fancy word for "high-speed."

You can find several types of broadband modem, depending on the method used to connect to the Internet:

- ✔ Cable
- ✔ Cellular
- ✔ DSL
- ✔ Satellite

The modem may be provided by your ISP, such as the cable company renting you a cable modem, or you can buy your own modem.

The broadband modem is a part of the computer network. See Chapter 13 for basic network information, but also check Chapter 15, which covers the broadband Internet connection specifically.

Cellular modems, also known as digital cellular modems, use the same wireless network as smartphones do for accessing the Internet. The cellular modem can dwell internally on your laptop or attach to a USB port or use a PC Card. Also see the later section "The smartphone tethering trick" for information on using your cell phone as your laptop's cellular modem.

Dialup modems

Traditional dialup modems are included as part of the main circuitry on most laptops. In fact, the only evident part of the modem is the hole into which you plug the phone cable. That's about as technical as it gets.

A dialup modem makes phone calls just like a human does: It dials a number, and then it screeches its unmelodic tones at the other computer, which also screeches back. After a few noisy moments, your laptop is connected.

✔ You need a landline for the dialup modem. They don't use cell phones, though it wouldn't surprise me if an enterprising nerd has managed to hook up a dialup modem to a cell phone.

✔ Not every laptop has a dialup modem. Apple dropped the dialup modem from its Macintosh laptop line years ago. Few PC Ultrabooks and net-books feature modems.

✔ You can always add a dialup modem to your laptop as a USB peripheral.

✔ The only part of the modem you're likely to see is the hole, or *jack,* into which the phone cord plugs. Refer to Chapter 6 for information on locating the thing.

✔ No, you cannot use the same phone line when the dialup modem is using it.

✔ Long-distance charges apply to modem calls just as they do to regular phone calls. Hotel surcharges apply as well.

✔ Some countries charge extra for modem-made phone calls. When you're traveling overseas, be sure to inquire about any extra fees before you use the phone.

The smartphone tethering trick

Modern smartphones, such as the iPhone or the popular Android phone, feature their own cellular modem. In fact, the modem is what makes a mere mortal cell phone into a "smartphone." It's possible to use that modem with your laptop by employing a trick known as smartphone tethering.

Smartphone tethering involves connecting your cell phone to the laptop by way of a standard USB cable.

After the smartphone is connected, Windows should recognize it instantly and set up the cellular modem for you. In fact, Windows automatically interprets the connection as another valid Internet connection. You'll be online in moments.

The only drawback to using your smartphone as the laptop's modem is that most cellular providers charge extra for the service. Not only that, but most cell phone data plans charge by the gigabyte, which means that using your smartphone as the laptop's modem can be an expensive proposition.

✔ Not every smartphone is capable of tethering to a laptop. If you attach your smartphone to the laptop and the laptop recognizes only the digital photos (or music) on the cell phone, it probably cannot be used for tethering.

✔ If you plan to tether the Internet connection quite often, consider instead obtaining a cellular modem for your laptop.

Modem Setup

Your laptop's modem is one of the last computer devices you'll ever use that must be configured before you can use it. Yes, there's a certain amount of "dumb" in a modem. Because the modem dials the phone just like a human, the basic setup operation includes telling the modem how to dial the phone, which numbers are long distance, and how to dial long-distance numbers.

Welcome to 1998.

Finding modem control

To do the initial modem setup, pay attention to these steps:

1. **Open the Control Panel.**

2. **Choose Large Icons from the View By menu in the upper-right corner of the Control Panel window.**

   The easiest way to get to modem control is to forgo Category view.

3. **Open the Phone and Modem icon.**

   In Windows Vista, it's the Phone and Modem Options icon.

   If you see the Location Information dialog box, continue setting up your modem. Otherwise, carry on with the later section "Setting modem properties."

   The questions presented in the Location Information dialog box deal with setting up your laptop modem's dialing rules for your home location or wherever you plan to use the modem the most.

4. **Choose your country or region from the drop-down list.**

5. **Enter your home location's area or city code.**

6. **Enter a carrier code, if one is required.**

   I have no idea what a carrier code is, so I left it blank.

7. **Enter the number you need in order to access an outside line, if necessary.**

   For example, if you need to dial an 8 or a 9 to escape the local PBX, enter that number; otherwise, leave the box empty.

   To insert a pause in dialing, use the comma. For example, if you have to dial 9 and then pause, type **9,** (the number 9 and then a comma) in the box.

8. **Choose whether you need to use tone or pulse dialing.**

9. **Click OK to continue.**

After you complete these steps, the laptop is now satisfied that you know where you are and that the modem knows how to dial the phone from that location. The next thing you see is the Phone and Modem Options dialog box, which is covered in the next section.

Setting modem properties

The Phone and Modem dialog box, shown in Figure 16-1, is where you configure the modem as well as edit your location information and add locations. The dialog box is the first thing you see after your initial modem setup (covered in the preceding section).

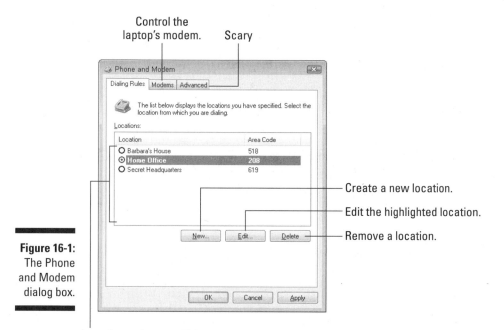

Figure 16-1:
The Phone
and Modem
dialog box.

To open the Phone and Modem dialog box, follow Steps 1 through 3 from the preceding section.

- ✔ The Dialing Rules tab (refer to Figure 16-1) lists the locations where you use your modem to dial up a connection.
- ✔ The Modems tab is where the modem is controlled and can be adjusted.
- ✔ The Advanced tab is just too terrifying to discuss in this or any other book.

Other sections in this chapter cover the various things you can do in the Phone and Modem dialog box.

Silencing the modem

Most people enjoy hearing the modem make its hideous noise as an online connection is being made. If you don't, you can mute the modem. Quietly follow these steps:

1. **Open the Control Panel.**

2. **Ensure that either Large Icons or Small icons is chosen from the View By menu.**

   The View By menu is found in the upper-right corner of the Control Panel window.

3. **Open the Phone and Modem icon.**

   The Phone and Modem dialog box appears. (Refer to Figure 16-1.)

4. **Click the Modems tab in the Phone and Modem dialog box.**

5. **Choose the laptop's modem from the list.**

6. **Click the Properties button.**

7. **In the modem's Properties dialog box, click the Modem tab.**

8. **Use the volume slider control to set the modem's volume.**

   Loud is on the right. Soft is toward the left. Off is all the way over on the left.

9. **Keep clicking the various OK buttons to close the various dialog boxes.**

You can put away those noise-reducing headphones now.

Adding special modem-command settings

Some ISPs require you to give your modem special commands. You do this to improve the connection or, often, to troubleshoot a bad connection. The settings are entered into a text box labeled Enter Initialization Commands, on the Advanced tab of the modem's Properties dialog box.

To display the modem's Properties dialog box, follow Steps 1 through 6 in the preceding section. Click the Advanced tab to input special modem-command settings.

Suppose that you're told to use the modem command ATS58=33 to help set up the laptop's modem. If so, type that text into the box *exactly* as written. Click the OK button to close the dialog box and make this change permanent.

Dialing from other locations

When you first set up the modem, you told it how to dial the phone. You entered information for the laptop's primary location. But consider that you visit other locations where you use your laptop. If you plan to return to those locations, it pays to set them up permanently. That way, you can quickly configure the modem to dial from any of your favorite haunts.

To create a new location, tread these steps:

1. **Open the Phone and Modem dialog box.**

   Directions for accessing this dialog box (refer to Figure 16-1) are found earlier in this chapter.

2. **Ensure that the Dialing Rules tab is selected.**

   The Dialing Rules tab lists the locations where you use your laptop. My Location is your home base (unless you already renamed it).

3. **Click the New button.**

   The New Location dialog box appears. Use it to customize the way the modem dials the phone from any location.

4. **Enter a name for the location.**

   For example, type **The Twilight Zone**.

5. **Select whichever country where the location is found.**

   I believe that the Twilight Zone is in Canada.

6. **Enter the area code.**

7. **Fill in the Dialing Rules area.**

   For example, when you're creating a location for a hotel and it requires you to dial an 8 before making a local call or a 9 for making a long-distance call, put those numbers into the appropriate boxes.

   You can leave these items blank when no rules are required.

8. **To disable call-waiting while the modem is online, select the To Disable Call Waiting Dial check box. Then select the proper code sequence from the drop-down list.**

   The call-waiting signal disconnects an active modem connection. You select this box to disable call waiting on a per-phone-call basis.

9. **Select whether your connection requires tone or pulse dialing.**

   Select the Pulse option only if your area is limited to pulse dialing. You'll be painfully aware of this annoyance; otherwise, you can choose Tone.

10. **Click OK to save the settings.**

When your laptop visits the location, simply choose it from the Phone and Modem window. When you go to another location to dial out, choose that location as well. You need to do this for each location where you use the laptop's modem.

You can use these steps to rename your home location from My Location. Just select the My Location item and click the Edit button. Type a new name using the Edit Location window — for example, Home Office. Click OK.

Dialing area codes

You have to follow rules about dialing area codes. You may not know them all, but you certainly know the frustration when the automated voice says, "You do not need to dial a 1 . . ." or, equally as often, "You must first dial a 1 or 0 . . ." Who really knows what to dial? And why, if they know whether you need to dial a 1, doesn't the phone company do it for you automatically?

When you set up a location for your laptop's modem, you also have the opportunity to explain to the computer all about dialing long-distance numbers, or how and when to use an area code. Here's what you do:

1. **Choose your current location in the Phone and Modem dialog box.**

   The directions for opening the Phone and Modem dialog box are concealed earlier in this chapter.

2. **Click the Edit button.**

3. **In the Edit Location dialog box, click the Area Code Rules tab.**

4. **Click the New button to create a new rule.**

   The New Area Code Rule dialog box appears, as shown in Figure 16-2.

   Filling in this dialog box is an art form. You need to know which prefixes for your area code require that the area code be dialed. Fortunately, if you're using a modem, you probably have only a couple of phone numbers that you'll dial anyway. If they require dialing an area code, place those prefixes into the dialog box by using the Add button.

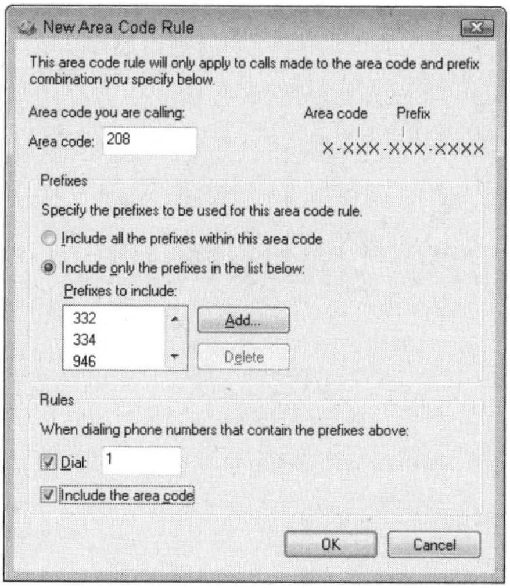

Figure 16-2:
Making up
a new area
code rule.

If you're calling locally and you need to enter the area code for only certain prefixes — the so-called local long-distance prefixes, or when you live in a large area covered by one area code and certain prefixes are long distance — add those prefixes in the dialog box.

Finally, if you have to always dial the area code, choose the option Include All the Prefixes Within This Area Code, and select the two check boxes at the bottom of the dialog box. That way, every time you dial any local number, the modem automatically prefixes 1 and your area code to the number.

5. Click OK to add the new rule.

To put these dialing rules into effect, you select the Use Dialing Rules check box whenever you enter a new phone number for the modem to dial.

Yes, you can ignore and forget about all these things! Rather than create rules all the time, simply type the full number to dial every time you set up a new modem connection. But, if you're dialing a lot of numbers in different locations, setting up the rules can make things far easier.

Setting up calling card info

The rightmost tab in the Edit Location dialog box is for entering calling card information. This tab lets Windows automatically blast out the calling card information as the modem connects, allowing you to charge, for example, a specific call at a business center to your company's credit card.

To enter calling card information, edit the location information as described in previous sections. Click the Calling Card tab, and you see a buncha options. Fill them in with the information you need in order to use the calling card, and leave irrelevant items blank.

Drat Those Disconnect Time-Outs!

Just like when you're hanging up a phone, you should always remember to manually disconnect the modem when you're done using it. Even if you forget, the modem eventually hangs up by itself. That's because Windows runs a time-out clock on the modem. After a period of inactivity, the modem eventually hangs up itself.

Yes, it's a good thing that the modem can time-out and hang up. That may save you money on pricey calls. But it's also a bad thing when the time-out hits unexpectedly. To ensure that the modem doesn't time-out on you when you don't want it to, consider checking two separate places in Windows.

Setting the general time-out

The general modem-time-out value is set in the modem's Properties dialog box. Refer to the section "Silencing the modem" (found earlier in this chapter) for the steps required to display the modem's Properties dialog box. After you're there, heed these steps:

1. **In the laptop modem's Properties dialog box, click the Change Settings button on the General tab.**

   You need to either type the administrator password or click the Continue button if you see the User Account Control warning.

   A second, more complex modem Properties dialog box appears.

2. **Click the Advanced tab.**

3. **Click the Change Default Preferences button.**

4. **Select the Disconnect a Call If Idle for More Than check box, and then enter a time-out value into the text box.**

   Yes, if you leave this item deselected, no general time-out takes place.

5. **Click OK and close the various open dialog boxes.**

Oh, but you're not done — there are *two* locations for setting time-outs. The second location is covered in the next section. Be sure to check both!

Setting time-outs for each session

Time-outs are also set for each connection you make with the modem. These connections are discussed in Chapter 15. Here's how to reset the time-out for each connection:

1. **Open the Control Panel.**

   You can return to Category view if you switched to Icon view in other sections in this chapter.

2. **Choose Network and Internet.**

3. **Choose the Internet Options link.**

   The Internet Options dialog box shows up.

4. **Click the Connections tab.**

5. **Choose the dialup connection you want to modify.**

6. **Click the Settings button.**

   The dialup connection's Settings dialog box appears. But, oh, you're not anywhere close yet.

7. **Click the Properties button.**

8. **In the Properties dialog box, click the Options tab.**

9. **Set the time-out value next to the item Idle Time Before Hanging Up.**

   To disable the time-out, choose Never from the menu.

10. **Click OK and close the various open dialog boxes and windows.**

If you want to set the time-outs for each dialup connection, repeat Steps 5 through 10. Have fun!

Chapter 17

Online Safety

*T*he Internet was designed to withstand a nuclear attack. Sadly, it wasn't designed to withstand an attack from an antisocial teenage programmer who craves negative attention. He, and millions like him, is the scourge of the Internet, wreaking havoc with viruses, scam web pages, spyware, and a host of nasties. You have to deal with these threats with your laptop out there on the Internet. This chapter shows you how.

✔ Also see Chapter 21 for information on keeping your laptop's data and hardware secure.

✔ Also refer to my book *Troubleshooting & Maintaining Your PC All-in-One For Dummies* (Wiley) for more Internet security information and tips.

The Windows Action Center

Using a laptop on the Internet with no form of security is like smearing your body with honey and walking nude through the bear cage at the zoo. It's just not safe out there! Fortunately, Windows comes with an armada of tools to keep you safe, unbuttered, and fully clothed.

The main location for your defense against the bad guys is the *Action Center* window, shown in Figure 17-1. To see this window, open the Control Panel, and click the Review Your Computer's Status link found beneath the System and Security heading.

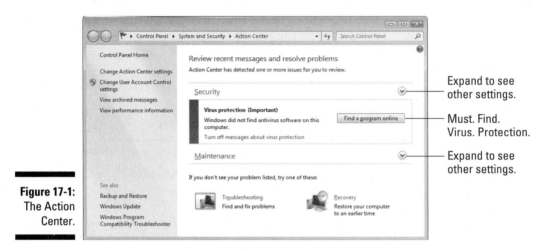

Figure 17-1: The Action Center.

Immediately, the Action Center tells you of any pending problems in your computer. For Windows 7, two issues that might pop up immediately are your laptop's lack of an antivirus program (shown in Figure 17-1) and a backup (not shown in Figure 17-1). Links in the Action Center help you to deal with those situations, and later sections in this chapter offer the details.

✔ For more information on backing up your laptop, see the section in Chapter 21 about backing up your data.

✔ You can expand the areas in the Action Center to view specific information about your laptop's security status. (Refer to Figure 17-1.)

✔ The Action Center also sports a wee little icon in the notification area. The icon looks like a pennant and features an X whenever an issue occurs. Click the icon to see more information.

✔ In Windows Vista, the window to visit for security information is the Windows Security Center: Open the Control Panel, and click the Check This Computer's Security Status link beneath the Security heading.

Antivirus Software

The most evil threat to your laptop's security is the computer virus. Its preferred method of delivery is in an e-mail attachment, though you can also invite a computer virus into your laptop from a shady web page. Rather than worry about such things happening, just employ antivirus software to protect your laptop. It's a must.

- ✔ The most successful viruses use the concept of *human engineering* to ply their evil craft. This technique fools you into doing something you would otherwise avoid, such as open a suspect e-mail attachment or click a misleading link on a web page. Be safe and be smart, and you'll avoid most of the viral scourge that's out there.

- ✔ Viruses have many names. There are *worms* and *Trojan horses,* for example. The generic term *malware* describes malevolent (or malicious) software. Basically, it's all bad stuff. The way to deal with it is to use antivirus software on your laptop.

- ✔ Antivirus software is only one of many tools that you need to keep your PC secure. I also recommend using a firewall, covered in the later section "Behind the Firewall," as well as antispyware software, covered in the later section "Sneaky Spyware."

Checking for an antivirus program

The antivirus program that comes with Windows is Windows Defender. It protects against malware as well as spyware. Beyond Windows Defender, third-party antivirus programs are available. They include popular choices such as Norton AntiVirus, McAfee VirusScan, and AVG. One of these programs may have come preinstalled on your laptop in addition to Windows Defender.

To confirm that your laptop already sports an antivirus program, visit the Action Center or Windows Security Center as described earlier in this chapter. (In Windows Vista, the antivirus program is listed under the Malware Protection category in the Windows Security Center window.)

Getting a free antivirus program

When your laptop lacks antivirus protection or you simply don't trust Windows Defender, you can easily obtain a free program. Here are some suggestions:

- ✔ **Avast! Antivirus:** www.avast.com
- ✔ **AVG Anti-Virus:** www.grisoft.com
- ✔ **Kaspersky antivirus protection:** www.kaspersky.com

Scanning for viruses

You can scan for viruses on your laptop in two ways: actively or passively.

To *actively* scan for viruses, the antivirus program does a complete scan of memory, the storage system, and, finally, individual files. Everything is checked against a database of known viruses.

A *passive* virus scan is done as files are received into your computer. Every file coming in is individually scanned and then checked against the virus database. Most virus programs are configured to do this automatically. For example, when you receive an e-mail message with a virus attachment, your antivirus software alerts you and immediately destroys or "quarantines" the bad program.

Obviously, each antivirus program does things differently. You have to refer to the documentation that comes with your antivirus software program to see how things work. For Windows Defender, follow these steps to perform an active scan:

1. **Start the Windows Defender program.**

   In Windows 8, summon the Charms bar by pressing the Win+C keyboard shortcut. Choose the Search charm, and type **Windows Defender**. Click or touch the Windows Defender tile that appears on the left side of the screen.

   In Windows 7, from the Start menu choose All Programs⇨Windows⇨Windows Defender.

   In Windows Vista, from the Start menu choose All Programs⇨Windows Defender

2. **In Windows 8, choose the type of scan — Quick, Full, or Custom.**

   If you've never scanned your laptop for viruses, choose the Full option. It takes longer, but it's thorough. Otherwise, the Quick option is best.

3. **Click the Scan or Scan Now button.**

   In older versions of Windows Defender, the Scan button is found on the toolbar.

After the scan is complete, you see a summary screen. If any malware is detected, you see directions on what to do next.

As Windows Defender is normally configured, it always scans passively, so there's no need to worry about setting up the type. To confirm that passive scans are enabled in the Windows 8 version of Windows Defender, click the

Settings tab and ensure that a check mark appears by the item Turn On Real-Time Protection (Recommended). In older versions of Windows, follow these steps in Windows Defender:

1. **Choose the Tools button on the toolbar.**

2. **Choose Options.**

3. **Ensure that a check mark appears by the item Automatically Scan My Computer (Recommended).**

   You can further set up the scheduled time at which the scans take place.

4. **Click the Save button if you've activated the scan or changed the schedule.**

Ensure that the automatic scan takes place at a time when your laptop will be on and you won't be busy doing anything else.

✔ Sometimes, it helps to have and run *two* antivirus programs, though not at the same time: Do an active scan with the first program and shut it down, and then do an active scan with the second program. The second one may catch things that the first one misses.

✔ If you use two antivirus programs, ensure that the passive scan is turned off for one of them. Too many antivirus programs doing passive scans can slow down your laptop.

✔ Some antivirus programs require paid subscriptions. You don't pay for the program, but rather for accessing and updating the antivirus database, or *signature,* files. Believe me: The cost of the subscription is *worth it!* Don't delay in updating your antivirus database!

Disabling the antivirus program

Sometimes, you're asked to turn off your antivirus software. For example, the installation directions for adding new software to your laptop may suggest turning off antivirus protection. Doing so helps the installation proceed smoothly and doesn't distress the antivirus program, which may believe that a new virus, and not a new program, is being installed.

My advice is to disable the antivirus program only if an installation program asks you to.

To temporarily disable your antivirus software, locate its icon in the notification area. Right-click the icon and choose the Disable, Exit, or Quit option.

This action temporarily shuts down the antivirus software, allowing your new software to be installed.

For Windows Defender, disable automatic scanning by following the steps at the end of the previous section; remove the check mark by the option to turn on automatic scanning.

After the software installation is done, restart your computer. That also restarts the antivirus software.

Protecting your laptop from the viral scourge

Malware happens to good people, but it also happens to fools who don't heed good advice, such as

- Don't open unexpected e-mail file attachments, even if they appear to be from someone you know and trust. If you weren't expecting something, don't open it!

- When I send something that someone isn't expecting, I first send a heads-up message. The first message lets the person know that the second e-mail has a legitimate file attached.

- Avoid especially any file attachment that can be run as a program, including any file ending in the letters BAT, COM, EXE, HTM, HTML, PIF, SCR, or VBS.

- Avoid opening compressed zip files, or Compressed Folder attachments, specifically when they require a password to open them.

- A plain-text e-mail message cannot contain a virus. But a virus may be in an e-mail signature or attachment!

- Viruses cannot be hidden inside pictures or images attached to e-mail messages.

- Odds are good that if you leave the attachment unopened and simply delete the message, your computer will not be infected.

- Disable the feature that makes your e-mail program automatically save e-mail file attachments. Only save attachments manually.

- The best protection against nasty programs in e-mail is to use both your common sense and your antivirus software.

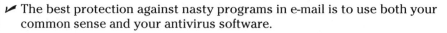

TIP

The social networking threat

Social networking sites such as Facebook and Twitter are tremendously popular but also a common source of computer infection and compromise. The problem isn't the sites themselves, but rather the add-ons you find on the sites as well as links shared by others. Often times, those add-ons can turn out to be scams, or the links your friends share with you can lead to infected web pages.

My advice is to not let down your guard. If you don't expect that your friend Al is the kind of guy to share a get-rich-quick-on-the-web type of link, *don't click the link!* Likewise, be mindful when you play a game or use an add-on for a social networking site. Remember: There's no need to give out your password or cell phone number to find out how well you scored on a trivia test. It simply isn't worth the risk.

Behind the Firewall

In the real world, a firewall is a specially constructed part of a building designed to impede the progress of a blazing inferno. The firewall acts as protection for whatever lies on the other side.

On the Internet, a *firewall* keeps nasty things from either coming into or escaping from your laptop. It does that by monitoring the Internet's virtual doors, called *ports*. Each port is an individual connection used by an Internet program. The firewall monitors everything that travels into or out of the ports.

The reason a firewall is necessary is that many of the Internet's ports are left open. Just like leaving a door open, an open port invites unwanted guests. The firewall software not only helps close those ports but also alerts you whenever anything unexpected knocks on the port's door and wants in or out.

✔ Without a firewall in place, your computer is wide open to attack from any number of nasties on the Internet.

✔ The best firewall is a *hardware* firewall. Most network gateways (routers) come with this feature installed and are more than capable of defending your Internet connection, as well as all computers on the local network, from incoming attacks.

✔ The survival time of an unprotected, nonfirewalled Windows computer on the Internet averages only a few minutes. After that length of time passes, your laptop *will be* infected and overrun by nasty programs sent from the Internet.

✔ A firewall cannot protect your computer from a virus. It may prevent the virus from replicating itself on other computers, but it doesn't stop the virus from coming in. You should use *both* antivirus software and a firewall.

Finding the firewall

In Windows 8 and Windows 7, the firewall is configured to be on and working all the time. Therefore, it's not easy to turn off. I recommend that you simply not mess with it.

To view the status of the Windows Firewall, obey these steps:

1. **Open the Control Panel.**

2. **Choose System and Security.**

3. **Choose Windows Firewall.**

   You can review the status of the Windows Firewall, shown in Figure 17-2, or turn it on or off by using the links found on the left side of the window.

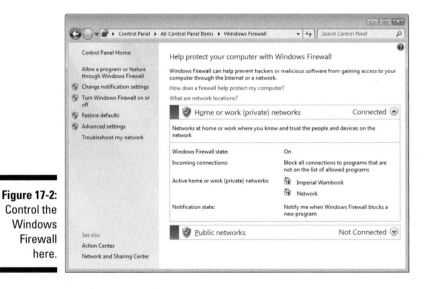

Figure 17-2:
Control the
Windows
Firewall
here.

4. **Close the Windows Firewall window when you're done.**

The key to setting the level of protection offered by Windows Firewall is to properly configure the laptop's network. See Chapter 13 for details. When you use a home network, the firewall is at its lowest setting. On public networks, the firewall is on full-bore.

You can use the steps in this section to find Windows Firewall in Windows Vista as well. Unlike in more recent versions of Windows, you must activate the firewall for Windows Vista: After Step 3, click the Turn Windows Firewall On or Off link found on the left side of the Windows Firewall window. In the dialog box that's displayed, choose the On option and then click OK.

Getting a firewall warning

Windows Firewall lets you know when suspicious Internet access is taking place. A pop-up message appears, similar to the one shown in Figure 17-3, alerting you that a program is attempting to access your computer from the Internet or from your computer to the Internet.

Figure 17-3: Is it okay for this program to access the Internet?

When the warning appears, *read it.* The name of the program is listed. In Figure 17-3, the name of the program trying to access the Internet is provided. It's Microsoft Windows Fax and Scan. Because I was trying to send a fax at the time the message appeared, the access is okay.

✔ Take the firewall warning seriously! It's not a panic situation, because nothing bad has happened. Yet! Still, don't let yourself develop the habit of automatically clicking the Allow Access button.

✔ No, the firewall doesn't warn you incessantly. As you tell it what's allowed and what's denied, it learns. After you train it awhile, the firewall alerts you less often.

✔ Various firewall programs use different terms in their warning boxes. I've seen Allow and Deny as well as Unblock and Keep Blocking. The messages are all basically the same type.

Sneaky Spyware

Spyware is a specific category of evil computer software, or *malware*. It sounds innocent: *Spyware* software monitors your activities on the Internet in order to target you with better, more appropriate advertising. In fact, many people willingly sign up for these services. The fools!

The problem is that spyware is often installed without your permission or knowledge. Often, the spyware is disguised as another program, computer utility, or cute little game. It purports to do one thing, but it's secretly monitoring your Internet activity.

To help fight spyware, you can use the Windows Defender utility — the same one used to fight other malware. It works automatically to stop spyware. There's nothing more for you to do; the program is configured and updated automatically.

✔ Antivirus software traditionally doesn't check for or remove spyware programs. If you're using something other than Windows Defender for malware protection, you need to either keep Windows Defender turned on or get specific, antispyware software.

✔ Your firewall cannot protect against spyware. That's because you typically invite spyware into your computer (whether you're aware of it or not). The firewall does, however, detect when the spyware uploads its vital information back to its mothership; a good firewall stops this type of activity from taking place.

Safe and Private Browsing

Internet Explorer features tools that are useful for web browsing without your having to worry whether anyone is snooping on you or trying to pull a fast one. The tools are part of the InPrivate Browsing feature and, coupled with a few other new features, can soothe your furrowed brow over any concerns you may have about your identity, character, or reputation being compromised on the Internet.

Summoning an InPrivate Browsing window

When you activate an InPrivate Browsing window, Internet Explorer ensures that none of the traditional ways that information is tracked on the Internet is being used. Items such as cookies, history lists, toolbar add-ons, and other tracking features are disabled when you open an InPrivate Browsing window.

To start an InPrivate Browsing window, press the Ctrl+Shift+P keyboard shortcut. This shortcut works for all recent releases of Internet Explorer (versions 8 and earlier), whereas the specific menu commands are different.

After you activate an InPrivate Browsing window, a new web browser window appears, which is required in order for InPrivate Browsing to work. At that point, you can browse the web and know that none of the tracking information normally used to monitor your activity is being stored.

InPrivate

- ✔ The InPrivate Browsing window features the InPrivate button on the left side of the address bar.
- ✔ To end your InPrivate Browsing session, simply close the InPrivate window.

Checking a suspect web page

I was a fool, once. I received an e-mail from what I thought was eBay, explaining that I could redeem a voucher by clicking a suggested link. Because I had just purchased an item at eBay, I obediently clicked the link, went to the web page, typed my eBay password, and suddenly realized that I was *not* on eBay.

Yes, that's how human engineering works. Normally, I'm not that gullible, but I've learned! To help you avoid making a similar mistake, you can use a feature in Internet Explorer to determine whether a web site is legitimate. It's the Smart Screen Filter.

To use the SmartScreen Filter in Internet Explorer 10, click the Safety button on the toolbar. (It looks like a gear icon.) Choose Safety⇨Check This Website. If prompted, click the OK button. Immediately, Internet Explorer checks a vast database of suspect web pages. If the page you're visiting has been marked, you're alerted immediately.

✔ In older versions of Internet Explorer, click the Safety button on the tool-bar, and then choose Smart Screen Filter⇨Check This Website.

✔ You can also confirm whether a web page is legitimate by looking at the address bar; Internet Explorer highlights the web page domain in bold text. Then you instantly know whether the site you're visiting is truly eBay or Yahoo! or a phony site that's trying to scam you.

Deleting your web browsing history

O those places you've been! Who knows? Well, Windows knows everywhere you've been on the web. It keeps your history. The purpose of the history list isn't to incriminate you, of course. It exists so that you can easily go back and visit a website that you wandered into some time ago.

The browse history feature is handy, and one of the earliest web browsing program features. But it can also be embarrassing, or even a security risk, when you don't want others using your computer to know where you've been.

There are two solutions to removing the History feature's electronic bread crumbs.

First, you can browse the web using the InPrivate window, as described in the section "Summoning an InPrivate Browsing window," earlier in this chapter.

Second, you can burn your entire web history with the zeal of a Third World dictator. Heed these steps:

1. **Press the keyboard shortcut Ctrl+Shift+Del, where Del is the Delete key on the laptop's keyboard.**

   The Delete Browsing History dialog box appears. It's chock-full of items that are recorded as you visit websites.

2. **Ensure that the History item is selected.**

   It's the only option you should zap; choose other items in the window at your own peril.

3. **Click the Delete button.**

   History is gone and doomed to be repeated!

Windows Update

One key to your laptop's software security that you might not think of directly is keeping Windows up-to-date. That means installing the various updates and patches released by Microsoft to ensure that your laptop's operating system has all the latest security information and can meet any known, current, or looming threats.

Confirm that your laptop is configured to update Windows by following these steps:

1. **Open the Action Center window.**

   Refer to the section "The Windows Action Center," at the start of this chapter.

2. **From the links on the left side of the window, choose Windows Update.**

   You're alerted to any pending updates. My advice is to always install the important ones.

3. **Click the Change Settings link found on the left side of the window.**

   Review how and when the automatic updates are installed.

   I recommend that you choose the option Download Updates but Let Me Choose Whether to Install Them. The reason is that you don't want to be out in the middle of somewhere and need to leave, only to discover that you cannot shut down your laptop because an update is installing. Been there. Done that. Hated it.

4. **Click the OK button if you've made any changes.**

5. **Close the Windows Update window.**

Though I recommend updating Windows, I do not recommend that you install a new version of Windows on your laptop. That's because, despite the best efforts of Microsoft, an update simply cannot be configured as well as the original operating system that comes with your laptop.

Because the lifespan of the average laptop is around five years, I recommend waiting and getting the newer version of Windows when you buy a new laptop.

Chapter 18

Portable Web Browsing and E-Mail Tips

*O*h, pish! There really isn't any difference in browsing the web on a laptop and browsing the web on a desktop. That is, unless your laptop can't make an Internet connection. Wireless networking might be everywhere, but it isn't *everywhere*. Not yet. And, what about e-mail? Can you receive e-mail on the road like you can at home? Does it really work the same way?

Puzzle not your weary head. There are subtle differences between using a laptop for Internet access and using a desktop, especially when the laptop has no Internet connection. This chapter offers you a slew of tips and tricks for using the web and accessing e-mail when your laptop is far, far away from the Internet.

Web Browsing When You're Out and About

I have only one suggestion for web browsing on the road, especially if you're away from an Internet connection for some time (such as on an airplane): *Save your web pages!*

For example, before you wander from your beloved high-speed Internet connection, quickly browse a few of your favorite web pages. As you do, save those web pages to the laptop's mass storage medium for offline reading while you're away. Here's how it works in Internet Explorer:

1. **Press the F10 key to summon the menu.**

2. **From the menu, choose the Save As command.**

   A typical Save As dialog box appears, though it's titled Save Webpage.

3. **Use the gizmos in the dialog box to find a location for the web page.**

   Unless you specify a folder, the web page is saved in the My Documents folder for your user account. That's fine.

   Keep the name that's given to the web page, which is the same as the web page's title.

4. **Choose the format Webpage, Complete for saving the web page.**

   This option, chosen from the Save As Type drop-down list, saves everything on the web page, including graphics, sounds, and fun stuff like that. It takes up quite a bit of storage space, creating a special folder to hold all graphics and nontext items referenced by the web page.

5. **Click the Save button to save the web page.**

Continue browsing to other web pages you want to save for reading later. I often stock up on my favorite opinion writers and bloggers before I leave on a trip. That way, I have plenty of reading material on the plane.

To view the web pages later, open the Documents folder for your account. Then open the icon representing the web pages you saved. The pages are displayed in Internet Explorer, where you can read them just as though you're connected to the Internet.

✔ The steps described in this section do not work for the tile version of Internet Explorer that's available in Windows 8. Use Internet Explorer on the desktop instead.

✔ None of the links on the web page you save are active. Only when you reconnect to the Internet does clicking the links lead somewhere.

✔ If you keep seeing a prompt to connect to the Internet, click the Tools button and choose Work Offline from the menu.

✔ Some images may not appear on the web page. That's okay. The Web Page Complete option isn't *totally* complete.

E-Mail Tips Galore

Things are as bad on the road as they were in the old days. I remember staying at one hotel in San Francisco in the early 1990s. To retrieve my e-mail, I had to disassemble the phone jack in the wall. Using alligator clips, I manually connected my laptop's modem to the hotel's phone system. That was a fun, nerdy thing to do, but those days are long over.

Now that the Internet is everywhere, reading your e-mail on the road is no longer something that only MacGyver can do. Even so, this section contains a bunch of e-mail tips and suggestions you may find handy during your laptop journeys.

- ✔ If you have a broadband (high-speed) connection at home, using the Internet on the road with a broadband connection works exactly the same way. See Chapter 15.
- ✔ Refer to Chapter 16 for information on using a modem in strange and wonderful places away from home. Though, when Wi-Fi is available, your laptop can use it instead of the dialup modem.

Reading e-mail on the road

Your e-mail program should work from any remote location. There's no need to change anything, except for two weird exceptions.

First, you might be able to receive mail but not send it. That's because (brace yourself for nerd talk) the SMTP server you normally use may not be accessible from your remote location. One solution is to determine the *local* SMTP server's name and recajigger your e-mail connection to use it. Yes, it's a pain. Another solution is to use web-based e-mail while you're away, in which case all this SMTP-acronym stuff doesn't matter.

The second weird exception happens when you use dialup access. In that case, you can incur the long-distance phone charges to directly access your local ISP; follow my advice in Chapter 16. Or simply use a web-based e-mail service.

Yeah, it looks like the bottom line is to use web-based e-mail while you're on the road. See the next section.

- ✔ Using dialup on the road makes you incur long-distance charges, which can be outrageous in a hotel room.
- ✔ Check with your ISP to find information about its web-based e-mail service before you take off for the road.

Opening a web-based e-mail account

A free, web-based e-mail service makes e-mail available to you anywhere you can find Internet access. Using these services is easy and, best of all, free. When you use web-based e-mail, you never have to worry about connecting to your ISP's e-mail account. Your e-mail is available anywhere you have web access — even if you don't have your own computer with you.

Here are some of the more popular web-based e-mail services you might consider:

- **Gmail:** `http://gmail.google.com`
- **MyWay Mail:** `http://mail.myway.com`
- **Windows Live (Hotmail):** `http://mail.live.com`
- **Yahoo! Mail:** `http://mail.yahoo.com`

Just because you have a web-based e-mail account doesn't mean that you need to abandon your ISP's e-mail account. Many people often juggle more than one e-mail account. For example, you can open a free account on Yahoo! Mail and either tell everyone to send your mail to that account when you're on the road or have your regular mail forwarded to it. (Forwarding e-mail is covered later in this chapter.)

Some people even use their web-based e-mail accounts as their public accounts and keep their primary accounts, the ones they have at their ISPs, secret or reserved for private e-mail. That way, the main account remains relatively spam-free. And, when the public, web-based e-mail account becomes overwhelmed with spam, it can be discarded and replaced by a new, free, web-based e-mail service.

Accessing e-mail from a friend's computer

I don't believe that Miss Manners covers this topic: What do you do when you're visiting friends or relatives and the urge to check your e-mail hits you?

If you have a laptop and your friends or relatives have their own network, you can easily hook into it and use your laptop that way (assuming that they're open to the idea — always ask and be prepared for a "No" answer).

Your friend or relative may offer to set up an account for you on his computer. That's nice, and it's a good thing to do for security reasons. But all you need in order to pick up your e-mail is a computer with Internet access. Then you can use your ISP's web-based e-mail system to peruse your mail or visit any mail waiting for you on a web-based e-mail system (Gmail or Yahoo!, for example).

✔ I don't recommend setting up your own e-mail account on a friend's or relative's computer. It's just too much of a security risk.

✔ The best option is to pray that your friends or relatives have a wireless connection and then use your laptop's wireless network adapter to hook into their network for full Internet access.

✔ Yes, I've taken a wireless router with me to visit relatives. By plugging the router into their broadband connection, I give myself wireless access throughout their home without having to trouble them by asking for permission. (Well, I ask permission to hook up the wireless router.)

✔ If Internet access is disallowed, you still have the library option. Cybercafés and wireless hot spots also have Internet access that you can consider.

Forwarding your messages

It's possible to send all your incoming e-mail to another e-mail address. This service is known as *e-mail forwarding,* and your ISP may offer it for free, or your company or business may have it available as a feature. When you know that you're going to be away for a spell, you can have your e-mail forwarded to another account.

For example, if you know that you're going to be out for three weeks, you can have your e-mail forwarded to your web-based e-mail account for that length of time. Any e-mail coming into your regular account is immediately redirected to the other account. That way, you don't miss a thing.

You face, sadly, a problem with forwarding your e-mail, which is why you may not find it available as an option. Occasionally, e-mail gets stuck in the space-time continuum, in what's scientifically referred to as an *endlessly forwarding loop.* Your mail is forwarded to you, which then reforwards the mail back to you, which then repeats the process. Eventually, the system becomes clogged with e-mail, and when the IT guys figure things out, they simply delete your e-mail account to fix the situation. That's a bad thing.

So, if e-mail forwarding is an option, look into it. But be careful to ensure that your e-mail is being forwarded to a real account and isn't lost in the Twilight Zone. In fact, test the system by forwarding all your e-mail a day or so before you're set to leave so that you can ensure that everything works.

✔ Sometimes, you can set up e-mail forwarding for yourself, such as by choosing a forward-my-mail option on the ISP's e-mail website. At other times, someone there may have to complete the configuration for you. And sometimes, forwarding just isn't available.

✔ Don't forget to stop forwarding your e-mail when you return.

Setting up an autoresponder

An *autoresponder* lets you answer your e-mail when you're away from the office or utterly unavailable. It's a single message that you set up, one that's sent to everyone who sends you e-mail. It says, "I'm out of this dreary office and in Tahiti for a month. Don't bother e-mailing me until March!" Or something.

Check with your ISP to see whether an autoresponder is available. Often, you can set one up yourself on the ISP's e-mail website.

You still receive your mail when you configure an autoresponder. It's just that the messages are replied to and the sender knows not to expect a real reply from you for a while (if ever).

Dialup E-Mail Tips

Indeed, I shall pity you if you have the misfortune of being forced into using a dialup connection to check your e-mail. It happens. When it does, you can refer to the tips in this section to see how to get the most from e-mail when using a dialup connection.

Disconnecting after picking up e-mail

When you're using a dialup account, you don't need to be connected to the Internet all the time while you read your e-mail. Especially given how much battery power the modem draws, I recommend having your e-mail program immediately hang up (or disconnect) after sending or receiving e-mail. Here's where to check those settings in Windows Live Mail:

1. **Press Alt+M to summon the menu, and choose the Options command.**

   In Windows Mail or Outlook Express, choose Tools⇨Options.

   The Options dialog box duly appears.

2. **Click the Connection tab in the Options dialog box.**

3. **Put a check mark by the option Hang Up After Sending and Receiving.**

4. **Click OK.**

You may also want to disable automatic checking, as covered in the next section.

✔ This setting isn't needed for broadband access.

✔ Similar settings are available for other e-mail programs. Search the program's Help index for the term *hang up*.

Disabling automatic checking

On a laptop with a dialup connection, you probably don't want the battery to systematically drain every ten minutes when your e-mail program attempts to collect new messages. To fix this situation, you can direct the laptop not to automatically pick up your e-mail. Here's how it goes:

1. **Start Windows Live Mail.**

   These steps apply to Windows Mail as well as to Outlook Express.

2. **Summon the menu by pressing Alt+M, and choose Options.**

3. **In the Options dialog box, click the General tab (if needed).**

4. **Deselect the Check for New Messages Every [blank] Minutes check box.**

5. **Choose the Do Not Connect option from the If My Computer Is Not Connected at This Time drop-down list.**

   Setting this option ensures that merely starting your e-mail program doesn't cause it to try to dial in to the Internet.

6. **Deselect the check box next to the option Send and Receive Messages at Startup.**

   This setting prevents the program from immediately contacting the Internet when you open it. That way, you can read pending messages and then connect with the Internet when you're ready.

7. **Click OK.**

Making these settings saves time and battery power only when you use the dialup modem to retrieve your e-mail.

Sending everything in one batch

As you peruse your e-mail, you read messages and reply to messages and then click the Send button to send those messages. On a broadband connection, that's fine. But when you're not connected to the Internet or you're using a dialup connection, the send-as-you-go option isn't practical. Instead, you should configure your e-mail program to send everything in one batch.

Here are the directions for setting up Windows Live Mail to send messages all at one time:

1. **Press Alt+M to open the menu, and choose Options.**

   Options is found on the Tools menu in Windows Mail and Outlook Express.

2. **In the Options dialog box, click the Send tab.**

3. **Deselect the Send Messages Immediately check box.**

4. **Click OK.**

The messages now sit in the outbox and wait until you click the Sync button on the toolbar. In older e-mail programs, click the Send button.

Chapter 19

Between the Desktop and Laptop

*T*he trend these days is to use only a laptop computer. That's fine for most people, but plenty of us still have both desktop and laptop computers. This combination can be highly useful, as long as both systems can get along. Proper sharing must take place between the two computer systems, a thread of harmonious cooperation. This chapter covers the desktop-laptop link and the issues that are involved when you have both stationary and portable computers.

Data from Here to There

Ever since the first protonerds of the pre-digital age developed two different and utterly incompatible computers, exchanging information has been an issue. The goal is to move information from one computer into another. The solutions are various — some simple, some complex, some fast, some slow. This section covers the gamut.

Sneakernet

The traditional way of moving information from one computer to another is to place the information on some type of removable media and swap the media between the computers. In the olden days, the media was magnetic or paper tape. Then came floppy disks, optical discs, and now media cards and thumb drives. The information exchange works like this:

1. You save or copy information from a computer to removable media.

2. You walk (in your sneakers) to the other computer.

3. You plug the media into the second computer.

4. You open the media (assuming that the second computer can read it in the first place).

In four steps, that's the process of *sneakernet,* or the physical, human-powered moving of data from one computer to another.

Sneakernet exists today, even when the laptop and desktop are sitting next to each other and footwear isn't an issue, but it's neither the fastest nor bestest way to exchange information.

Ugly octopus net

Before a networking standard appeared, computer users could connect their desktop and laptop computers by using both systems' serial or printer ports. To accomplish this feat, an ugly cable octopus was used, similar to the one shown in Figure 19-1.

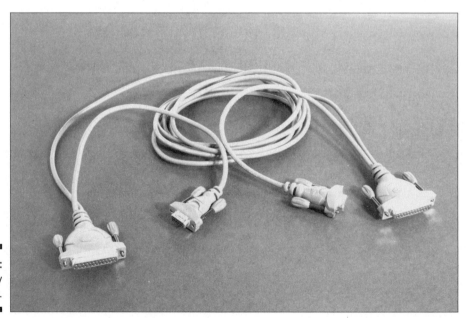

Figure 19-1:
The ugly
cable thing.

The ugly cable octopus connects the desktop system and laptop systems. Then special software is used to connect the computers and exchange information. Although this method was more automatic than sneakernet, the complex hardware setup and software requirements meant that using such a thing was a major pain in the butt.

Ethernet

The simplest way to send files between laptop and desktop is to place them both on the same computer network. After they're configured and connected properly, you can share and access folders on the storage system of both desktop and laptop to easily exchange files.

After the network connection is made, copying files between systems works just like copying files on a single computer. In fact, Windows comes with something called the Sync Center, which makes the process easy. (Refer to the next section.)

✔ Networking is the preferred way to connect two computers. Even if all you have is a desktop and a laptop, I highly recommend getting networking hardware to make connecting the two a snap.

✔ Refer to Chapter 13 for more information on networking your desktop and laptop computers.

Internet sharing with Dropbox

My preferred way to share files between my various computers is to use a utility called Dropbox. What it does is set up folders on your computer that are automatically duplicated on any other computer (or mobile device) that has the Dropbox software installed and shares your Dropbox account. When you create a file in your Dropbox folder (or one of its subfolders), the file is echoed on all your computers. It's a great way to share.

You can obtain a free copy of Dropbox by visiting www.dropbox.com.

✔ Files stored in your Dropbox folder are accessed instantly between your computer and laptop. There's never any need to copy anything; Dropbox does the work for you.

✔ I find Dropbox a much better solution for desktop-laptop synchronization than the dratted Windows Sync Center.

✔ Your Dropbox files can also be accessed online at the Dropbox website.

✔ If you have a mobile device — cell phone or tablet — you can access your Dropbox files there as well. All you need is the Dropbox app.

✔ As long as you don't have a lot of data to share, Dropbox can be used for free. Larger quantities of data require a subscription.

✔ Windows 8 features an app, similar to Dropbox, called Windows Sky Drive. It lets you save files to "the cloud" on the Internet, which you can then access from other devices that can access the Sky Drive. Perhaps Sky Drive may one day be as popular as Dropbox, but until then I know that Dropbox works and is more widely available than Sky Drive.

Synchronized Bliss

Coordinating files between desktop and laptop computers should be simple, right? After all, computers are supposed to make things easier. They love repetitive tasks. One of those tasks is synchronizing files between two computers, such as your desktop and laptop. In Windows, this chore is handled by the Sync Center.

Though Sync Center comes with Windows, and it's the operating system's approved method of synchronizing files, it's not the easiest thing to use. In fact, I strongly recommend using a file sharing utility, like Dropbox (covered earlier in this chapter), if you find that any of this Sync Center nonsense causes you unexplained woe.

✔ The Sync Center works on computers that are networked with each other, either wired or wirelessly.

✔ Refer to Chapter 13 for information on networking as well as on sharing files and folders.

✔ The ability to sync network files as described in this section isn't available on all versions of Windows.

✔ The Sync Center is designed for mobile devices, such as MP3 players, personal information managers (PIMs), smartphones, and other portable USB gizmos. It can, however, be used to help manage files between a desktop and laptop computer, which is what I concentrate on here.

Visiting the Sync Center

Synchronizing files between two computers is done in the everything-but-the-kitchen Sync Center. To visit the Sync Center, follow these simple steps:

1. **Open the Control Panel.**

2. **Switch to Small Icon view.**

   Use the View menu in the upper-right corner of the Control Panel window to choose the Small Icon item.

3. **Open the Sync Center icon.**

The Sync Center window opens, but it's probably bereft of any sync partnerships, so I didn't insert an obligatory illustration here. Simply put, the links on the left side of the window help you deal with the Sync Center, and any partnerships that are set up between your laptop and desktop appear as icons in the larger part of the window on the right. Close your eyes and picture it now.

✔ In older versions of Windows, you can Find the Sync Center on the Start button menu: Choose All Programs➪Accessories➪Sync Center.

✔ In Windows Vista, you need to choose the Classic View item from the left side of the Control Panel window to see the Sync Center icon.

✔ When syncs have been set up in the Sync Center, you see a weensy Sync Center icon in the desktop's notification area, similar to the one shown in the margin.

✔ Double-clicking the Sync Center icon in the notification area opens the Sync Center window.

✔ The Sync Center can be accessed from the Windows Mobility Center. In Windows 8, you can summon the Windows Mobility Center from the Windows shortcut menu; right-click the mouse in the lower-left corner of the screen, and choose Mobility Center. In older versions of Windows, you can quickly summon the Mobility Center window by pressing the Win+X keyboard shortcut.

Using the Sync Center

The Sync Center works by comparing files from two locations. For a laptop user, that means a folder on your laptop computer as well as a folder on the desktop PC. When you sync the folders, newer files from one folder are updated in the other folder.

For example, when you leave on a trip, you can sync your desktop and laptop so that important files from your Work folder on the desktop computer are up-to-date with those on your laptop. Ditto for when you return: Sync the computers so that your files are always current.

Setting up a sync partnership

Assume that you have a desktop computer and a laptop computer. Presently, they're both in your home or office, and both are on a network. You're about to leave for That Important Business Trip. It's time to set up and use a sync partnership. Here's how:

1. **Open the Network window.**

   Specific directions can be found in Chapter 13.

2. **Browse to the computer that has the folder you want to sync to.**

   For this example, it's your desktop computer.

3. **Open the computer's icon.**

   The Network window displays a list of folders being shared by that computer.

4. **Right-click the folder you want to sync with.**

5. **From the shortcut menu, choose Always Available Offline.**

   Windows dawdles, impressing you with a busy-looking dialog box while it does who-knows-what. Just wait a few. (When Windows is done, the Cancel button becomes dimmed.)

6. **Click the Close button.**

   Or Windows may voluntarily close the window for you.

7. **Close the network computer's window.**

You can confirm that the sync is ready by reviewing the sync partnership in the Sync Center window. This topic is covered in the next section. You're not done yet!

Before you flee down the road, you must first sync your files. This topic is covered in the section "Synchronizing files," a little later in this chapter.

Reviewing sync partnerships

No, don't call it a *sync*. If you say "sync," people hear "sink," and that term has too much potential for humor to be a computer topic. Instead, say "sync partnership." There.

The Sync Center window displays devices and folders that your laptop is partnered with when it first opens. To see the details, you open the Offline

`Files` folder found in the Sync Center window. Doing so displays a list of network folders that your laptop is synced with. It's a boring list of icons, so, once again, I didn't add a silly figure here.

Synchronizing files

To synchronize files, coordinating them between your laptop and desktop, follow these steps:

1. **Open the Sync Center window.**
2. **Choose the View Sync Partnerships task from the left side of the window (if necessary).**
3. **Click the Sync or Sync All button.**

   You can wait and watch (grab some popcorn and a beverage) or go off and do something else while Windows synchronizes the files in the sync partnership folder.
4. **Close the Sync Center window when you're done.**

You can review the results of the operation by choosing View Sync Results from the task list on the left. Any problems are most likely unavailable files and folders or Access Denied errors.

Your laptop must be connected to the network and the shared folders accessible for a sync operation to be successful.

Accessing synced files

You're gone. You're on the road. You're away. Now comes the time to access the files you synchronized with your desktop computer. Here's what you do:

1. **Open the Sync Center window.**
2. **Choose View Sync Partnerships from the left side of the window (if necessary).**
3. **Open the Offline Files folder.**
4. **Open the folder for the files you need to access.**
5. **Open a file.**

   The file opens on your computer, ready for you to use it.

If the file isn't available, the computers didn't completely sync their information. Refer to the preceding section.

> ✔ Unavailable files appear with a ghostlike, dimmed icon. Scary.
>
> ✔ Yes, you can copy the file from the synced folder to another folder of your hard drive. But the file doesn't stay synced unless you copy it back when you're done.

Syncing a new file

If you're on the road and you create a new file that you want to sync back to your desktop computer, you should follow these steps:

1. **Save the file as you normally do.**

   For example, save it in the `Documents` folder in your user account area.

2. **Open the folder in which you saved the file,**

3. **Click to select the file.**

4. **Press Ctrl+C to copy the selected file.**

5. **Open the Sync Center.**

6. **Open the `Offline Files` folder.**

7. **Open the sync partnership folder in which to save the file.**

8. **Press Ctrl+V to paste the file, placing a copy in the sync partnership folder.**

Only with the file in the sync partnership folder is it properly synchronized with your desktop computer.

Frustrated? Refer to the earlier section "Internet sharing with Dropbox" for information on using the Dropbox utility, which I find works far, far better than Windows Sync Center.

Ending a sync partnership

If the need ever arises to stop syncing with a network resource, follow these steps:

1. **Open the Network window.**

2. **Browse to the network location where you have sync partnerships.**

3. **Right-click a sync partnership folder.**

   Remember that this type of folder sports the little green Sync Center flag on its icon.

4. **Choose Always Available Offline to remove the check mark.**

5. **Click the Close button to dismiss the Always Available Offline dialog box.**

   Windows may automatically close the window for you.

6. **Close the Sync Center window when you're done.**

Your PC from Afar

A truly amazing feat that your laptop is capable of is accessing your desktop computer for serious remote-control action. It's amazing. From any location where the Internet is available, you can simply *phone home* and use your desktop PC as though you were sitting in front of it and not while you're pretending to work on your screenplay in that L.A. coffee hot spot where Robert De Niro is rumored to hang out.

Although remote access is truly something, it's also a security risk. Do you really want every creep on the Internet using your desktop PC? It can happen! Therefore, I strongly advise that you try the tricks in this section only with a well-established firewall in place — specifically, one designed to let in only your laptop and not any other computer system. (You may need the abilities of a computer security expert to set it up, but that's good. This task isn't something to try casually.)

Setting up for Remote Desktop

The tool to use for accessing one computer from another, on either the local network or the Internet, is Remote Desktop. It's not available for Windows XP, and it might also not be available on laptops running the Starter, Home Basic, or Home Premium versions of Windows 7.

Follow these steps to configure your desktop computer for remote access from a laptop. These steps should take place on your desktop computer:

1. **Press Win+Break on the keyboard to open the System window.**

2. **Take note of the computer's name.**

   You use this name when connecting to the computer on the network.

3. **From the list of tasks on the left side of the window, choose Remote Settings.**

4. **If prompted with the User Account Control dialog box warning, click the Continue button or enter the administrator password to continue.**

   The System Properties dialog box appears, with the Remote tab up front.

5. **In Windows 8, choose the item labeled Allow Remote Connections to the Computer. In Windows 7 and Windows Vista, the item is labeled Allow Connections Only from Computers Running Remote Desktop with Network Level Authentication (More Secure).**

6. **If a warning dialog box appears, click OK to dismiss the warning.**

7. **Click OK to close the System Properties dialog box.**

8. **Close the System window.**

The computer is now open to sharing its desktop remotely with another computer on the network.

Accessing Remote Desktop on the network

After you coerce a computer into the idea of a remote connection, the next step is to use a second computer, such as your laptop, to access the first computer and use it remotely on the network. Yes, this sounds like mind control, and I purposefully avoid any talk radio references in this book.

To access the other computer's desktop, heed these directions:

1. **Press Win+R to summon a Run dialog box.**

2. **Type** mstsc **and click the OK button.**

   Or if you have a version of Windows that's not Windows 8, you can find the Remote Desktop program on the Start menu: Choose All Programs⇨Accessories⇨Remote Desktop Connection.

   The Remote Desktop Connection dialog box appears.

3. **If the computer you want to connect to is available from the drop-down list, choose it. Otherwise, type the computer's name, which you remembered to write down after reading the preceding section.**

   The computer must already have been configured to accept a remote desktop connection; refer to the previous section.

4. **Click the Connect button.**

   You must log in to the remote computer by using your user account name and password on that computer.

5. **In the security window, type your username and password, just as though you were logging in to the other computer.**

6. **Click OK.**

   Wait a few seconds.

7. **You may see a security warning; click the Yes button.**

   Eventually, the laptop's screen changes. What you see displayed is the other computer's desktop. In Figure 19-2, my laptop's screen is displaying the desktop PC's desktop.

   Your clue that you're using another computer comes from the banner at the top of the screen. In Figure 19-2, it says `janus`, which is the network name of my desktop computer.

8. **Use the remote computer.**

   When the remote desktop is set up and connected, you see on your computer's screen the display of another computer on the network. Moving the mouse on your computer moves the mouse on the other one, and ditto for the keyboard. It's just as though you're sitting at that computer, when you're actually working things from a remote location.

Figure 19-2:
Remote
Desktop in
action.

9. **To break the connection, click the X button in the strip at the top of the screen.**

   Refer to Figure 19-2.

10. **Click OK to confirm the disconnection.**

    The connection is broken, and you're using only your own PC again.

Note that any programs you started or any activities you run on the remote desktop continue to run after you disconnect. You must specifically stop them before you disconnect, if that's what you want.

- ✔ After the connection is made, the remote computer might log off any user and display the Welcome screen. That's normal.

- ✔ The remote desktop can be displayed in Full Screen mode or in a window. In Full Screen mode, a strip appears across the top of the screen and acts as a sort of window control. In Window mode, the remote desktop appears in a window on your computer's screen.

- ✔ Sadly, you cannot copy files and folders between the remote system and your own computer by dragging items into and out of the remote desktop's window. The Remote Desktop connection is more of a control-and-access feature than a file exchange utility.

- ✔ Remote Desktop Connection works best on the local network. When you need to access your desktop PC from the Internet, I recommend using the program Real Virtual Network Computing, abbreviated VNC. (If you find the missing *R* in the abbreviation, let me know.) This product was once free but now costs money, so I don't write about it in any detail. For more information, visit `www.realvnc.com`.

Part V
The Laptop Goes Elsewhere

In this part . . .

*I*t's trendy, and it's a cute thing to have in your den, but that laptop was designed for going on the road. No, you don't need to take the laptop to the south of France and take a picture of yourself, on the terrace at 6:30 a.m., checking your e-mail back in the States (not that I've ever done such a thing). You simply need to realize the potential: Thanks to wireless networking, you can take your laptop anywhere. Get up! Get out! Get your laptop on the road!

Chapter 20

O the Places You'll Go

You can take your laptop here. You can take your laptop there. You can take your laptop everywhere.

Take your laptop to the park. Laptop, laptop, after dark.
Use your laptop on a plane. Take your laptop down the lane.
Laptop with your cousin Ned. Use a laptop when in bed.
Laptop, laptop in Nantucket, on a hill or on a bucket.
Take your laptop where you please. Take your laptop overseas.
Use your laptop in the car. Use your laptop in a bar.
Laptop with a cup of joe. Laptop, laptop, on the go.

Laptop here! Laptop there! Laptop, laptop, everywhere!

On the Case

Time for a confession: You need a laptop case not because it makes you look cool to have one. Nope, you need a laptop case because your mobile, digital lifestyle demands that you carry with you more junk than just the laptop. Admitting that, you can go forth and find yourself a quality carrying thingy for your laptop.

Features to look for in a laptop case

I've been toting around laptop computers for over 25 years. Here's what I've learned during that time about finding a case for toting around a laptop computer:

- ✔ Does your laptop fit? This question doesn't imply that the case needs a compartment designed to fit your specific laptop. Instead, you want to ensure that your laptop fits comfortably inside the case and that the case can zip up or close easily with the laptop inside.

- ✔ Actually, you *don't* want a case with a compartment designed to fit your specific laptop. You may not be using the same laptop years from now, but it's nice to keep using the same case.

- ✔ Get a soft case, not something hard, like the traditional briefcase. I think that a soft case holds the laptop more securely, whereas a laptop tends to jostle around inside a hard case.

- ✔ Does the case have plenty of pouches? You need pouches for storing accessories, office supplies, discs, manuals, Altoids, year-old receipts, and other things you plan to carry around with you. The pouches can also be used for smuggling.

- ✔ I recommend a case that opens to display two large and separate areas. You can slide your laptop into one and put paper, notepads, or computer accessories into the other area.

- ✔ Zippers are preferred over snaps, buckles, or latches. Be sure, however, that the bag isn't so snug that the zipper can damage the laptop. In that case, look for those Velcro or "touchless" zippers.

- ✔ Having an easy-access pouch on the case's outside helps with storing important documents, such as airline tickets, and other information that you need to grab quickly.

- ✔ A carrying handle is a must, but a shoulder strap is better.

- ✔ A backpack makes a great laptop carrying case. The bonus here is that shouldering the backpack keeps both your arms and hands free. That way, you can hold your boarding pass in one hand and coffee in the other and still carry the laptop with you.

- ✔ If you know that you have to carry lots of stuff (extra material for your job or perhaps something heavy, like a printer or video projector), consider getting a laptop case with wheels and a retractable handle.

- ✔ As far as size goes, keep in mind that the bag needs to fit beneath the seat in front of you on an airplane. Don't get something too big.

✔ Avoid a laptop case that's too tiny! Some trendy cases hug the laptop like a thong on a stripper. That's ineffective! (Well, for the laptop, not for the stripper.) You need a laptop case with some extra room in it. Think sweatpants, not hot pants.

✔ Avoid a laptop case that is too bulky or contains too much padding.

✔ Avoid a case that has your laptop manufacturer's or dealer's name on it. A laptop case with *DELL* on it may scream brand loyalty, but it also tells thieves that something worth taking is inside the case.

✔ The idea behind your laptop bag is to safely carry and protect the laptop while you're traveling; plus, it needs to carry all your laptop toys and other related goodies. Go nuts on the extra features, if you must. But, honestly, if you can find a solidly made case, bag, or backpack that does what you need, you're set.

Recommended brands

I've used an Eddie Bauer soft briefcase as my laptop bag for over 20 years. You can see a picture of this handy nylon bag in Figure 20-1. It has plenty of pouches, zippers, and storage compartments, plus room left over for me to toss in magazines and books or even a box of chocolates to take home. That bag has been all over the world with me.

Figure 20-1:
My trusty old Eddie Bauer soft case.

For longer trips, I use a backpack instead, primarily because it's roomier but also because thieves don't suspect backpacks to contain laptops as much as they suspect briefcases. If you choose a backpack, ensure that it's well put together, with reinforced seams on heavy-duty material.

The following list shows brand-name bags that I can recommend or that have been recommended to me. If you have an outlet mall or retail location near you, pay the place a visit and peruse the stock. Don't forget to take your laptop with you for a test fitting!

- www.ebags.com
- www.eddiebauer.com
- http://oakley.com
- www.targus.com
- www.thenorthface.com

- If you can find one, get one of those CIA bags. It's designed with a locking zipper so that spooks can carry secret stuff around the world. But no one in the CIA uses it because it's so dang obvious. If you can pick one up on eBay or from a retired federal employee, do so at once!

I'm-Leaving-On-a-Jet-Plane Checklist

You may not be jetting across the country. Perhaps you're just walking over to the neighborhood coffee bistro. Either way, consider this section your laptop checklist.

Things to do before you go

Here are some things you should consider doing before you toddle off with your laptop:

- Charge the battery! In fact, this task is probably something you want to do long before you leave. For example, I typically charge my laptop the night before I leave on a trip.
- If you're lucky enough to have a spare battery, charge it as well.
- Synchronize your laptop with your desktop. Refer to Chapter 19 for more information.
- Back up your important files. See Chapter 21.

✔ Remove any discs from the optical drive. By doing so, you avoid having the drive spin into action when you start up the laptop on battery power. Also, put that disc with your other discs so that you don't forget about it or neglect it.

✔ Go online and save a few web pages to your hard drive for offline reading while you're away. (Refer to Chapter 18.)

Things to pack in your laptop bag

A good laptop case is useful for holding more than the laptop. Otherwise, it would be called a laptop *cozy* and not a case. When you're at a loss about what to put into your laptop case, consider this list for inspiration:

✔ Two words: office supplies. Pens. Paper. Sticky notes. Paper clips. Rubber bands. Highlighter. And so on.

✔ Pack the power cord and AC adapter!

✔ Bring any extra batteries you possess.

✔ When you're traveling overseas, remember to bring along a power conversion kit or an overseas power adapter.

✔ Bring a phone cord if you plan to use the laptop's modem.

✔ Bring a 6-foot Ethernet cable — even if you don't plan to use a network.

✔ Bring headphones if you plan to listen to music or watch a DVD. Wearing them is more polite than sharing the noise with people sitting next to you.

✔ If you're making a presentation, don't forget the presentation! If you need your own video projector, pack it too.

✔ Pack any necessary peripherals: mouse, keyboard, PC Card, and external storage, for example.

✔ Ensure that you have some screen wipes.

✔ Bring a deck of cards. (You need something to play with after the battery drains.)

✔ If you're taking along a digital camera, don't forget the camera's computer cable or a memory card reader. Then you can save those digital images directly to the laptop when you're away.

Also take a look at Chapter 27 for more goodies you may want to take with you.

Looming Questions at the Airport

Taking a laptop onboard a commercial airliner today is about as normal as bringing onboard a paperback book and a sack lunch. That's good news. It means that taking your laptop on a commercial airline flight isn't unusual and that the airlines are willing to accommodate your needs and not consider you an oddball exception.

Is your laptop case one carry-on bag or half a carry-on bag?

Sadly, your laptop's case is often your only carry-on luggage. Some airlines let you carry the laptop case plus the typical overnight bag — the same kind of bag that many folks try to jam into the overhead bins. Other airlines are less forgiving.

Do not check your laptop as luggage! You don't want to subject the laptop to the kind of torture that most checked bags suffer. You don't want your laptop to be stored in the subzero cargo hold, and you don't want to risk your laptop being stolen. Do not check your laptop!

When the plane is full and you've tried to sneak on too much carry-on luggage, check the luggage, not the laptop.

If you absolutely must check the laptop case, keep the laptop with you; check only its case.

Laptop inspection

Thanks to the takeover of airport inspections by the Transportation Security Administration (TSA), the security-screening procedures for laptop computers are standardized all over the United States. Here's what you need to do:

1. **Before you get into the inspection line, remove your laptop from its carrying case.**

   Yes, you're burdened with *stuff* for a few moments. You have to carry your boarding pass, picture ID, laptop case, coat, and carry-on bag — plus any small children, shoes, and whatnot. But it's only for a few moments.

2. **When you reach the X-ray machine, place your laptop in its own container and put the container on the conveyer belt.**

You can also put other electronics in the same bin with your laptop. For example, add your cell phone, tablet, or perhaps your car keys. The TSA just wants to see the laptop out by itself, not on top of or beneath other things.

3. **Mind your laptop through the X-ray machine.**

4. **Pick up your laptop on the other end of the X-ray machine.**

After the ordeal, you can put everything away, replacing the laptop in its case and storing all the other stuff that was disassembled or removed during the screening process. Then you're on your way to the gate.

- You can buy a special, approved laptop case in which to store the laptop for its journey through the X-ray machine. Though this idea sounds handy, the cases are skimpy and basically hold only the laptop. Stick with my case recommendations from the earlier section "On the Case."

- Watch your laptop! The X-ray machine is a popular spot for thieves! Refer to Chapter 21.

- The X-ray machine doesn't harm the laptop.

- You may be asked to turn on the laptop. That's a good reason to have its batteries fully charged. If they're not, be sure to pack the power cord. Most X-ray stations have a wall socket you can use.

All aboard!

After you board the plane, find your seat. Try to store the laptop under the seat in front of you. You can put it in the overhead storage bin, though I recommend instead underseat storage, which is easier to get to and avoids the peril of having latecomers jamming their steamer trunks and body bags into the overhead bins and crushing your laptop.

Keep the laptop in its carrying case! Wait until you hear the announcement that you can turn on your electronic devices before you whip out your laptop.

- Obviously, you should avoid bulkhead seats, which lack underseat storage.

- I prefer window seats for computing aloft. That way, I can control the window blind, to shield my laptop's screen from the sun. Plus, I can more easily angle the laptop toward me and away from prying eyes in other seats.

✔ When the airline offers an extended-legroom class, such as the exit row or United Economy Plus, take it! More room for legs means more room on the tray table for your laptop.

✔ 3M makes a special laptop display cover, the 3M Laptop Privacy Filter. It prevents peering eyes from seeing the information on your laptop screen, which is a problem on airplanes. The filter can be found at office supply and computer stores all over the place.

Airplane mode

Before the airplane takes off, and just before it lands, you'll doubtless be reminded by the crew to turn off all electronic devices. That includes laptop computers. Further, you're asked to disable any wireless transmission emitting from your electronic gizmos if you turn them on again.

For your wireless laptop, computing aloft means turning off the wireless network adapter. The simple way to do it is by using a hardware switch; many laptops come with a wireless on–off switch. If your laptop has this type of switch, be sure to turn off the wireless network adapter when you use your laptop in the air.

When a wireless network adapter switch isn't evident, follow these steps to disable the thing in Windows 8:

1. **Press Win+C to summon the Charms bar.**

2. **Choose the Settings charm.**

3. **Choose the Wireless Network button.**

   It's the upper-left button found in the bottom clutch of six buttons on the Settings screen.

4. **Click the button next to Airplane Mode.**

   When the text says *On,* as shown in Figure 20-2, the laptop is in Airplane mode.

If you use an older version of Windows, attempt these steps:

1. **Open the Network and Sharing Center window.**

   Refer to Chapter 13 for more information on opening this window.

2. **From the list of tasks on the left side of the window, choose Change Adapter Settings.**

   In Windows Vista, choose Manage Network Connections.

3. **Right-click the laptop's Wireless Networking Connection icon.**

4. **Choose Disable from the shortcut menu.**

   In Windows Vista, you need to deal with the UAC warning: Click the Continue button or type the administrator password.

5. **Close any open windows.**

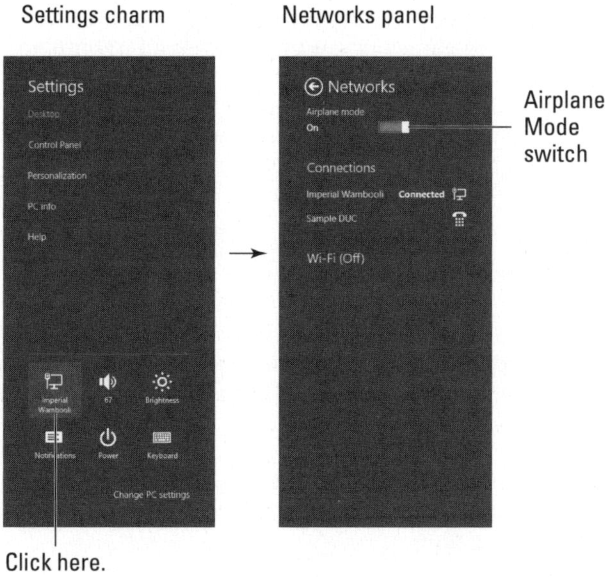

Settings charm   Networks panel

Airplane
Mode
switch

Figure 20-2:
Airplane
mode in
Windows 8.

Click here.

You can now use your laptop in the air without fear of its wireless network adapter interfering with the cockpit's instrumentation and the plane crashing into the ground in a film-at-11 type of fireball.

✔ Don't forget to reenable the wireless network adapter when you need it again. Repeat the preceding steps, but in Step 4 choose the Enable command.

✔ If your laptop sports Airplane mode, use that mode of operation when you compute aloft.

✔ Some laptops feature a keyboard combination to turn the wireless networking off or on. On my Lenovo laptop, the key combination is Fn+F5.

Up, up in the air

After the announcement is made allowing you to use your electronic devices in the plane, and after ensuring that the laptop's wireless network adapter poses no peril to your fellow passengers, you can whip out your laptop and . . . do whatever with it.

Of course, the conundrum is trying to find a place for the thing. Some seats are so close together that opening the laptop while it's sitting on your tray table is nearly impossible. And when the jerk in front of you lowers his seat, computer time is over! Well, unless you have a Tablet PC, in which case you flip over the display and keep computing. Likewise, most netbooks work on the tray table when the seat in front of you is reclined.

When you get the laptop open and running, the real choice becomes this: Do you get work done or play games or perhaps watch a DVD movie? Hmmm.

How long you can use the laptop depends primarily on its battery life and also on the flight's duration. When you hear the announcement to shut down electronic devices, shut down Windows and turn off (or hibernate) your laptop.

Air power

The airlines have heard your cries for help, or at least those cries for in-flight power. Many of them now offer AC power on many flights for use with your laptop. Three power plans are often available:

AC power: This is the type of power you're used to, provided with a standard U.S. or European power outlet. Sometimes it's a two-prong outlet, and sometimes there's a grounding plug.

DC "cigarette lighter" power: This kind of power is the same as the kind offered in your car, with what is still curiously called the *cigarette lighter*. You need a cigarette lighter power adapter to use this type of power with your laptop.

EmPower DC power: The most common type of laptop electricity available on airlines is EmPower. You need a special EmPower adapter to use this system, or you can use a cigarette lighter power adapter / EmPower adapter — an "adapter adapter."

 Power adapters aren't universal. You need to ask the airlines whether your flight has a power adapter you can use and, furthermore, whether your seat is near a power adapter. An extra fee may also be involved, though most of these adapters are in either the business or first-class section, so my guess is that you already paid the extra fee when you overpaid for your ticket.

Remember that your laptop comes with batteries. Use them whenever power isn't available. Just because the airplane lacks something to plug into for power doesn't spell doom for your laptop computing abilities aloft.

✔ Cigarette and EmPower adapters are available wherever laptop goodies are sold. Also check the iGo website: www.igo.com.

✔ AC means *a*lternating *c*urrent. It's the same type of power that comes from the wall in your home or office.

✔ DC means *d*irect *c*urrent, which is the type of power that comes from a battery.

✔ Shhhh! Apparently, the 747 aircraft has a standard U.S. wall socket located near one of its exit doors. The socket is used to plug in the vacuum for cleaning the plane, but you can probably sneak your laptop into that socket during a flight. Don't tell anyone I told you.

In-flight Wi-Fi

A recent development, proving that perhaps not all wireless signals are dangerous to air travel, is the availability of Wi-Fi Internet access on certain flights. It's not free (well, maybe in First Class), but it works for folks who are desperate to check their e-mail or update their Facebook status.

My advice is that if you really need to get on the Internet, go ahead and pay for the service. Especially on long flights, forking over $8 or so for several hours of Internet access can be worth it.

✔ Directions for accessing in-flight Wi-Fi are usually found in the seat pocket in front of you.

✔ As with other pay services, you need to fire up your laptop's web browser after making the wireless connection in the air. Obey the directions on the web page to sign up for the in-flight Wi-Fi service.

✔ The in-flight Wi-Fi providers don't like you using Skype or similar programs to make phone calls, but from my personal observations, that doesn't seem to stop anyone.

✔ Even though in-flight Wi-Fi is offered, that doesn't mean it works. There are spots where the signal drops off, such as remote locations and over the ocean when you're flying overseas. So if you're on a super-long flight to Europe, don't get suckered in to paying for in-flight Wi-Fi.

Café Computing

It used to be that you'd walk into a coffeehouse, order a cappuccino, sit around with artsy folks dressed in black, and discuss the plight of the common man. Today, you go to the coffeehouse, order your double-tall decaf machiatto, and discuss how to connect to the café's Wi-Fi. Whether the person sitting next to you is a common man makes no matter; if she knows the SSID and password, you can have a conversation.

This section mulls over a few of my observations while café computing:

- ✔ It doesn't have to be a café. In fact, a major U.S. city park soon became a hub of wireless activity with all sorts of people using their laptop computers. The reason? The new business next to the park set up a wireless network *without security*. So, laptop users were "borrowing" the free Internet access.
- ✔ You see one other difference between the cafés of yesterday and today: Whereas the café denizen of yesteryear could sit all day, the laptop user eventually gets up and leaves when the battery runs dry.

Where to sit?

Before visiting the counter to order your beverage and mystery scone, scout out the entire café for a good place to sit.

You want a table, unless you think that it's fun to balance a laptop on your knees while you sit on a sofa or an old sack of Columbian coffee beans.

Grab a table that's either away from the windows or facing the windows. You want to avoid having that bright light from the windows reflecting on your laptop screen and washing everything out. (You can tilt the screen to avoid the glare when you can find nowhere else to sit.)

Another suggestion: Be mindful of high windows and skylights. As a sunny day grows long, the sun sweeps a slow swath of bright light across some tables. You don't want to be sitting at a table that's in the path of the moving shaft of light. (The voice of experience is speaking here.)

When you really want to get work done, find a spot away from the door and away from the sales counter. Do the opposite if you prefer to be social.

Be a socket sleuth

Another important factor in determining where to sit in a café is the presence of wall sockets. Without trying to look like you're searching for bombs, duck down and look under tables or against walls for a helpful AC power source.

When you find a power source, great! Grab that table.

If you want to be honest about things, inquire at the counter whether it's okay to plug in. Otherwise, just sneak a cord over the socket as nonchalantly as possible.

Note that not all power sockets are on. My favorite coffeehouse in my hometown has a row of obvious wall sockets next to some nice tables. Those wall sockets, sadly, are usually turned off. You can tell when you plug in: Your laptop doesn't alert you to the AC power presence and continues sucking down battery juice.

When you do manage to plug in, try to arrange the power cord so that no one trips over it. If someone does trip over your cord, expect expulsion.

Other tips 'n' stuff

Always try to buy what they're selling when you're computing in a coffeehouse, diner, or café. Order a cup of coffee. Eat a biscotti. Buy a snack. The management at some places may enjoy having you there because your on-the-go electronic presence adds to the atmosphere, but these places are also in the business of making money. The courts have already established that you can be thrown out for using the wireless networking if you don't buy something, so buy something!

In my book *PCs For Dummies* (published by John Wiley & Sons, Inc.), the rule is simple: No beverages near your computer! It goes double for the laptop, where the keyboard and computer are in the same box. But who am I to deny you a warm, delicious cup of joe? If you want to drink and compute, pour your beverage into a heavy, hard-to-topple, ceramic mug. And grab yourself a nice, thick wad of napkins, just in case.

Never leave your laptop unattended! If you have to go potty, take the laptop with you. *Never* leave your laptop all alone at the table. It will be stolen. (Also see Chapter 21.)

Don't forget to pack a wireless mouse in your laptop bag! When I work on the road, especially in a spot where I'm setting up shop for a few hours, the external mouse is a blessing.

Sometimes, you may be asked to leave or relocate, especially when you're taking up an entire booth all by yourself. Be knowledgeable about this situation in advance. If you see the place filling up, move to a smaller table, or just pack up and leave.

In Your Hotel Room

These days, the hotel industry honestly expects you to have a laptop with you. The phone jack for the dialup modem is obvious. The directions for the wireless Internet are on the same table where you will, predictably, set your laptop. Now, the room service menu still has no Nerd Food section, but I expect that change to come along soon. Until then, peruse these hotel room laptop tips:

- ✔ If you're using a dialup modem, be sure to create a location and a set of dialing rules for the hotel. Especially if you plan to return, creating the location and rule set now saves you time in future visits. See Chapter 16.

- ✔ Many hotels have *broadband,* or high-speed, Internet access. If it isn't free, you're staying at a discount hotel or motel. In that case, you probably have to pay for broadband access, usually in 24-hour increments. After connecting to the network, open your web browser and follow the instructions on the screen to set things up.

- ✔ I recommend staggering the 24-hour periods that cheap hotels grant for Internet access. Start your 24-hour session at 6 p.m. That way, you can use the connection that evening, and then the following morning, and throughout the next day's afternoon.

- ✔ If you're planning to stay a week or more, see about negotiating a lower Internet connection rate. Also check to see whether any of your credit cards or the auto club offer free Internet access at that hotel.

- ✔ Some hotels provide an Ethernet cable; look for it either in the desk drawer or (oddly) hanging in the closet. Even so, I've noticed that the current trend at most hotels is for wireless Internet access only.

- ✔ Beware of digital phone lines! Do not plug the laptop's modem into anything other than a hole properly labeled *Modem*.

- ✔ Use the inexpensive printer: Send a fax to the hotel's fax machine. Refer to Chapter 11.

- ✔ Leaving your laptop set up in the hotel room is a security risk. It's not that the housekeeping staff will steal it; they probably won't. More likely, an information thief will get hold of your laptop to cull passwords and credit card numbers. See Chapter 21 about heeding security issues while in a hotel.

- ✔ Another security risk is the hotel's wireless network. Be careful when you're sending sensitive data — passwords, account numbers, credit card information, and so on — over the wireless (or even wired) network. Who knows how secure that network is or whether hackers are lying in wait nearby?

✔ Set the hotel's wireless network as a public network. See Chapter 14.

✔ Occasionally, I find the rare hotel room that lacks a sufficient number of power sockets by the desk. Note that unplugging a lamp or TV in a hotel can activate the security system. So if the hotel dick comes knocking at the door, be prepared to tell him that he can keep the lamp — you just want to use the wall socket. (And consider a more trustworthy hotel for your next trip.)

✔ I wrote this section in a hotel room.

Mind the Laptop's Temperature

One reason that your laptop doesn't have the latest, fastest microprocessor is heat. Even in a desktop PC, cutting-edge technology generates lots of heat. Managing this heat in a desktop is a huge chore, so you can imagine the things your laptop has to do to keep cool.

So many electronics are packed into the laptop's case that, when coupled with the battery, which heats as it discharges, there can be a whole lotta heatin' goin' on. The laptop comes with a wee li'l cooling fan, one that may even have two speeds for when the temperature gets too high. But that may not be enough! Do not let your laptop get too hot.

✔ Avoid putting your laptop where it sits in direct sunlight.

✔ Do not store the laptop in your car's trunk.

✔ Don't let the laptop run in a closet or in any closed environment where air cannot circulate.

✔ Do not block the little vents on the laptop that help it inhale cool air and expel hot air.

✔ When the laptop continually runs too hot, especially when the battery compartment becomes too hot to touch, phone your laptop dealer for service.

✔ As a suggestion, consider buying your laptop a cooling pad. Chapter 27 covers this and other gizmos.

Chapter 21

A More Secure Laptop

*T*here's a reason that no one has ever stolen the Statue of Liberty. I'm sure that someone has wanted to steal it; the thing would be impressive in any back yard, something to boast about. But I'm guessing the reason the statue hasn't been stolen is that it isn't portable. You see, thieves like to steal items that are portable, like laptops. This chapter explains some things you can to do to prevent it from happening.

The Hot Laptop

Sure, your laptop can get hot. Managing heat is one of the laptop hardware's primary duties. But this section's title has nothing to do with that kind of "hot." No, the topic here is hot as in stolen, pilfered, purloined. Bad Guys out there want your laptop more than you do.

Well, the Bad Guys don't want to use your laptop. They may want to steal it and sell it for drug money. Some Bad Guys want the data inside your laptop, stored on the mass storage system. The Bad Guys get what they want, mostly because the typical laptop owner doesn't think like a thief. Most of us are rather trusting people, and that trust is, sadly, what makes laptops so easy to steal in the first place.

First, the good news: Most laptops are forgotten and not stolen. As silly as it sounds, people leave their expensive laptops sitting around unattended more often than someone sneaks off with them. But don't let that trivial tidbit lull you into a false sense of security. Many laptops are stolen right out from under the eyes of their owners.

Think of the laptop as a sack of cash sitting around. To a crook, that's exactly what it is. Treat the laptop as a bag full o' money, and chances are good that you'll never forget it or let it be stolen.

The best way to protect your laptop is to label it. Specific instructions are offered later in this chapter. Keep in mind this statistic: Ninety-seven percent of unmarked computers are never recovered. Mark your laptop.

Other interesting and potentially troublesome statistics:

- ✔ The chance of your laptop being stolen is 1 in 10.
- ✔ Most laptop theft occurs in the office. That includes both coworkers and Well-Dressed Intruders, or thieves in business suits.
- ✔ Laptop theft on college campuses (from dorm rooms) is up 37 percent.
- ✔ A thief who steals a $1,000 laptop typically gets about $50 for it on the street.
- ✔ According to law enforcement, 90 percent of laptop thefts are easily avoidable by using common sense.

Before Your Laptop Is Stolen

Any law enforcement official will tell you that taking a few extra steps of caution can avoid a disastrous theft. Like any shopper, a thief enjoys convenience: If your laptop is more difficult to pinch than the next guy's, it's the next guy who loses.

Mark your laptop

You can help in the recovery of a stolen laptop if you mark your laptop by either engraving it or affixing a tamper-resistant asset tag. After all, the best proof that something is yours is your name on the item in question.

- ✔ You can use an engraving tool to literally carve your name and contact information on your laptop.

- ✔ I know some folks who are clever and merely write their names inside their laptops, either on the back of a removable door or inside the battery compartment or in other places a thief wouldn't check. Use a Sharpie or another indelible marker.

- ✔ Asset tags are available from most print shops. The tags peel and stick like any stickers do, but cannot be easily removed or damaged. For an investment of about $100, you can buy a few hundred custom tags, for not only your computers but also other valuable items (cameras, bicycles, and TVs, for example).

- ✔ The STOP program offers a bar-code asset tag that leaves a special tattoo if it's removed. The program also offers a recovery system that automatically returns stolen (or lost) property directly to your door. STOP stands for Security Tracking of _Office_ Property, although home users and (especially) college students can take advantage of the service. Visit www.stoptheft.com for more information.

Register the laptop and its software

Be sure to register your laptop; send in the registration card or register online. Do the same for any software you're using. If the laptop is then stolen, alert the manufacturer and software vendors. If someone using your stolen laptop ever tries to get the system fixed or upgraded, the company cares enough (you hope) to help you locate the purloined laptop.

Keep with you a copy of the laptop's serial number and other vital statistics — specifically, in a place other than in the laptop's carrying case. That way, you know which number to report to the police as well as to the manufacturer.

Be mindful of your environment

They say that a gambling casino is a purse snatcher's paradise. That's because most women are too wrapped up in gambling to notice that their purses are being pilfered. The purses can be on the floor, at their feet, or even in their laps. Thieves know the power of distraction.

When you're out and about with your laptop, you must always be mindful of where it is and who could have access to it. Watch your laptop!

For example, when you're dining out, put the laptop in its case beneath the table. If you need to leave the table, either take the laptop with you or ask your friends to keep an eye on it for you.

Take your laptop with you when you leave to make a phone call.

Keep your laptop with you when you visit the restroom.

Secure your laptop in your hotel room's safe. If the hotel lacks a room safe, leave it in the hotel's main safe at the front desk.

Be especially mindful of distractions! A commotion in front of you means that the thief about to take your laptop is behind you. A commotion behind you means that the thief is in front of you. Thieves work in pairs or groups that way, using the commotion to distract you while your stuff is being stolen.

Here's one place to watch out for a group of thieves pulling the distraction ploy: at the airport screening station! Just one raised voice or "the woman in the red dress" can divert your attention long enough for your laptop to disappear. Also be aware of distractions on crowded escalators, where the movement of the crowd can knock you down and someone can easily grab your laptop bag and take off.

Attach the old ball-and-chain

Chapter 6 takes you on a tour around your laptop's external places, pieces, and parts. One thing I point out over there is the place for the old ball-and-chain: a hole or slot into which you can connect a security cable. That hole has an official name: the *Universal Security Slot,* or *USS.*

The USS is designed to be part of the laptop's case. Any cable or security device threaded through the USS cannot be removed from the laptop; the cable itself must be cut (or unlocked) to free the laptop.

Obviously, the USS works best when the laptop is in a stationary place. Like using a bicycle lock, you have to park the laptop by something big and stable and then thread the cable through that big thing and the USS for the lock to work.

- ✔ The best place to find a security cable for your laptop is in a computer or office supply store.
- ✔ Some cables come with alarms. You can find alarms that sound when the cable is cut, plus alarms that sound when the laptop is moved.

Protect Your Data

Passwords protect only your laptop's data, not the laptop itself. Most thieves are looking to make a quick buck; generally, for drugs. They don't care about the contents of your laptop; they just want the cash it brings. But, a data thief wants more.

Data thieves feast on information. They want your passwords. They want credit card numbers, which are valuable to sell. Furthermore, they can use your own computer to order stuff on the Internet or to make transfers from your online bank account to their own.

The sad news is that password protection doesn't stand in the way of most clever data thieves. They know all the tricks. They have all the tools. At best, you merely slow them down.

This section offers various ways to protect the data on your laptop. These methods may not prevent a theft, but they help keep the information on your computer away from the weirdoes who want it.

Avoid the Setup password

Your laptop's Setup program allows you to specify a password that's required well before the operating system loads. Although this is the first line in data defense, I cannot recommend it, because of two issues.

First, if you forget the Setup password, you're screwed. Many people march forward with this Setup password scheme and then end up leaving the laptop on 24 hours a day and, over time, forgetting the password. That's bad.

Second, the Setup password can be circumvented because too many people forget it. Just about every manufacturer has a method of overriding the password, which essentially nullifies the reason for having it in the first place.

✔ If your laptop manufacturer has assured you that the Setup password cannot be circumvented, corrupted, erased, or overpowered, feel free to use it. But do not forget that password!

✔ You're prompted for the password every dang doodle time you start your laptop. That means turning on the laptop or waking it up after hibernation.

✔ Some data crooks simply yank the hard drive from the laptop so that they can steal the information from your hard drive by using their own, special equipment. Information can also be stolen directly from the laptop's memory chips. In either instance, the Setup password doesn't protect you.

Use a password on your account

Another method of providing reasonable protection is to ensure that your account on Windows has a password. True, you can use Windows without a password-protected account. Don't, especially on a laptop. You *need* a password on your user account and a *strong* password as well. (See the nearby sidebar "Strong passwords.")

Only older versions of Windows allow you to set up an account without a password. If you haven't set a password for your user account in Windows, do so now. Immediately obey these steps:

1. **Pop up the Start button menu.**

2. **Click your account picture at the top of the Start button menu.**

3. **In the User Accounts window, choose the link Create a Password for Your Account.**

4. **Type the same password twice, once in each box.**

   You type the password twice to ensure that *you* know the password.

5. **Type a password hint into the Password hint box.**

   Hint: The password hint should not be the same as your password. Just a hint.

6. **Click the Create Password button and close the User Accounts window.**

I recommend that you immediately log off Windows and log in again, just to get used to the password thing. (To log off Windows, choose the Log Off command from the Start button menu's Shutdown menu.)

✔ You must have a password for your Windows 8 account. Even if it's a silly password, it works. But check out the nearby sidebar, "Strong passwords."

✔ Computer security nabobs say that you should change your password every few months or so, and more often in high-security areas. In fact, if you use your laptop with a corporate account, you'll probably be pestered to change your password on a regular schedule.

✔ If you forget your password, you're screwed. It's possible to recover Windows, but all your account information may be utterly lost and not retrievable. Keep that in mind when you're choosing a password.

Strong passwords

Too many passwords are easy to figure out. Do you know what the most common password is? It's *password* — believe it or not! People use as passwords their own first names, pet names, simple words, single letters — all sorts of utterly unsecure things.

If you're serious about protecting your computer's data, create a serious password. The computer jockeys like to call it a *strong* password. It usually involves a mixture of letters and numbers using both upper- and lowercase letters.

The password should contain more than eight characters. You can even use a smattering of symbols in your password, such as the hyphen.

When you have trouble remembering your password, write it down! Just don't keep the password list near your computer. I know folks who write their passwords on their kitchen calendars or in their recipe books. Random words and numbers there may not mean anything to a casual onlooker, but they're helpful when you forget the password.

Tell Windows not to memorize Internet passwords

Even with a password locking up your user account, you may still want to take extra security precautions with other passwords you may use. For example, when a web page asks for your password, *do not* check the box to automatically remember the password later.

When Internet Explorer (or whichever web browser you're using) asks whether you want to remember a password, answer in the negative.

If possible, configure the e-mail program to require you to type the e-mail password every time you collect new messages. Yeah, this method is a pain, but when security is an issue for you, having to input that e-mail password every time you check for new e-mail is a good thing.

To configure your e-mail program to prompt for your e-mail password, follow these steps:

1. **In Windows Live Mail, press the F10 key to display the menu bar.**

   This step isn't necessary when using Microsoft Mail or Outlook Express.

2. **Choose Tools⇨Accounts.**

   The Accounts dialog box reports for duty.

3. **Click to select your e-mail account from the list.**

4. **Click the Properties button.**

   Your ISP's e-mail connection Properties dialog box appears.

5. **Click the Servers tab.**

6. **Erase your password from the Password text box, and deselect the Remember Password check box.**

7. **Click OK to make the change.**

   Repeat Steps 2 through 7 for each e-mail account listed.

8. **Click the Close button when you're done, and (optional) quit your e-mail program.**

After following these steps, you're prompted for your e-mail password every time you go to pick up e-mail. A dialog box appears. Just type your password and press Enter, and then you can pick up your mail.

Silly passwords

Data thieves steal passwords all the time. Recently, someone hacked into an online website's user database. The entire list of users and their passwords were compromised. When the Good Guys looked over the list, they discovered that far too many people were using very insecure passwords. In fact, most of the passwords were downright silly.

Here's a sampling of real passwords used by folks who should know better — no matter what, never use any of these passwords!

111111	iloveyou
1234	letmein
12345	master
123456	monkey
1234567	mustang
12345678	passw0rd
2000	password
654321	qwerty
696969	rockyou
abc123	shadow
baseball	sunshine
dragon	superman
football	trustno1

Disable the Guest account

The Windows Guest account allows anyone to enter your computer. Even considering that the Guest account is highly limited, it's just enough for a data thief to establish a foothold and start hacking away.

The good news is that Windows automatically disables the Guest account (but not in Windows XP). To confirm that the Guest account is disabled, follow these steps:

1. **From the Start button menu, click your account picture to open the User Accounts window.**

2. **Choose the link Manage Another Account.**

   In Windows Vista, click the Continue button or type the administrator password to proceed.

   In the Manage Accounts window, look at the Guest account icon. If the Guest account is already turned off, you're done; skip to Step 5.

3. **Click the Guest Account icon.**

4. **Choose the link Turn Off the Guest Account.**

5. **Close the Manage Accounts window.**

In Windows 8, you can confirm that the Guest account is disabled (and it is, unless you've turned it on). Follow these steps:

1. **Summon the Control Panel.**

2. **Choose the User Accounts and Family Safety heading.**

3. **Beneath the User Accounts heading, choose the Remove User Accounts link.**

4. **Ensure that the Guest account is turned off.**

   The account has the text *Guest Account Is Off* beneath it when it's disabled. If not, choose the Guest account, and on the next screen, click the Turn Off the Guest Account link.

Lock Windows

Windows has a unique locking command. By pressing the Windows key (Win) and then the L key, you can quickly lock the computer. Only by logging in again — which requires you to type your password — can you regain access.

If you plan to leave your laptop for a moment, consider locking it: Just press Win+L. This way, even if you trust the other folks with you, they're prevented from doing even harmless mischief.

Laptop, Phone Home

The reason that you've never lost your spouse or older child is that they have the unique ability to phone home when they're lost. Even a young child or the most intoxicated spouse can relay location information and then sit and wait for a speedy pickup. Believe it or not, your laptop can be just as smart.

The ability of a laptop to *phone home* was supposedly discovered accidentally: A programmer configured his work laptop to phone his home computer every night at about 8 o'clock. The two computers then exchanged data and updated each other.

One day, the laptop was stolen from work. But then a few days later, the home phone suddenly rang at 8 p.m. The programmer picked up the phone and heard the sound of his laptop's modem making the call. He immediately grabbed the incoming Caller ID and, long story short, the police nabbed the thief and the laptop was returned.

You don't need to be a programmer to set up a similar system for your own laptop. Many programs of this type do basically the same thing: They make the laptop phone home, or, often, they alert a tracking service over the Internet. The result is the same: A stolen laptop's cry for help is heard, and the laptop is quickly recovered.

For more information, refer to the following websites of companies that offer these phone-home services:

- www.absolute.com
- www.laptopcopsoftware.com
- www.ztrace.com

Your Fingerprint, Please

A popular craze in security devices is the fingerprint reader. It requires you to either slide or press a finger or thumb on a special gizmo as a form of identification. Laptops equipped with this type of device let you use your thumb or another popular digit to log in to Windows: Scan the correct digit and you're in.

If your laptop doesn't have a fingerprint reader on its case, you can buy an external USB device or, often, find a combination mouse/fingerprint reader. Of the two types, I prefer the fingerprint reader on the laptop's case, and I use it all the time to log in. The USB fingerprint reader I messed with was awkward; its cord was too long and the process too slow to be effective.

✔ Obviously, a fingerprint reader is a far more secure method of identification than a password. I mean, who ever forgets their hand?

✔ The fingerprint reader is configured using special software that comes with your laptop. You can often access that software from the Windows Mobility Center.

✔ You don't have to log in to Windows using your finger or thumb; you can click the Other Credentials button to choose your account and type a password.

✔ The fingerprint reader is part of a larger world of nonpassword security know as *biometrics*. In the future, your laptop's webcam might be used as your login, recognizing your smiling face as your valid login ID.

Back Up Your Data

You may not think of backing up your stuff as a form of security, but it is. If you ever lose your laptop, you lose not only the hardware but also all the stuff on your laptop. The best way to keep that stuff is to back it up; create a safety copy of all your data, files, videos, music, pictures, and so on. That's what backup is all about.

There are many ways to make a backup copy of data. I often copy information from my laptop to a network hard drive. I'm fond of using the Dropbox utility, covered in Chapter 19. Sometimes, I use a media card to back up important files. It's simple: I just drag the folders I use from the laptop's hard drive to the media card. There are, however, more sophisticated ways to back up your stuff. One of the best is to use a first-rate backup program.

✔ Windows 8 has a backup program, though it's called File History, not Backup.

✔ Not every version of Windows comes with a backup program. Only the more expensive versions come with a program called *Windows Backup*.

- ✔ There are also Internet backup utilities. Those programs automatically copy your important files to storage on the Internet.

- ✔ Backup programs, other than the Internet backup utilities, work best with external hard drives. If your laptop's data is important to you, get a small, portable external hard drive for backing up.

Preparing for backup

To make a backup operation work, you need a few things:

- ✔ Software, such as File History or Windows Backup
- ✔ A schedule
- ✔ External backup media

Your laptop comes with either the File History utility or the Windows Backup program. You can also find a third-party backup program, though I don't cover using other backup programs in this book.

The schedule helps keep the backup operation automatically updated. As long as your laptop is on and attached to the external backup media, and the laptop is on, backups happen automatically.

For external media, you need a storage device that's separate from the laptop. Although you can use an optical drive, that type of disc just doesn't hold enough information. Therefore, to make the process effortless, I recommend getting an external, USB hard drive for your laptop's backups.

- ✔ Western Digital makes inexpensive, external USB hard drives known as *My Book.* You can also get USB-powered drives, such as the Western Digital Passport, though they're a little more expensive.

- ✔ Your laptop's main mass-storage device is the hard drive. In Windows, it's referred to as *C:* or *Drive C.*

Finding that backup program

In Windows 8, the backup program is found in the Control Panel. Beneath the System and Security heading, click the link Save Backup Copies of Your Files with File History. The File History window displays any external storage devices your laptop can use for backing up. See the later section "Windows 8 File History" to configure the File History utility.

In Windows 7, the backup program is found on the Start button menu: Choose All Programs⇨Maintenance⇨Backup and Restore. The Backup and Restore window appears, as shown in Figure 21-1.

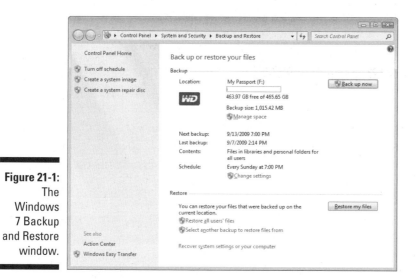

Figure 21-1:
The
Windows
7 Backup
and Restore
window.

If you've not yet backed up your laptop, you see a different Backup and Restore window from the one shown in Figure 21-1. To configure the backup, follow the steps in the later section "Configuring for backup."

Windows Vista has two similar locations for backing up. Rather than confuse you, from the Start button menu choose All Programs⇨Accessories⇨System Tools⇨Backup Status and Configuration. As with other versions of Windows, you need to configure the backup before you make a backup copy of your laptop's files.

Configuring for backup

If a backup has yet to be configured on your laptop, follow the steps in this section to set things up and back up the laptop's hard drive for the first time.

✔ Don't take the backup hard drive with you! It might be stolen. And, when you want to be truly security minded, lock up the backup drive in a fire safe when you're not using it.

✔ Windows displays a warning dialog box when you miss a regularly scheduled backup. It's an annoying but useful reminder.

Windows 8 File History

In Windows 8, follow these steps to configure the File History (backup) program:

1. **Open the Control Panel.**

2. **Click the link Save Backup Copies of Your Files with File History.**

   It's found beneath the System and Security heading.

3. **Ensure that the laptop's external hard drive appears in the Copy Files To area of the window.**

   If you don't see the drive there, you can't turn on File History; attach an external hard drive to your laptop.

4. **Click the Turn On button.**

   If the button says Turn Off, File History is already configured.

At this point, the File History utility is pretty much as configured as it can be. There's really little else that you're required to do.

Windows Backup

In Windows 7 and earlier versions of Windows, follows these steps to configure backup on your laptop:

1. **Open the Backup and Restore window.**

   Refer to the earlier section "Finding that backup program."

2. **Choose the link Set Up Backup.**

   In Windows Vista, click the Back Up Files button. Because the button is adorned with a shield icon, you can expect to see a User Account Control (UAC) warning.

3. **Choose the location for the backup — your laptop's external hard drive.**

4. **Click the Next button.**

5. **Keep the option Let Windows Choose (Recommended).**

   In Windows Vista, you get to choose the types of files to back up; I recommend keeping everything selected.

6. **Click the Next button.**

   You can click the Change Schedule link to set up a specific schedule for the backup, though I recommend leaving things as Windows suggests.

   In Windows Vista, you set the schedule on the next screen: Set a time when you know that the laptop will be connected to the external hard drive *and* when the laptop isn't turned off.

7. **Click the Save Settings and Run Backup button.**

   The backup proceeds. You can sit and watch, but it's boring. If you want, do something else with the laptop: Browse the Internet, catch up on e-mail, or actually get work done.

Eventually, the backup process is over and you can close the Backup and Restore Center window.

The only time to return to the Backup and Restore Center window is in the future, when you need to confirm that a backup has taken place or to run a restore operation.

- The first backup takes the longest. After that, Windows merely keeps the backup copy fresh, backing up only those files you added or changed since the last backup.

- You can modify the backup schedule by clicking the Change Settings link in the Backup and Restore Center window.

Backing up your stuff

The typical PC backup program backs up your laptop's stuff on a regular schedule; you have no need to manually back up or even to remember to back up.

When you miss a backup, such as when the laptop is turned off or you're away from the external hard drive during the scheduled backup time, you'll be reminded. Simply reconnect the external hard drive (the one you use for backup), and click the warning message to start the backup.

If you need to manually back up, open the Backup and Restore window (refer to Figure 21-1) and click the Back Up Now button. (Manual backups are not possible with the Windows 8 File History utility.)

Restoring from a backup

Having that safety copy of your data doesn't mean anything unless you can get at the data. The operation for retrieving backed-up files is *restore*. You can restore one file or all files on the entire laptop's hard drive. How it works depends upon which version of Windows is installed on your laptop.

Restore files with Window 8 File History

Despite all the things I dislike about Windows 8, file restore in the File History feature is pretty keen. Here's how it works:

1. **Start the File History program.**

   It's accessed from the Control Panel: Click the link Save Backup Copies of Your Files with File History, found beneath the System and Security heading.

2. **On the left side of the File History window, click the link Restore Personal Files.**

   The Home – File History window appears, as shown in Figure 21-2. It scrolls left and right to let you review changes to your personal files on the laptop.

Choose a file or folder to restore.

Figure 21-2:
Restoring
files in
Windows 8.

See older files.   See newer files.
Restore selected file.

3. **Scroll the list of file versions to the date or time from which you want to restore a** file.

4. **Choose from the window the file or folder you want to restore.**

   You can choose multiple files or folders to restore a whole batch at once.

5. **Click the Restore button.**

   Refer to Figure 21-2 for the location of the Restore button.

6. **Choose how to restore the file, if prompted.**

   You have three options:

Choose Replace the File in the Destination if you want to overwrite any existing file or folder with the older copy.

Choose Skip This File to ignore the operation and keep your existing file or folder as is.

Choose Compare Info for Both Files if you want to examine more details about the newer file that you're replacing with a backup.

You're prompted for each file you restore if another file with the same name already exists.

7. **Close the various File History windows when you're done restoring files.**

The File History restore procedure works only when you keep a backup drive attached to your laptop and you've enabled the File History feature in Windows 8, as described earlier in this chapter.

Restore files with Windows Backup

For versions of Windows that employ the traditional Windows Backup program, heed these steps to restore your files:

1. **Ensure that the external hard drive you use for backups is attached to your laptop.**

   You can't restore files unless the backup hard drive is available.

2. **Open the Backup and Restore window, as described earlier in this chapter.**

3. **Click the Restore My Files button.**

   In the next window, you have three choices:

   Search: This option works for restoring files when you know all or part of the name but not where the file was located on the laptop's storage system.

   Browse for Files: This option lets you restore individual files.

   Browse for Folders: This option is used to restore entire folders, which includes the contents of the folder, any subfolders, and all their contents.

   Knowing where the files are located on your laptop is helpful if you plan to use the Browse buttons.

4. **Choose the option to locate the files you want to restore.**

5. **To find the file, work the Search or Browse dialog box that's displayed.**

6. **Click OK, Add Files, or Add Folder when you've found the files or folders you want to restore.**

   You're building a list of files to restore. You can repeat Steps 3 through 5 to continue adding files as necessary.

7. **Click the Next button.**

8. **Choose In the Original Location.**

   When you choose this option, the file is restored to the location where it was lost. Otherwise, you can choose the option In the Following Location and then use the Browse button to locate the folder where the file will be restored.

9. **Click the Restore button.**

   When a copy of the file already exists at the location you're restoring to, you see a warning dialog box. My advice is to choose the Copy, But Keep Both Files option. Sort out the differences later.

10. **Click the Finish button and close the window when you're done.**

The odds of safely recovering all your laptop's data depend on how often you back up its hard drive. For my laptop, I back it up once a day. My play computer (which isn't only for games, by the way), I back up once a week.

Chapter 22

A Laptop for Work, a Laptop for Play

My favorite laptop ad of all time features a mountain climber. He isn't climbing and using the laptop at the same time (though that would be something). No, he's sitting on a ledge somewhere, typing on his laptop. That's because we all know how important it is to read your e-mail before rappelling down Half Dome in Yosemite. Actually, the image was more of a "Here's a rugged individual who can go anywhere, and he uses such-and-such laptop." Whatever.

Despite the folly of taking a laptop on a climb, the guy was rather smart. If climbing mountains was his job, then he had the right device. If climbing a mountain was his hobby, then he still had the right device. You can use your laptop for both work and for play. This chapter offers suggestions for both environments.

Presentation Information

Yes, I've given PowerPoint presentations using my laptop — many times. A laptop with PowerPoint software on it, coupled with a video project, can be a persuasive, informative tool. It can also induce narcolepsy. Regardless, you might find the information in this section useful.

The dog-and-pony show

To inform the masses, you need a laptop with *PowerPoint* software installed — it's the presentation application that often comes with Microsoft Office.

PowerPoint creates documents generically referred to as *slide shows.* Each slide can contain text, graphics, or pictures, or any combination. You can add animations and sound effects plus interesting fades and transitions between slides.

Of course, the PowerPoint program isn't the point. The point is the information you put on the slides. If you're clever, you can assemble your important information in an informative, entertaining, and memorable way. As someone who has slept through, and been bored by, hundreds of PowerPoint presentations, I know that doing things well is the exception, not the rule.

PowerPoint is fairly easy to figure. Even schoolkids use it with no fuss to make reports and, generally, waste time — just like professional salespeople! Often, better! Here are some generic PowerPoint suggestions and tips:

✔ PowerPoint must be installed on your laptop. Although . . .

✔ . . . Microsoft offers PowerPoint Viewer, which lets you play, but not edit, PowerPoint presentations. The viewer comes in handy when you create a presentation using your desktop PC and then copy it to your laptop for a road show. This viewer program can be obtained from the Microsoft website (www.microsoft.com), in the Downloads area.

✔ PowerPoint takes advantage of sounds, fonts, and animation on your computer. When you create a presentation on your desktop, ensure that the same font or sound files exist on the laptop; otherwise, your presentation won't look the same.

✔ My advice is to create the PowerPoint presentation on the same laptop you plan to use for making the presentation. If that's not possible, don't employ special fonts or sounds in your presentation.

✔ One trick I use to keep a presentation from becoming too boring is to engage the audience during the show. Ask questions or have the audience fill in the blanks. This strategy not only makes the show more lively but also helps keep people awake and on their toes.

✔ Avoid creating a slide show that you simply read to your audience. That's the most boring thing you can do, and the audience will walk away thinking that you've wasted their time. Instead, put your facts on the slide, and supplement the information with your presentation dialogue.

✔ A great way to spread the word is to provide hard copies of the slide show. You don't need to put one slide on each page. Instead, put six slides on a page to save paper. (This technique also avoids the crush of fans who want a copy after the presentation.)

✔ The first slide of any presentation I make isn't the first slide shown. Instead, the first slide is used to help set up the laptop and video projector (covered in the next section). On that slide, I have a logo or my contact information to test the focus. It also helps to employ some sort of sound effect so that I can test the audio system.

✔ Yes, creating a backup copy of your presentation on an optical disc or media card is an *excellent* idea. That way, if you lose the laptop or suddenly discover an incompatibility, you can use the disc or media card with someone else's computer to deliver the talk.

✔ These days, it's often not necessary to bring a laptop to a presentation. Merely having the presentation files on an optical disc or a media card is sufficient. Simply slide the media with the presentation file into the video projector and the program runs — assuming, of course, that the video projector is equipped to read such information. (Not all models have this ability.)

Set up your presentation

I suppose that the most nerve-wracking part about giving a presentation is ensuring that everything works. When the laptop, projector, and software work correctly, the speech itself should go smoothly, right? Even when well prepared, few folks enjoy speaking before large groups, especially groups of businessfolk who are used to — and often unimpressed by — computer presentations.

PowerPoint keyboard shortcuts

Display next slide: Spacebar; Enter; N; down arrow; right arrow

Redisplay previous slide: Up arrow; left arrow; P; Backspace

Go back to the first slide: 1, Enter (press 1 and then the Enter key)

Go to slide number *n*: *n*, Enter

Display a black screen: B; . (period)

Display a white screen: W; , (comma)

Cancel the show: Esc; – (hyphen)

Hide the pointer or navigation box: A; = (equal sign)

In most circumstances, you're allowed to set up your laptop and run a test to ensure that everything works before giving your presentation to an audience. A technician might be available and even do everything to set it up for you. That's great. But it still doesn't make the situation any less nerve-wracking.

For a presentation before a handful of people, viewing the PowerPoint slide show on your laptop screen and sitting at the end of a table is perfectly fine. Most of the time, however, you connect your laptop to a video projector. The video projector works like a combination second monitor and projector.

Modern laptops automatically assume that they have two monitors. The second monitor is available via the VGA expansion port, found on the side or back of your monitor. Refer to Chapter 6, and specifically Table 6-1, for more information.

In versions of Windows before Windows 8, the easiest way to connect to a video projector is to use the Connect to a Projector program, found on the Start button menu. Choose All Programs➪Accessories➪Connect to a Projector. Then choose how you want to extend the desktop from the options displayed, as shown in Figure 22-1.

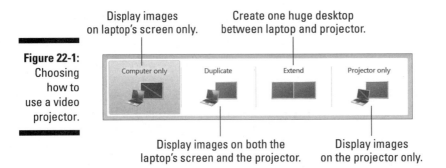

Display images on laptop's screen only.   Create one huge desktop between laptop and projector.

Figure 22-1: Choosing how to use a video projector.

Display images on both the laptop's screen and the projector.   Display images on the projector only.

When the Connect to a Projector command is unavailable, you can connect your laptop to a video projector or an external monitor by following these general steps:

1. Turn on your laptop!

Plug it in, if you can. Start it up. Log in.

2. Connect your laptop's external video connector to the video projector.

The video projector determines the connection you use. It may be the standard VGA connector, digital video, display port, S-Video, or what-have-you.

3. **Connect the laptop's audio-out port to the projector or to the location's sound system.**

   Chapter 6 helps you find the audio-out jack. Note that it might also double as the headphone jack.

   At this point, your laptop might be smart enough to instantly use the external monitor. The laptop's desktop shows up as the projected video image. If so, that's great. You're done. If not, you may need to coax your laptop into using the external monitor exclusively or in a dual-monitor setup. Continue:

4. **Right-click the desktop and choose Screen Resolution from the pop-up menu.**

   In Windows Vista, choose the Personalize command and then choose Display Settings in the Personalization window.

   Use the window or dialog box that opens to configure the external monitor, which is really the video projector.

5. **Check the projected image.**

   At first, the projector may show only the Windows desktop. That's not why people are coming to the meeting, though. Still, it proves that the image shows up.

6. **Run your PowerPoint presentation.**

   Take your presentation for a "pre-run." Load the main slide, and ensure that it shows up on the screen.

   If your presentation has sound effects, preview them as well to ensure that the sound system is working.

7. **Close the laptop's lid, and go mingle or sit at the dais and wait to be introduced.**

   I leave my laptop at the podium, lid closed, ready to go. When I open the lid, the presentation is ready to run. Only when too many people are around and security is a concern do I take the laptop with me.

Some laptops sport a special function (Fn) key on the keyboard, used to activate the external video port. You may need to press this key to switch the display over to the video projector.

Here's another tip (but without the Tip icon): Consider getting one of the professional presentation gizmos. It's a combination laser-pointer-and-computer-input device. The gizmo connects wirelessly to your laptop and allows you to stand at a distance and give the presentation, using buttons on the device to move through the slides back and forth. Such devices can be found at any office supply or computer store.

Video projector suggestions

Most locations where you give presentations might already have video projectors. If not, you need to bring your own. As with buying a laptop, choosing a video projector can be frustrating and intimidating — not to mention expensive. Here are my suggestions:

✔ You need a more powerful video projector when you frequent larger auditoriums. Most low-end projectors handle small rooms well. The key word here is *lumens*. The more lumens, the better the projector is for a larger venue.

✔ Resolution is an issue. If you plan to project to a larger screen, you need a resolution higher than 1024 by 768. Then again, don't go overboard with very high resolutions (greater than 2048) when your presentations don't need it.

✔ Buy an extra bulb — if you can afford it. Nothing sucks more than having a bulb burn out before a presentation. But, dang, those bulbs are expensive. Half of what you pay for the projector is probably the price of the bulb. And, you cannot find replacement bulbs in the hotel's sundry store.

Laptop Music

I had to chuckle as I saw the person next to me on a recent air trip. The poor fellow had to fix his MP3 player, and then, after getting it all set up, he plopped down his tray table and began to unfold his laptop. Me? I just flipped open my laptop, plugged in my headphones, and started listening to music. I was set.

Your laptop can play music, just like an iPod but without the "Aren't I cool?" Apple logo. All you need is a set of headphones or earbuds and you and your music are anywhere the laptop is.

Playing a CD

The simplest way to hear music on your laptop is to slide a musical CD into its optical drive slot (or tray) and listen to the music play. Windows is configured to automatically play any musical CD you insert into the drive. In fact, you might even see the album's artwork appear in the music-playing window, as shown in Figure 22-2.

When you're done listening to the CD, eject the disc by pushing the eject button on the laptop's optical drive.

Album artwork   Rip CD   View library

Figure 22-2:
Playing
some Huey
Lewis.

Play
controls

Volume
control

In Windows 8, you can use the Music app to listen to music, but I believe that the app is designed to get you to purchase music online from Microsoft. Even so, when you insert a musical CD in Windows 8, the Windows Media Player window appears. (Refer to Figure 22-2.)

Loading some tunes

The music-playing program that comes with Windows is Windows Media Player, illustrated in Figure 22-3. It's not the best digital music jukebox out there, but it comes with Windows, so I feel compelled to write about it.

One of the best ways to use Windows Media Player is to copy, or *rip,* music from a CD and store it on your laptop for the long term. To do so, follow these steps:

1. **Start the Windows Media Player program.**

   The least painful way to start the Windows Media Player in Windows 8 is to press Win+R to summon the Run dialog box. Type **wmplayer** into the box and click the OK button. This method also works for older versions of Windows, though you can also find the Windows Media Player on the Start button menu: Choose All Programs⇨Windows Media Player.

2. **Insert the music CD into the laptop's optical drive.**

   The disc should begin to play immediately. That's okay; you can pause the playback or rip while the disc plays, though the playback may pause as the tracks are ripped.

3. **Click the Rip CD toolbar button.**

   If you don't see the button, you need to close the tabs found in the upper-right part of the window: Click a tab to close it.

   The ripping is complete when you see the text *Ripped to Library* appear by each track on the album.

4. **Eject the CD when you're done ripping.**

   Press Ctrl+J to eject the disc.

Media Library

Current media playing in drive

Create a CD

Sync with MP3 player

Tabs

Figure 22-3: Windows Media Player.

Play and volume controls

Now Playing view

The music you rip is stored on the laptop, available in Windows Media Player anytime you want to hear it.

✔ Get some quality headphones, as opposed to listening to music on the laptop's tiny and awful speakers.

✔ Windows Media Player deals primarily with music, but you can also use it to view any videos, pictures, or recorded TV stored on the laptop's hard drive.

✔ The Windows Media Player program is different from the program Windows Media Center. The Media Center program provides a full-screen interface for multimedia computers and PCs connected to digital television.

> ✔ If you use an iPod, you'll want to use the iTunes music-playing program to manage your laptop's music files. iTunes is a similar program, designed to interface primarily with the iPod.

Configuring Windows Media Player to automatically rip a CD

You can set up Windows Media Player to automatically rip any CD inserted into the laptop's optical drive. Heed these steps:

1. **Click the Organize button on the toolbar.**
2. **Choose the Options command from the Organize button's menu.**
3. **In the Options dialog box, click the Rip Music tab.**
4. **Place a check mark by the option Rip CD Automatically.**
5. **Click OK.**

After you save the music on the laptop's mass storage system, you can listen to it any time: Open Windows Media Player and choose Music from the Media Library.

Load up some music before you leave on a trip.

Videos on the Laptop

The family vacation can be a stressful event, especially when traveling by car. One way to entertain the kiddies in the back seat is to give them a DVD player. Those portable DVD players are popular, and they almost look like laptops. But why bother with such a thing when your laptop itself can be used to play DVDs and other videos? Considering that most folks travel with their laptops anyway, there's no point in bothering to take anything extra.

Watching a DVD movie

Viewing a video on your laptop is as easy as listening to a music CD: Simply insert the DVD movie into your laptop's optical drive. In seconds, the optical disc is recognized, and the movie plays on the full screen using Windows Media Player.

✔ Window 8 doesn't allow DVDs to be played in Windows Media Player. Instead, a specific DVD-playing program may run when you insert a DVD into your laptop's optical drive.

✔ You cannot copy a movie from a DVD to long-term storage on your laptop's hard drive. That's because DVD movies are copy-protected, and the movie studios consider *any* copying illegal. So if you plan to watch a slew of DVDs on your laptop during vacation, you need to bring the various DVDs with you.

Viewing other video files

You can watch video you've created yourself or downloaded from the Internet on your laptop, just as you can view video files on a desktop computer. The files can be transferred from a video camera or copied from another PC. You view the files by opening them in Windows, which displays their contents in Windows Media Player or whichever video-viewing program you use on your laptop.

When your laptop is connected to the Internet, you can visit the YouTube website to view videos: www.youtube.com. Commercial television programs are available on Hulu: www.hulu.com.

Using the webcam

You can use your laptop's webcam to create videos or capture still shots, though normally the webcam is used for video chat, which is covered in the later section "Doing video chat." The software that performs these feats most likely came with your laptop or, if you're using a USB webcam, with the camera itself.

You can look in the Control Panel for webcam options, found in the Hardware and Sound category. You might also find a Scanners and Digital Cameras icon, if you use the Control Panel's Icon view.

✔ The webcam is activated by software; you run a program that uses a webcam to turn it on and capture an image or a video.

✔ A built-in webcam often features a lamp, which is turned on when the webcam is active. The lamp ensures that the captured image has enough light; plus, it's your clue that the webcam is taking your picture.

Sayonara, Cell Phone

If you recall laptop history (found in Chapter 1), you know that one pillar of laptop technology is communications. That means not only computer communications, networking, and modem use, but also people communications. Yes, it's possible to use your laptop as a phone. This section explains how.

Making a phone call with your laptop

You need these three things to turn your laptop into a telephone:

✔ An Internet connection

✔ A headset, or at least a good microphone and set of speakers

✔ A VoIP program

Making the Internet connection is something that the laptop does naturally. See Chapter 15 for more information. You can always buy a nice headset, which I recommend not only for voice communications but also for playing games and listening to music. That leaves only the VoIP thing.

VoIP stands for *Voice over Internet Protocol,* or using the Internet as a telephone. To make it happen, you use special software that lets you chat it up with others on the Internet, as well as connect with traditional phone services.

Most VoIP is done with stationary converters, such as for the home or office. For communicating on your laptop, you'll probably use the Skype program, which can be downloaded from the Internet at www.skype.com. Skype lets you communicate with other Skype users at no cost, but you need to pay a fee to dial up real phone numbers. Skype works with both voice and video communications; see the later section "Doing video chat."

✔ VoIP: Say "voyp," not "vee oh eye pee."

✔ VoIP might also be known by other terms, most of them involving the word *telephony.*

✔ You can "call" any other computer in the world by using Skype with your laptop, though that second computer should also have Skype installed. Millions of people make Skype calls every day, saving lots of money over traditional long-distance and international dialing rates.

✔ All laptops come with speakers, though your laptop may have a built-in microphone. In that case, you don't need a headset (though I still recommend one).

Doing video chat

They promised everyone back in the 1960s that something modern and wonderful would happen soon: It was the *picture phone,* and it would bring new meaning to picking up a phone call while stepping out of the shower.

Seriously, the picture phone is here today, and it uses old-fashioned modem technology to send video images over standard phone lines. Using your laptop and a broadband Internet connection, you can do much better, sending live, smooth video to other users on the Internet. It's *video chat.*

Most online chatting programs feature a video option, allowing you to see a person as well as type messages to them. Some programs even let you connect with multiple humans, each of them appearing in a teeny window while you do with your laptop what people once did in person: meet up. In Figure 22-4, you see the Skype video chat interface in action.

Figure 22-4:
Chatting it up visually with Skype.

✔ See the earlier section "Making a phone call with your laptop" for more information on Skype.

✔ Another popular video chat program is Google Talk. You can get a free copy at `www.google.com/talk`.

✔ One weird thing about video chat is that you don't really look into each other's eyes, as would happen with real human interaction. That can throw off some folks, making their chat partners appear disinterested. My advice is to look into the camera when you're talking and then look at the screen when the other person is talking. Just don't feel weirded out when the other person isn't looking right at you.

eBooks on Your Laptop

If you're reading this book on an eBook reader, raise your hand. There. Don't you feel silly, sitting there with your hand up? Has anyone asked you whether you have a question? If not, you can put your hand down.

Just in case anyone did ask whether you have a question, the question would be, "Why would I pay a few hundred dollars for an eBook reader when I have a laptop that is more than up to the task?" The answer is that some people think it's cool to use an eBook reader, similar to the way driving a Prius somehow makes you care about the environment more than the guy driving the Jeep next to you. It's all about perception.

Perceive this: Save some money and use your laptop as an eBook reader.

Understanding the eBook thing

It seems to be a recent fad, yet one of the most popular gizmos these days is the eBook reader. It's essentially a customized computer that displays text and graphics on a large screen, kind of like a Tablet PC. Actually, it's more like the Dynabook concept, which began the whole laptop computer craze.

The eBook reader lets you peruse text in a handy way, like having an electronic book — which is where the term *eBook* comes from. The reader is simply hardware, though. The software lets you buy or download current and classic books as well as articles from newspapers and magazines.

Because the eBook reader is highly customized and lacks the power and expandability options of a modern laptop computer, it's lighter and costs less. It's also quite the trendy accessory for the "I want to look cool" set.

✔ The most popular eBook reader is the Amazon Kindle, though other companies are coming out with their own eBook readers even as you read this sentence.

✔ E-book readers offer longer battery life than traditional laptops. They're also about the size and shape of a typical book.

✔ Most eBook readers also feature some form of wireless networking, which is how the books are transferred into the reader and how newspapers and magazines are loaded.

Reading an eBook on your laptop

You can use your laptop to read an eBook, and you don't need to go through any extra gyrations to do so. The only thing you need to do is find a source for obtaining the electronic copy of a book.

First, and best, are the free books available on the Internet. I provide some links. Second, you can buy an electronic copy of any book (including this one), save it to your laptop, and read it on the road.

The bottom line: Get that electronic book onto your laptop.

✔ You can get the Kindle app for your laptop, which allows you to read Kindle eBooks. Visit:

```
www.amazon.com/gp/kindle/pc/download
```

✔ A good place to look for books is Google Books at `http://books.google.com`. The book can be read while you're online, or you can click a link to buy it.

✔ A bonus for getting the Kindle app or Google Books is that your entire online library follows you wherever you go. So if you have a tablet or phone with a Kindle or Google account, you get access to the same titles on your laptop.

✔ A resource for public domain (older) books is Project Gutenberg at `gutenberg.org`. When you see a book you like, click the link to display the entire book in the web page window, and then save the web page to your laptop's storage system.

✔ See Chapter 18 for more information on saving web pages.

Part VI
Troubleshooting and Maintenance

The 5th Wave   By Rich Tennant

"I tell him many times—get lighter laptop. But him think he know better. Him have big ego. Him say 'Me Tarzan, you not!' That when vine break."

In this part . . .

I'm not going to lie to you and say that using your laptop is a worry-free topic and that your laptop will function flawlessly for decades with little effort on your behalf. No, that would not only be dishonest — I would also be depriving some copywriter of their job writing laptop advertising.

Laptops are robust little fellows, but they do require care and attention. As with any computer, regular maintenance is a must. In your role as computer operator, you must attend to the laptop's needs. When trouble brews, it helps if you know what to do. The chapters in this section help you help the laptop in times of woe and offer tips on how to reward a well-behaved laptop with an upgrade or two.

Chapter 23

Laptop Troubleshooting

- -

- -

*T*here is one thing, and only one thing, that causes trouble in any computer. That thing is *change*. The change consists of new hardware, new software, or a setting or configuration you've just made. Of course, not all change causes a computer to go bonkers. But chances are good that when you have trouble, it was change that led to the trouble.

Computer troubleshooting generally involves discovering what has changed in your computer. Oh, and there are random acts of God as well. Regardless, this chapter helps you to hunt down the change, fix the trouble, and get your laptop back up and running in working order.

✔ Changing or modifying data files (such as Word documents or MP3 or JPEG files) isn't the type of change that causes trouble. No, changing or modifying programs or parts of Windows is what can lead to trouble.

✔ For more information on PC troubleshooting, I highly recommend my book *Troubleshooting & Maintaining Your PC All-in-One For Dummies,* published by Wiley, and available exclusively on Planet Earth.

The Universal Quick-Fix

Before dropping into that deep pit of high-tech despair, you should try one thing first: Restart your laptop. Oftentimes, restarting the laptop unclogs the drain and allows your computer to work properly again. If there were a "take two aspirin and call me in the morning" laptop fix, restarting the laptop would be it.

Refer to Chapter 5 for information on restarting your laptop.

No, you don't need to reinstall Windows

Industry-wide, the average call for tech support is less than 12 minutes. When the call reaches 10 minutes, tech support people are often advised to end the call. One way they do that is simply to say that you need to reinstall the Windows operating system to fix your problem. Does this advice fix your problem? That's not the issue. It fixes *their* problem, which is to get you off the phone.

I've been troubleshooting and fixing computers for years. Only a handful of times has reinstalling Windows been necessary to fix a problem — and that's usually because the user deleted parts of the Windows operating system, either accidentally or because of a virus or another computer disaster. Beyond that, with patience and knowledge, any computer problem can be solved without replanting the operating system.

Reinstalling Windows is like rebuilding your home's foundation when all you need to do is fix a leaky faucet. When someone tells you to reinstall Windows, run. No, better: Scream, and then run. Try to find another source of help. *Remember:* Only in drastic situations is reinstalling Windows necessary. If you can find someone knowledgeable and helpful enough, he can assist you without having to reinstall Windows.

The Windows Troubleshooter

Windows comes with a handy troubleshooter (as shown in Figure 23-1), which should be the first stop in your laptop-fixing journey. This statement assumes, of course, that you can get the laptop started and operating to the point where you can follow these steps:

1. **Open the Control Panel window.**

2. **From beneath the System and Security heading, click the Find and Fix Problems link.**

3. **Choose a category or click a link to begin troubleshooting.**

4. **Follow the directions on the screen.**

   The directions vary, depending on what exactly you're troubleshooting.

You may have to restart Windows after troubleshooting certain items.

The Troubleshooter can also be accessed by clicking the Troubleshooting icon, found at the bottom of the Windows Action Center. See Chapter 17 for more information about the Action Center.

Neither Windows Vista nor Windows XP features the Windows Troubleshooter.

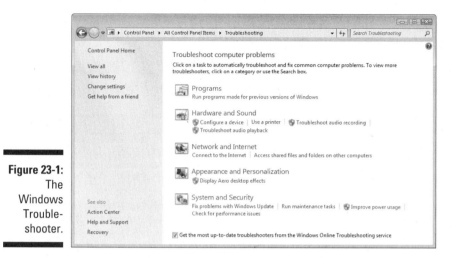

Figure 23-1:
The
Windows
Trouble-
shooter.

System Restore to the Rescue!

Windows employs a program named System Restore, which can be used to rescue Windows, especially after a software upgrade or configuration change. You simply restore Windows to an earlier point, back before the trouble started.

System Restore works automatically. It sets *restore points* regularly, especially before installing new software or updating Windows. (Unlike in older versions of Windows, there's no need to manually set a restore point.) All you need to do is use System Restore when you need to recover from a weird or unusual event. To do so, follow these steps:

1. **Press the Win+Break key combination to summon the System window.**

   The Break key and Pause key are the same on your laptop's keyboard. The key may be labeled Pause/Break or simply Pause. I've also seen the Break key shared with the End key.

2. **On the left side of the System window, choose the System Protection link.**

   In Windows Vista, click the Continue button or type the administrator password to get past the User Account Control dialog box.

3. **Click the System Restore button.**

   The System Restore program runs. Depending on which version of Windows you have, different things happen. Your goal is to choose a restore point date from which the system will be restored.

In some versions of Windows, you select a restore point from a list. Other versions display the most recent date but show an option for picking additional (older) dates.

4. **Click the Next button and obey the directions on the screen to restore the system.**

The System Restore program works to bring back older versions of installed software, drivers, or simply your settings. That takes some time, and you should be careful not to do other things while System Restore is working.

Eventually, your laptop restarts. Again, obey the directions on the screen.

When the laptop starts up again, System Restore isn't quite complete. Go ahead and log in, but wait until you see the confirmation message that the system has been restored. At that point, you can check to see whether the issue has been resolved.

- ✔ If the issue hasn't been resolved, try running System Restore again but use an earlier restore point.

- ✔ System Restore doesn't delete any new files you created. It affects only the operating system and installed software.

- ✔ System Restore lets you reset the system to only a few days or so earlier. Attempts to use a restore point older than a week earlier generally don't meet well with success.

- ✔ System Restore is a great way to return some of your personalized settings — desktop background, screen saver, window colors — when things get really fouled up. I get e-mail all the time from readers whose grandkids or other annoying relatives have screwed up their computer settings. System Restore is the solution.

- ✔ You also have an emergency start-up System Restore option. You may see a text menu when the laptop restarts, identifying a potential problem. If so, choose the option Last Known Good Configuration or whichever option allows for a System Restore operation.

Safe Mode

When you need to do serious troubleshooting, Windows offers the special mode of operation named *Safe mode*. I question the name. Doesn't it imply that normally Windows is *not* in Safe mode? What is it then? *Unsafe mode?* But I digress. . . .

Safe mode helps determine one major thing: whether the problem lies with Windows or with other software. In Safe mode, only the most basic programs required to run Windows are loaded on start-up. The rest of the stuff — those troublesome things called *drivers* — aren't loaded. Then, if the problem is gone in Safe mode, the problem is *not* to be blamed on Windows.

Entering Safe mode

Safe mode happens in a number of ways. Most annoyingly, your laptop starts in Safe mode when something is awry and Windows cannot start normally. See the later section "Testing in Safe mode" to find out what to do, as well as the even later section "My laptop always starts in Safe mode!"

If your laptop features multiple operating systems, you need to press the F8 key immediately after choosing which operating system to start.

Testing in Safe mode

In Safe mode, Windows doesn't load common device drivers or other software extensions to the operating system. Therefore, the screen has a very low resolution, and some hardware features you're used to working with aren't available, such as networking or the webcam.

Your job in Safe mode is to try to repeat the error. Do whatever it is that's causing your trouble. If the problem persists in Safe mode, it's most likely a Windows problem. If not, and when everything seems okay, the problem is caused by something else on your computer — a software program or piece of hardware.

When you're done troubleshooting, restart Windows. If the problem has been fixed, the laptop starts normally.

- A *device driver* is a program that Windows uses to access special hardware features. For example, your laptop's graphics are controlled by a device driver, as is the touchpad, the network interface, and other pieces of hardware. In Safe mode, Windows uses only the most necessary hardware.

- Do not try to use your computer in Safe mode. Don't get work done; don't run your word processor. Don't play a game. Safe mode is for fixing the problem, not for doing anything else.

✔ When the problem is in Windows itself, which is evident in Safe mode, you should visit the Windows tech support website to find the solution. Restart the computer in Normal mode, and visit the Microsoft Knowledge Base:

```
http://support.microsoft.com
```

Type a few keywords to search the Knowledge Base for your problem. A solution should quickly be at hand.

"My laptop always starts in Safe mode!"

When your laptop starts in Safe mode, it means that something is wrong. A piece of hardware or software has told Windows that it just can't function, so the system starts in Safe mode — first, to alert you to the problem, and second, to give you the opportunity to fix things.

In most cases, the problem's description appears on the screen, and you can address the issue by reading the text that's displayed.

Common Problems and Solutions

It would be nearly impossible for me to mention every dang doodle problem your laptop can experience. So, rather than list every dang doodle one of them, or 1,000 or even 100, I've narrowed the list to 5. Each of them is covered in this section.

Also, I wrote a computer troubleshooting book (and I promise not to mention it again in this book) for those desperate times when you need more help. Check out *Troubleshooting & Maintaining Your PC All-in-One For Dummies*, which has extensive laptop coverage.

"The keyboard is wacky!"

This problem happens more often than you would imagine, based on the e-mail I receive. The solution is generally simple: You accidentally press the Num Lock key on your keyboard, and half the alphabet keys on your keyboard start acting like numbers.

The solution is to press the Num Lock key and restore your keyboard to full alphabetic operation.

Touch pad touchiness

Some laptop touch pads seem to operate merely by looking at them. I call them touchy touch pads. Rather than be frustrated, simply adjust the touch pad's sensitivity. Visit the Mouse Properties dialog box to fix things: Switch the Control Panel over to Icon view and open the Mouse icon. In the Mouse Properties dialog box, you can adjust the touch pad.

You don't have to use the touch pad. You can disable it in the Mouse Properties dialog box. If so, use an external mouse, which will probably make you happier.

Making the mouse pointer more visible

When you're having trouble seeing the mouse pointer on your laptop's screen, visit the Pointers tab or Pointer Options tab in the Mouse Properties dialog box. Refer to directions in the preceding section on how to summon this dialog box. The following suggestions can help you make the mouse pointer more visible:

- ✔ On the Pointers tab, you can choose larger mouse pointers than the set normally used by Windows. In the Scheme drop-down list, choose Windows Standard (extra large) for some supersize mouse pointers.

- ✔ On the Pointer Options tab, use two of the options in the Visibility area to help find the mouse pointer on the screen. Specifically, try Pointer Trails or the Ctrl-key click option.

- ✔ Pointer Trails adds a comet-tail effect to the mouse in Windows, helping you locate the mouse pointer as you move it around.

- ✔ When the mouse plays *Where's Waldo?,* you can find it with the Ctrl-key click option by pressing either Ctrl key on your keyboard. A series of concentric rings surrounds and highlights the mouse pointer's location.

"My laptop won't wake up"

A snoozing laptop can mean that the battery is dead. Consider plugging in the laptop and trying again.

When the laptop has trouble waking from Stand By mode — and you have to turn it off and then turn it on again to regain control — you have a problem with the power-management system in your laptop. See the next section.

Power-management woes

When your laptop suddenly loses its ability to go into Stand By or Hibernate mode, it means that you might have a problem with its power-management hardware or software.

First, check your computer manufacturer's web page to see whether you can find additional information or software updates.

Second, ensure that power management is properly enabled, as described in Chapter 10.

Finally, confirm that other hardware or software isn't interfering with the power-management software. If so, remove the interfering software or hardware or check for updates that don't mess with your laptop's power-management system.

"The battery won't charge"

Batteries die. Even the modern smart batteries are good for only so long. When your battery goes, replace it with a new one. When the battery goes unexpectedly, consider replacing it under warranty if it proves defective.

Rules and laws govern the disposal of batteries. Be sure to follow the proper procedure for your community to safely dispose of or recycle batteries.

Chapter 24

Laptop Maintenance and Upgrading

· ·

· ·

*T*he desktop PC owes its success to the fact that it can be easily upgraded. New hardware can be added to a computer with ease. Sadly, the laptop computer isn't quite as versatile. Laptops are designed for portability, not for internal expansion. Still, the potential for an upgrade exists in some types of laptops.

This chapter is about upgrading your laptop. You can upgrade the hardware, usually by adding more memory. Oh, well, and yes, you can always update software as well. I suppose that falls under the category of upgrading. And just to be sure I don't leave anyone out, I've also tossed in the topic of laptop maintenance.

New Laptop Hardware

Internal expansion options are somewhat limited on laptops. Even so, on many laptops, it's possible to replace or upgrade the hard drive and memory (RAM). Most other items on the laptop cannot be upgraded; the processor, video circuitry, networking adapter, modem, and other hardware are often all integrated into the laptop's main circuitry board, or *motherboard*. Buying an entirely new laptop is cheaper than trying to upgrade anything inside the laptop.

If your laptop is equipped with a handy method for adding more memory, do so! Memory chips are available far and wide, though my favorite place to shop for RAM is the online memory store at www.crucial.com. The site has a configuration program that helps you select the exact amount of memory you need. The program is very handy; plus, the memory chips come with good instructions on how to install them.

Some laptops allow for the hard drive to be replaced or upgraded. The easiest way to do this is when the laptop has a drive bay option. For example, you can use an optical drive, a media card reader, or a hard drive in the drive bay. So, if your computer came with an optical drive and you want to replace the drive with a second hard drive, the operation is not only possible but also relatively easy to accomplish. The bad news is that the extra drives are available only from the manufacturer and are often quite pricey.

Beyond these few basic items, your laptop is essentially a closed box, and no further upgrades are offered. Don't despair! Refer to Chapter 12 for various ways to expand your laptop without using a screwdriver.

- ✔ Ultrabooks and netbooks rarely have the capacity for a hardware upgrade. The trade-off between weight and size usually means that prying open the case and adding or changing something just isn't possible.

- ✔ Refer to the documentation that came with your hardware to find out exactly how to configure it. Note that the hardware you're adding might sometimes require its software to be installed first. Other times, it's vice versa.

How 'bout Some New Software?

Generally speaking, I don't recommend upgrading software. In the olden days, upgrades were necessary to add new features and expand the abilities of older programs. But today's software is so advanced that even a program developed half a dozen years ago would still serve you well.

Upgrading your software

I recommend upgrading your software only when a newer version of the program offers features you need or fixes problems you have. Otherwise, my motto is "If it ain't broke, don't fix it!"

I'm serious: You can avoid a lot of trouble by not upgrading. I've seen too many stable computers become unstable after simple upgrades. I've seen printers suddenly not work. Worse yet, I've seen the chain reaction of having to upgrade more than one application just to keep things compatible. That can be expensive, but it's a tough choice: The newer version of the application can boost your productivity. The key is to be prepared for anything.

✔ Upgrading is as easy as sticking the new program's disc into your laptop's optical drive. Everything after that should run automatically, with your input required in order to answer a few simple questions.

✔ You don't need to uninstall the previous version of a program when you're installing an update. The only exception is when you're specifically advised to uninstall any older versions.

✔ Refer to Chapter 9 for information on removing software from your computer.

Upgrading to a new version of Windows

I highly recommend against upgrading your laptop's operating system. Specifically, I recommend against upgrading Windows. Once upon a time, upgrading the operating system was a good idea. But the improvements and changes that upgrades make to Windows now are too great to risk the stability of your computer — specifically, a laptop.

Rather than upgrade Windows, the next best thing is simply to wait until you need to buy a new laptop. Then get the latest version of Windows preinstalled. That way, you're assured that all the hardware is compatible with the new version and that it's robust enough to handle the new version of Windows. When you're upgrading an older computer, you can't be assured of these things, so it's a risk. I don't recommend risking the investment you've made in your laptop.

✔ One thing you might not get with the update are *drivers,* or specific software that controls various parts of your laptop. These parts include the mouse pad, the wireless and Ethernet network adapters, the display, the power-management hardware — essentially, all the things that make your laptop easy to use.

✔ Sure, if you want to upgrade Windows, go ahead. I can't stop you. But I highly recommend against upgrading Windows.

✔ There's a difference between upgrading Windows and *updating* Windows. My advice is to *update* Windows, which is to keep Windows up-to-date. See Chapter 17 for more information on using the Windows Update program.

Upgrades versus updates

Computer jargon can be confusing enough without having to deal with vague terms that also exist in English. Prime examples are the words *upgrade* and *update*. They might seem like the same thing, but in the computer world, they're not.

Upgrade means to install a newer version of a program you already own. For example, you upgrade from version 2.1 of a program to version 2.2. Specifically, that's referred to as a *minor* upgrade. Moving from version 4.0 to version 5.0 is a *major* upgrade.

Update means to improve an existing program but not change its version or release number. For example, Microsoft routinely releases security updates for Windows. These updates, or *patches,* are applied to your version of Windows to improve features, address security issues, or fix bugs.

In some universe somewhere, this stuff all makes sense.

Laptop Maintenance

As with all things in the computer universe, there are two sides to laptop maintenance: hardware and software. This section covers both.

Maintaining software

There's really nothing to laptop maintenance: Most common maintenance chores happen automatically, since Windows Vista. These tasks include running disk tune-up and defragmentation programs. As long as you haven't disabled any of these activities, consider your laptop's storage system to be adequately maintained.

- For more software maintenance information, pick up a copy of my book *Troubleshooting Your PC For Dummies* (Wiley).

- Also see Chapter 21, which covers backing up your files in Windows. Backing up is yet another aspect of good, ongoing computer maintenance.

- No, unlike with an automobile, you have no reason to take your laptop into the dealer or a repair place for regular check-ups. When someone tells you that you need such a thing and nothing is otherwise wrong with your laptop, you and your money will soon be parted (if you catch my drift).

Keeping it clean

Laptops are robust beasts. They can go through a lot without cleaning. Well, any man will tell you that carpets can go for months with no vacuuming. But I digress.

After you've been around with your laptop a few times, you should do some clean-up. Look at those fingerprints! Yikes! If only your mother could see it. . . .

- Consider washing your hands from time to time.

- Turn off the laptop before you start cleaning it.

- You need a sponge or lint-free cloth as your cleaning tool.

- Isopropyl (rubbing) alcohol is also a good cleansing agent, but not for the screen. (More on cleaning the screen in a few pages.)

- If your laptop manufacturer has any specific cleaning instructions, directions, or warnings, please refer to them first before following the information offered here.

Sprucing up the case

The best way to give the case a bath is with a damp sponge. You can use standard dishwashing liquid, by mixing it at about one part detergent to five parts water. Soak the sponge in the mixture and then wring the sponge clean. Use it to gently wipe the laptop's case.

When you're done with the sponge, wipe off any excess moisture or dust by using a lint-free cloth.

- Ensure that the sponge is dry enough that it doesn't drip liquid into the laptop.

- You might also want to use cotton swabs to clean some of the gunk from the cracks.

- Do not clean inside any disk drive openings or the PC Card garage. Never spray any liquids into those openings, either.

- Avoid using detergent that contains strong chemicals (acid or alkaline). Don't use abrasive powders.

Grooming the keyboard

Every so often, I vacuum my laptop keyboard. I use the little portable vacuums, with either the tiny (toothbrush-size) brush or the upholstery-cleaning attachment. This effectively sucks up all the crud in the keyboard. It's amazing to watch.

Some people prefer to clean the keyboard by using a can of compressed air. I don't recommend this method, because the air can blow the crud in your keyboard farther inside the laptop. Instead, use a vacuum.

Cleansing the screen

I've found the techniques used for cleaning an LCD screen, whether it's for a desktop or laptop computer, to be filled with controversy! Generally, no one recommends using liquids, because they can damage the LCD's delicate surface. Even so, you gotta have something to rub with if you ever plan to get that sneeze residue off the thing.

First, for general cleaning, get a soft, lint-free cloth. Use it to wipe the dust off the monitor. For laptops with a touchscreen, use the lint-free cloth to help wipe off the finger smudges.

Second, dampen a sponge or lint-free cloth with water. Be sure to wring out all excess moisture. Rub the screen's surface gently, and don't get any excess liquid on or inside the monitor.

Let the monitor dry completely before closing the lid!

✔ Oftentimes, the keyboard creates a shadow stain on the screen. It's difficult to avoid and impossible to clean off. To help prevent the stain, place a soft, lint-free cloth — like one you'd use to clean the monitor inside the laptop — between the keyboard and screen when the laptop is closed.

✔ Office supply stores carry special LCD screen cleaners as well as the lint-free wipes you can use to clean your screen and the rest of your laptop.

✔ One product I can recommend is Klear Screen, from Meridrew Enterprises (`www.klearscreen.com`). No, it's not cheap. You want *good,* not cheap.

✔ Avoid using alcohol- or ammonia-based cleaners on your laptop screen! They can damage the LCD screen. Worse, they can render that expensive multi-touch monitor useless.

✔ Never squirt any cleaner directly on a laptop's screen.

Part VII
The Part of Tens

The 5th Wave   By Rich Tennant

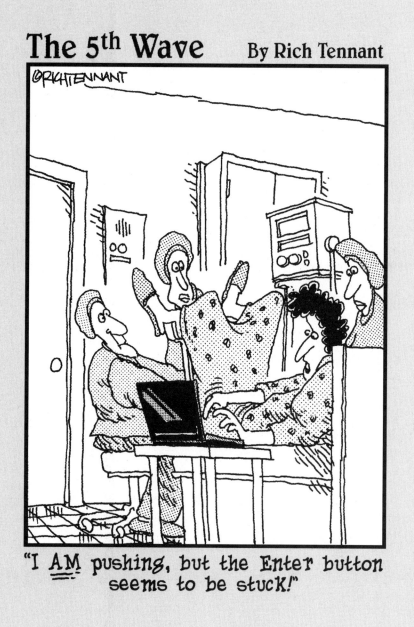

"I **AM** pushing, but the Enter button seems to be stuck!"

In this part . . .

They say that ancient man counted this way: One, two, many. Beyond two of anything, the word to describe any quantity was *many*. So whether it was a herd of three mammoths or a multitude of mammoths, our ancestors figured it was the same number. I'm also guessing that high school math in those days was less traumatic. Regardless, our civilization has advanced to the point where ten is an easy number to grasp, even for high school students.

There's nothing like wrapping up a *For Dummies* book with a part full of lists, where each list contains ten items. It's a tradition, and *Laptops For Dummies* is no exception. The chapters in this part list tricks and hints and helpful laptop info, all organized by lists of ten. Here is your Part of Tens.

Chapter 25

Ten Battery Tips and Tricks

Without a battery, your laptop would be merely a tiny, overpriced PC. You need the battery to give the laptop its power of portability. There also comes a battery of battery issues, most of which involve squeezing the largest amount of life out of a limited supply of battery juice. This chapter contains ten battery tips and tricks.

Don't Drop the Battery, Get It Wet, Short It, Play Keep-Away with It, Open It, Burn It, or Throw It Away

Enough said.

Scary lithium-ion battery trivia

Lithium-ion batteries are what many of us humans aspire to be: smart and popular. But the lithium-ion battery has a scary side. Consider this frightening lithium-ion battery information designed to literally shock you away from any thought of messing with your laptop's battery:

- ✔ When a lithium-ion battery is overcharged, it gets hot. Then it explodes.

- ✔ The lithium metal in the battery burns when it comes in contact with water.

- ✔ The acid inside the battery is not only highly caustic, it's also flammable.

- ✔ I'm sure that the acid is poisonous as well, but — golly — that last sentence had me at *caustic*.

- ✔ You cannot recycle a used lithium-ion battery, so don't ever think of buying or using a "recycled" battery.

Turn Down the Monitor's Brightness

To save a bit on battery life on the road, lower the brightness level on your monitor just a hair — or perhaps as low as you can stand. That definitely saves the juice.

- ✔ Buttons near the laptop's LCD monitor control the brightness.

- ✔ Sometimes, the brightness is controlled by using special Fn-key combinations.

- ✔ Your laptop's power manager might automatically dim the screen when the laptop is on battery power.

- ✔ Screen dimming can be done in the Windows Mobility Center. Look for this item in the Hardware and Sound category. In versions of Windows before Windows 8, the Win+X key combination summons the Windows Mobility Center.

- ✔ Check the Power Options window to see whether your laptop has any advanced or specific settings for disabling or saving power used by the display. See Chapter 10.

Power Down the Disk Drives

The motors in your laptop consume the most power — specifically, the motors that keep the hard drive continually spinning. When you're using a program that continually accesses the hard drive, such as a database, keeping the drive spinning continually is more efficient. But when you're working on something that doesn't require constant disk access, save some juice by "sleeping" an idle hard drive.

> ✔ Also consider turning off or disabling the laptop's optical drive.

> ✔ Refer to Chapter 10 for more information on hard drive time-outs.

Add RAM to Prevent Virtual Memory Disk Swapping

One way that the hard drive conspires with the operating system to drain the battery quickly is when the virtual memory manager pulls a disk swap. The way to prevent it is to add memory (RAM) to your laptop.

Virtual memory has nothing to do with virtue. Instead, it's a chunk of hard drive space that Windows uses to help supplement real memory, or RAM. Mass chunks of information are swapped between RAM and your laptop's hard drive, which is why you never see any Out of Memory errors in Windows. But all that hard drive memory swapping drains the battery.

Windows does a great job of managing virtual memory. Although you can fine-tune the virtual memory manager, I don't recommend it. Instead, test the virtual memory manager this way:

1. **Run three or four of your most-often-used programs.**

   Start up each program and get its window up and ready on the screen, just as though you're about to work on something. In fact, you can even load a document or whatever, to ensure that the program is occupied.

2. **Watch the hard drive light; wait for it to stop blinking.**

   Wait until the hard drive light on the laptop (refer to Chapter 5) stops blinking. That means hard drive access has stopped and the computer is simply waiting.

3. **Press Alt+Esc.**

   The Alt+Esc key combination switches from one program (or window) to another.

4. **Watch the hard drive light.**

5. **Repeat Steps 3 and 4 until you cycle through all programs and windows at least once.**

   What you're looking for is hard drive access. If you detect a noticeable pause or the hard drive light blinks as you switch between programs, it can be a sign that virtual memory is being used, by swapping from RAM to disk. Yes, your system is working harder than it should, and it affects battery life.

The idea isn't really to adjust virtual memory as much as it is to add RAM to your laptop and prevent virtual memory from ever taking over in the first place.

✔ A good amount of RAM to have with Windows is 1GB, although 2GB is even better. If you truly love your laptop, get 4GB.

✔ The Alt+Esc key combination switches between desktop applications in Windows 8. It doesn't switch between apps that are run from the Start screen.

✔ To see how much memory is installed in your laptop, view the System window. (Press the Win+Break key combination.) The amount of memory that's installed appears along with other information about your computer.

Keep RAM Empty

Even when you cannot add to RAM to your laptop, battery life can be extended by economically using the RAM you have.

To optimize performance, I recommend running only a few programs at a time on your laptop when you're using the battery. For example, you might be reading e-mail in your e-mail program, browsing the web, editing a document in your word processor, and keeping a game of Spider Solitaire going in another window. All that activity is unnecessary, and shutting down the programs you're not using helps save battery life.

It may seem trivial, but when you don't set a background image or wallpaper, Windows spends less time updating the screen. And, time is battery life! Consider setting a solid-color background image on your laptop: Right-click the Desktop and choose Personalize. Then choose a solid background color by using the Desktop Background link in the Personalization window.

Guard the Battery's Terminals

Like a big-city airport or a bus station or Frankenstein's neck, your laptop's battery has terminals. People don't traverse a battery's terminals; but, like Frankenstein's neck, electricity does. The terminals are usually flat pieces of metal, either out in the open or recessed into a slot.

✔ Keep your battery in the laptop.

✔ Outside the laptop, keep the battery away from metal.

✔ Keep the terminals clean; use a Q-tip and some rubbing alcohol. Do this whenever you succumb to the temptation to touch the terminals, even though you shouldn't be doing that.

- ✔ Do not attach anything to the battery.

- ✔ Do not attempt to short the battery or try to rapidly drain it.

- ✔ The terminals appear in different locations on the battery, depending on who made the battery and how it attaches to the laptop.

Avoid Extreme Temperatures

Batteries enjoy the same type of temperatures you do. They don't like to be very cold, and they don't like hot temperatures, either. Like Goldilocks, the battery enjoys temperatures that are *just right*.

Store the Battery If You Don't Plan to Use It

Don't let a battery sit. If you keep the laptop deskbound (and nothing could be sadder), occasionally unplug the thing and let the battery cycle, just to keep it healthy. That's the best thing to do.

When you would rather run your laptop without the battery inside, or when preparing a spare battery for storage, run down the battery's charge to about 40 percent or so and then put the battery in a nonmetallic container. Stick the container in a nice, cool, clean, dry place.

- ✔ Like people, batteries need exercise! Try to use your laptop battery every two months or so whether you're using the laptop remotely or not.

- ✔ The recommended storage temperature for lithium-ion batteries is 59 degrees Fahrenheit or 15 degrees Celsius.

- ✔ Also refer to the next section.

- ✔ A lithium-ion battery has an expiration date! After several years, the battery dies. This is true whether you use the battery or store it.

Understand That Batteries Drain Over Time!

No battery keeps its charge forever. Eventually, over time, the battery's charge fades. For some reason, this surprises people. "That battery was fully charged when I put it into storage six years ago!" Batteries drain over time.

Yet, just because a battery has drained doesn't mean that it's useless. If you stored the battery properly, all it needs is a full charge to get it back up and running again. So, if you store a battery (see the previous section), anticipate that you'll need to recharge it when you want to use it again. This process works just like getting the battery on the first day you buy your laptop; follow those same instructions for getting the stored battery up and running again.

Deal with the Low-Battery Warning

Thanks to smart-battery technology, your laptop can be programmed to tell you when the juice is about to go dry. In fact, you can set up two warnings on most laptops. (Refer to Chapter 10.) The idea is to act fast on those warnings when they appear — and to take them seriously! Linger at your own risk. It's your data that you could lose!

The real trick, of course, is to ration the battery power you have. Here's a summary of tips, some of which are found elsewhere in this book:

- **Be mindful of power-saving time-outs.** Setting a 15-minute Stand By time-out may work well in the office, but on the road you may want to adjust those times downward. Refer to Chapter 10.

- **Modify the display to use a lower resolution or fewer colors on the road.** In fact, for most computing, a resolution of 1024 x 768 is fine. This setting uses less video memory, which requires less power to operate and keep cool.

- **Mute the speakers!** This strategy not only saves a modicum of power but also prevents the ears of those next to you from hearing the silly noises your laptop makes.

- **Disable unused devices.** If you don't need the optical drive, remove its disc. Speaking of which:

- **If your laptop's optical drive is removable, consider removing it when you go on the road.** This strategy saves a bit on weight as well as on power usage.

- **Save some stuff to do when you get back home or reconnect to a power source.** Face it: Some things can wait. If that 20MB project file upload isn't needed immediately, save it for when you're connected to the fast Internet line back at your hotel or office.

- **Hibernate!** When time is short and your laptop has the Hibernation smarts, just hibernate. Refer to Chapter 10.

Chapter 26

Ten Handy Laptop Accessories

The spending doesn't stop after you buy the laptop. Nope, there are many, many laptop toys you can buy. Beyond software are gizmos and gadgets galore. Some are standard computer peripherals, like printers or media cards, but most are wonderful and useful items you can get to enhance your laptopping experience. This chapter has ten suggestions for you.

Laptop Bag or Travel Case

Buy yourself and your laptop a handsome traveling bag. Chapter 20 offers some useful suggestions and recommendations.

Spare Battery

Nothing cries "Freedom!" to the laptop road warrior more than an extra battery. Having a bonus battery doubles the time you can compute without that AC wall-socket umbilical cord. Some laptops even let you hot-swap from one battery to another while the laptop is still running, which means that the total length of time you can use your battery greatly exceeds your capacity to do work.

Ensure that the spare battery is approved for your laptop, coming either directly from the manufacturer or from a source that is reliable and guarantees compatibility. Using the wrong battery in your laptop can be disastrous.

Webcam

When your laptop lacks its own built-in webcam, run — don't walk — to the computer store and fetch yourself a nice USB webcam. You can do too many interesting and useful things with a video camera on a computer these days to be wandering this dry earth without a webcam on your laptop.

Cooling Pad

The ideal accessory for any well-loved laptop is a cooling pad. It's a device, similar to the one shown in Figure 26-1, on which your laptop sits. The *cooling pad* contains one or more fans and is powered by either the laptop's USB port or standard AA batteries. Your laptop sits on the pad, and the fans help draw away the heat that the battery and microprocessor generate. The result is a cooler-running laptop, which keeps the laptop happy.

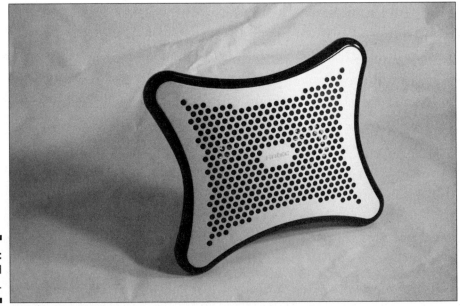

Figure 26-1:
A cool
cooling pad.

✔ Note that the cooling pad runs from the power supplied by the USB port or from its own batteries. That means it's portable.

✔ If you're getting a USB-powered cooling pad, try to buy a model that has a pass-through USB port so that you don't lose a USB port when you add a cooling pad.

✔ Some cooling pads also double as USB hubs.

Minivac

Useful for cleaning your laptop, especially the keyboard, is the minivac. This item is found in most office supply stores, and many are portable (battery powered). You'll be surprised (and disgusted) by the gunk that the minivac can suck from your laptop.

USB Lamp

Your laptop's LCD screen is illuminated and even shows up in the dark. Sadly, however, most laptop keyboards don't light up. To help you see the keyboard as well as other important areas around your laptop, you can light things up with a USB-powered lamp.

The lamp plugs into a standard USB port on your laptop. It has either a stiff, bendable cord or a clamp so that you can position it. Flip the switch and let there be light!

Note that some laptops might already have built-in keyboard lights. Some Lenovo models, for example, feature a lamp mounted atop the LCD screen; pressing the key combination Fn+Page Up turns the lamp on or off.

Full-Size Keyboard

Although you might not want to tote one around with you, there's a certain pleasure to be had when you're using a laptop with a comfy, full-size keyboard. Especially if you rely on the numeric keypad, for either numbers or cursor control, it's a joy to use a full-size, USB keyboard on a laptop.

In addition to (or perhaps, instead of) using a USB full-size keyboard, you can select any of a number of fun and different keyboards for your laptop. You can find keyboards with special Internet buttons, ergonomically designed to make typing easier on the human bod, as well as wireless keyboards. Because your laptop didn't come with a full-size keyboard, it's a buyer's paradise as far as choosing one for your laptop. Or, if all you need is a numeric keypad, you can get special USB numeric keypads for your laptop.

External Mouse

The only problem I have with using an external mouse on my laptop is that I neglect it. I'm so trained to use the touch pad that I forget about the full-size, comfy, and easy-to-use mouse right next to my laptop.

As with a keyboard, you aren't limited to your choice of an external mouse. You can get a basic mouse; a space age, optical glowing mouse; a mouse with lots of buttons; a weird mouse you can hover in the air and use like a TV remote; a wireless mouse; a trackball mouse; a tiny laptop mouse — the list goes on and on.

Although you can disable the touch pad on your laptop, I recommend keeping it active when you use an external mouse. When I'm browsing the web or reading a document, I typically revert to the touch pad rather than use the external mouse. (I'm hard to train.)

ID Card or Return Service Sticker

Way back when, your mom would probably write your name on your laptop, just like she wrote your name on your underwear. Today, you know why that process is important, and you can probably guess why it's necessary.

Businesspeople commonly just tape their business cards somewhere on the inside of their laptops, such as slightly to one side of the touch pad.

The idea here is not only to claim ownership of the laptop but also to pray that if the laptop is ever lost or stolen, it will be recognizable as your own. A good citizen will phone you and offer to return the laptop that he or she found with your name emblazoned on an ID card.

- ✓ While you're at it, attach a business card to other portable devices you might leave behind, like portable printers, power supplies, or video projectors.

- ✓ A better solution is to use a return service and take advantage of its tamper-resistant asset tags. Refer to Chapter 21 for more information.

Theft-Prevention System

The perfect gift for your dear laptop: some type of cable to keep it from walking off, one of those annoyingly loud my-laptop-has-been-moved alarms, or that special software that tries to "phone home" when the laptop is purloined. Ease your fears! Refer to Chapter 21 for more information on laptop security — specifically, these types of devices.

Chapter 27

Ten Things to Throw in Your Laptop Case

. . . .

In This Chapter

▶ The laptop's power cord

▶ A spare battery

▶ An external mouse

▶ Something to clean the laptop

▶ Security devices

▶ Removable media

▶ A set of headphones (or two)

▶ General supplies

▶ Cables, cables, and more cables

. . . .

I'm hoping that you follow my advice in Chapter 20 and purchase yourself a handsome laptop case. Now that you have the case, and all that room, what are you going to put in it? Well, yes, of course: The laptop goes into the case. Duh. What else? Anything you truly need? Anything you might forget? Here's a list of ten items you should consider throwing (or gently tossing) into your laptop's case.

Power Cord and Brick

This item is one that even I forget. Sometimes I think, "Oh, I'm only going to be gone for an hour, and the battery lasts for three hours, so I don't need the power cord." Then an appointment is canceled and I have more time but regret not taking the power cord with me.

Always take your power cord and its adapter, or "brick," in your laptop case. You just never know when a wall socket will appear. Take advantage of it!

Spare Battery

If you're blessed with a spare battery for your laptop, bring it!

✔ Don't forget to charge the spare battery before you leave.

✔ Also refer to Chapter 10 for more information on your laptop's battery.

Mouse

Anyone who's used to a real mouse probably won't forget to throw it in the laptop's case, but you never know. I highly recommend using a real (*external, not furry*) mouse with your laptop, especially if your laptop sits somewhere on a table or desk with room for the mouse. Better: Get a cordless mouse. I use a Microsoft Bluetooth mouse. Logitech makes a cordless mouse that holds the USB wireless base inside the mouse. It's darn convenient.

Screen Wipes and Cleaner

Go to the office supply store and buy some LCD screen wipes. Toss 'em in your laptop bag and keep them there. Make them a permanent part of your laptop bag.

Laptop Lock

Don't forget your laptop's antitheft device. Whether it's a cable you can connect to something solid or one of those loud, loud audio alarms, you probably want to pack it in your laptop bag. Refer to Chapter 21 for more information on laptop security.

Removable Media

Saving your stuff to the laptop's primary storage system often isn't enough. It helps to have an assortment of alternatives to get that information out of the computer, especially when your laptop isn't connected to a network for easy file transfer. Two such options are optical discs and media cards.

- ✔ I often toss a few DVD-R discs into my laptop bag when I'm away for a while. For short trips, I use a Secure Digital card. (Of course, my laptop features a Secure Digital media card reader.)

- ✔ The discs or media cards can also be used for backing up important data.

- ✔ When your laptop lacks a media card reader, get a USB thumb drive.

Headphones

The computer is a musical machine! Why bring along an MP3 player when all you really need is that digital music? Having the music on your laptop, plus some basic earbud headphones, means that your music is wherever you and the laptop are.

I also pack an audio splitter in my laptop case, plus a second pair of headphones. That way, when I go traveling with a companion, we can share the audio from the laptop and enjoy music or a movie together.

Office Supplies

Yeah, this is supposed to be the "paperless" age. Whatever. You still need a pad of paper and a writing implement, despite the redundancy and its overall anti-21st-century nature. I keep two pens, one highlighter, sticky notes, a small pad of paper, and a legal pad in my laptop bag. Although it's not intentional, my laptop bag has also collected various paperclips and rubber bands.

Another must-have item: business cards.

Also consider copies of your presentation (if you're making one) and perhaps some magazines or reading material — especially if you don't pay attention in Chapter 22, where I discuss eBook readers for your laptop.

Cables, Cables, Cables

Cables are good. When you can, bring spare Ethernet, phone, USB, S-Video, power, and any other type of spare cables you can muster. You might never use them, but then again, you never know.

✔ You never know where the Internet lurks! Taking along a goodly length of Ethernet cable with your laptop is always a good idea. Then you can instantly connect to any available Ethernet network without having to wait for or (worse) rent a cable.

✔ A goodly length is about 6 feet.

✔ Cables don't have to be all tangly, either. If you don't like wrapping up your cables, look for those cables that come with retractable spools at any office supply store.

✔ Another cable to have, if it's available for your laptop, is an automobile "cigarette lighter" DC adapter.

Not the End of the List

You can pack your laptop bag full of so much stuff that the bag will eventually weigh more than you do. There's only so much you can take: portable printers, USB hubs, PC Cards, external disk drives — and the list goes on.

The items mentioned in this chapter are good to *always* have in your laptop bag. Add the other stuff as you need it. Or, when you're traveling, consider putting those things in your checked luggage so that you're not toting their extra weight.

Index

● **T** ●

Notes

Notes

Math & Science

Algebra I For Dummies,
2nd Edition
978-0-470-55964-2

Biology For Dummies,
2nd Edition
978-0-470-59875-7

Chemistry For Dummies,
2nd Edition
978-1-1180-0730-3

Geometry For Dummies,
2nd Edition
978-0-470-08946-0

Pre-Algebra Essentials
For Dummies
978-0-470-61838-7

Microsoft Office

Excel 2010 For Dummies
978-0-470-48953-6

Office 2010 All-in-One
For Dummies
978-0-470-49748-7

Office 2011 for Mac
For Dummies
978-0-470-87869-9

Word 2010
For Dummies
978-0-470-48772-3

Music

Guitar For Dummies,
2nd Edition
978-0-7645-9904-0

Clarinet For Dummies
978-0-470-58477-4

iPod & iTunes
For Dummies,
9th Edition
978-1-118-13060-5

Pets

Cats For Dummies,
2nd Edition
978-0-7645-5275-5

Dogs All-in One
For Dummies
978-0470-52978-2

Saltwater Aquariums
For Dummies
978-0-470-06805-2

Religion & Inspiration

The Bible For Dummies
978-0-7645-5296-0

Catholicism For Dummies,
2nd Edition
978-1-118-07778-8

Spirituality For Dummies,
2nd Edition
978-0-470-19142-2

Self-Help & Relationships

Happiness For Dummies
978-0-470-28171-0

Overcoming Anxiety
For Dummies,
2nd Edition
978-0-470-57441-6

Seniors

Crosswords For Seniors
For Dummies
978-0-470-49157-7

iPad 2 For Seniors
For Dummies, 3rd Edition
978-1-118-17678-8

Laptops & Tablets
For Seniors For Dummies,
2nd Edition
978-1-118-09596-6

Smartphones & Tablets

BlackBerry For Dummies,
5th Edition
978-1-118-10035-6

Droid X2 For Dummies
978-1-118-14864-8

HTC ThunderBolt
For Dummies
978-1-118-07601-9

MOTOROLA XOOM
For Dummies
978-1-118-08835-7

Sports

Basketball For Dummies,
3rd Edition
978-1-118-07374-2

Football For Dummies,
2nd Edition
978-1-118-01261-1

Golf For Dummies,
4th Edition
978-0-470-88279-5

Test Prep

ACT For Dummies,
5th Edition
978-1-118-01259-8

ASVAB For Dummies,
3rd Edition
978-0-470-63760-9

The GRE Test For
Dummies, 7th Edition
978-0-470-00919-2

Police Officer Exam
For Dummies
978-0-470-88724-0

Series 7 Exam
For Dummies
978-0-470-09932-2

Web Development

HTML, CSS, & XHTML
For Dummies, 7th Edition
978-0-470-91659-9

Drupal For Dummies,
2nd Edition
978-1-118-08348-2

Windows 7

Windows 7
For Dummies
978-0-470-49743-2

Windows 7
For Dummies,
Book + DVD Bundle
978-0-470-52398-8

Windows 7 All-in-One
For Dummies
978-0-470-48763-1